The Elusive Self

The Elusive Self

Archetypal Approaches to
the Novels of Miguel de Unamuno

Gayana Jurkevich

University of Missouri Press
Columbia and London

PQ
6639
.N3
Z745
1991

Library of Congress Cataloging-in-Publication Data

Jurkevich, Gayana, 1953–
   The elusive self : archetypal approaches to the novels of Miguel de
Unamuno / Gayana Jurkevich.
      p.   cm.
   Includes bibliographical references and index.
   ISBN 0-8262-0757-X (alk. paper)
   1. Unamuno, Miguel de, 1864–1936—Biography—Psychology.   2. Men
in literature.   3. Self in literature.   I. Title.
PQ6639.N3Z745   1991
863'.62—dc20   91–15631
                                                                                              CIP

This work is brought to publication with the assistance of
The Program for Cultural Cooperation Between Spain's Ministry
of Culture and United States Universities.

Designer: Elizabeth K. Fett
Typesetter: Connell-Zeko Type & Graphics
Printer: Thomson-Shore, Inc.
Binder: Thomson-Shore, Inc.
Typeface: CG Plantin

For Thomas Mermall

Contents

Preface

I begin with a few words about what this book aims to do, what ground it does *not* cover, and how it is organized. The premise of this study is my belief that an understanding of don Miguel de Unamuno y Jugo's psychological constitution, about which so little has been written with any thoroughness, can be inferred if one accepts the notion that his novels are most unabashedly autobiographical, and that the complexes, archetypes, and neuroses presented by his male protagonists would therefore reflect a similar psychological makeup operating at the level of the author's personal unconscious. Since I focus exclusively on the male protagonists, my book does not include any substantive discussion of the three novels in which the protagonists happen to be women: *La tía Tula*, *Dos madres*, and *El marqués de Lumbría*. Consideration of these novels necessarily requires a distinct critical orientation which falls outside the scope of this study.

I express my gratitude to Miguel de Unamuno Adárraga for allowing me to quote from the Escelicer edition of Unamuno's *Obras completas*, edited by Manuel García Blanco. For the convenience of those who do not read Spanish, I provide English translations of material I feel is indispensable to a clear understanding of my argument. Unless otherwise indicated, all translations are my own.

I also wish to express my gratitude to Princeton University Press for granting me permission to quote from *The Collected Works of C. G. Jung*, translated by R.F.C. Hull, edited by Herbert Read, Michael Fordham, Gerhard Adler, and William McGuire, copyright © Princeton University Press; and from *Selected Works of Miguel de Unamuno*, translated by Anthony Kerrigan, annotated by Martin Nozick, copyright © 1967–1984 by Princeton University Press.

My thanks also go to the editors and publishers who granted me permission to reprint some of my previously published work. Portions of Chapter 1 appeared in the February 1991 issue of *Comparative Literature* as "Unamuno's *Intrahistoria* and Jung's Collective Unconscious: Parallels, Convergences, and Common Sources." An abridged version of Chapter 5 was published as "Archetypal Motifs of the Double in Unamuno's *Abel Sánchez*" in the May 1990 issue of *Hispania*.

Thanks also to my friend and colleague Marshall J. Schneider of Baruch College/CUNY for his patient and close reading of the manuscript, and to John Coleman of New York University, whose keen observations led to the writing of my first chapter. A substantial part of this book was completed in the home of my parents, Dr. Igor and Marianna Jurkevich. My gratitude to them, and to the steadfast companionship of my dear friend Vassily.

Abbreviations

Quotations from the works of Unamuno are from *Obras completas*, ed. Manuel García Blanco (Madrid: Escelicer, 1966–1971), cited parenthetically by volume and page numbers. The following abbreviations indicate specific works within *Obras completas*:

AC   *La agonía del cristianismo* (The Agony of Christianity)
AP   *Amor y pedagogía* (Love and Pedagogy)
CSN   *Cómo se hace una novela* (How to Make a Novel)
DI   *Diario íntimo* (Private Diary)
ETC   *En torno al casticismo* (On Authentic Spanish Tradition)
N   *Niebla* (Mist)
NM   *Nada menos que todo un hombre* (Nothing Less Than Every Inch a Man)
PG   *Paz en la guerra* (Peace in War)
SMB   *San Manuel Bueno, mártir* (Saint Manuel Bueno, Martyr)
STV   *Del sentimiento trágico de la vida* (The Tragic Sense of Life)

Quotations from *The Collected Works of C. G. Jung*, trans. R.F.C. Hull, edited by William McGuire et al., Bollingen Series xx, will be cited parenthetically in the text by volume and appropriate page numbers.

Quotations from *Selected Works of Miguel de Unamuno*, trans. Anthony Kerrigan and annotated by Martin Nozick (Princeton: Princeton University Press, 1967–1984), will be cited parenthetically as "K-N," followed by the appropriate volume and page numbers. Where I have interpolated a reading preferable to that offered by Kerrigan-Nozick, such adjustments shall be enclosed within brackets: [ ].

The Elusive Self

Introduction

Y además, lo repito, ¿no son, en rigor, todas las novelas que nacen vivas, autobiográficas y no es por esto por lo que se eternizan?

(Unamuno, 8:732)

And besides, strictly speaking, are not all novels which are born alive autobiographical, and is this not why they become eternal?

Miguel de Unamuno y Jugo lost his father before reaching his sixth birthday. Carlos Feal Deibe refers to this event as Unamuno's "crisis of 1870," and implies that it anticipated the crises that occurred in Unamuno's life in 1897, and then again in 1924–1925.[1] Don Miguel's works of fiction attest to the absence of a strong father figure, if, in fact, such a figure is present in his novels at all. Recent Unamuno scholarship suggests that the entire corpus of the author's work be viewed as a gargantuan effort to substantiate the paternal, or masculine, figure.[2]

It is the aim of the present volume to offer a Jungian study of the manner in which Unamuno attempted to make concrete in his major novels the process of masculine individuation, and to examine the recurring networks of archetype and metaphor that Unamuno employed to create a personal myth through fiction. Leon Edel refers to creative writing as a masquerade that, through symbol and myth, retells an author's life story. "All literature," he observes, "is a form of disguise, a mask, a fable, a mystery: and behind the mask is the author."[3] Unamuno corroborates Edel's thesis when he observes, "Y él que queremos ser y no el que somos es nuestro yo íntimo" (8:491; And the one we want to be, and not the one who we are, is our most intimate self). An essential point of literary psychology is the study of the dichotomous relationship between the self an author might present to his public and the private self as he lives it intimately or

1

biographically.[4] The potentially destructive opposition between one's public and private selves is particularly relevant to an evaluation of Unamuno's literary characters, who are often engaged in conflicts of this type. It appears that Unamuno himself chose to offer the outside world an aggressively willful persona, behind which he concealed a relatively insecure man, dependent upon maternal shelter.

I begin my study with a consideration of *En torno al casticismo*. The five essays which comprise this collection owe a great deal to Unamuno's profound knowledge of late nineteenth-century psychology. To substantiate his sociological argument, Unamuno not only utilizes theories promulgated by the then "establishment" psychology, but he anticipates key elements fundamental to the school of analytical psychology founded by C. G. Jung early in the twentieth century. The rather surprising coincidences in point of view between Jung and Unamuno appear to have common sources in Romantic "psychology" and philosophy, as well as in the idea of a "national spirit" elaborated by German ethnopsychologists in the mid–1880s.

Unamuno's first three novels, *Paz en la guerra*, *Amor y pedagogía*, and *Niebla* explore the process of masculine individuation in which a youthful male protagonist struggles to free himself of the unconscious chthonic, maternal element. As described by Jung, the process of individuation aims to achieve the wholeness of self through a resolution of antithetical elements in the personality, and through the acceptance and integration to male consciousness of the female, or anima, archetype.

A man in whom the mother archetype remains dominant tends to maintain infantile relationships with women. For the male neurotic specifically, the general characteristics of the matriarchal world are rather pronounced.[5] In the case of Unamuno's male protagonists, as in Unamuno himself, the "liberation" of the anima archetype from the mother-imago is never carried through to its desired conclusion. Rather than encountering the anima archetype in his spouse, the Unamuno hero projects the mother-imago directly onto his wife, who is then unable to assume her appropriate function as an independent and complementary entity. She is thus fated to remain the perennial wife-mother, or virgin-mother, to her husband.

The second group of Unamuno novels, *Abel Sánchez*, the *Tres novelas ejemplares*, and *Cómo se hace una novela*, illustrates a progressive disintegration of male personality. Attempts at individuation are no longer made, almost as if hope for their completion no longer exist. It seems that the fragmented male characters of these novels, perhaps reflecting Unamuno's own mounting anguish and inability to resolve the polarities of his psyche, explode into full-blown neuroses, often accompanied by pathologically morbid symptoms. In some cases, such as that of Joaquín Monegro, the ego is in direct competition with a rejected shadow personality, while in *Nada menos que todo un hombre* a strong, publicly assumed *persona* threatens the protagonist's ego with complete eradication.

Finally, I discuss *San Manuel Bueno, mártir* as symbolic of an uneasy truce, possibly due to psychic exhaustion, among the multiple selves found in a single personality. The notion of *intrahistoria* (intrahistory), which Unamuno first introduced in *En torno al casticismo* as the bearer of past generations into the present and the future, is reaffirmed most assertively in this novel as the only possibility for never-ending life left to man.

In approaching Unamuno's prose fiction from a psychological point of view, I am especially concerned with isolating the networks of recurring metaphor, image, and unconscious association that lie beneath the metastructure of the novels in question. The origin, form, appearance, and disappearance from usage of these repetitious *structures obsédantes*[6] serve as the basis from which Unamuno's unconscious personality, and the elaborate construction of his personal myth, can be isolated.

All of Unamuno's work shows an extraordinary contact with what C. G. Jung terms the archetype, or primordial image. Jung considered the archaic symbolism of the archetypes to be universal in nature and to have existed from the most remote of times in the collective unconscious of all men. Jung further observed that archetypal activity was especially prevalent in states of mind predisposed to creative imagination, fantasy, and artistic elaboration.[7] Being the highly creative individual that he was, it is not at all unlikely that Unamuno, in his attempt to wrestle with the problems of identity and selfhood in his literature, would have made contact with the archetypes of the collective unconscious. Unamuno was, furthermore, a Hellenist by profession. Given the fact that the archetypes frequently express themselves through mythology, the Unamuno novel lends itself especially well to a critical analysis based on Jungian psychology, informed as it is by the symbolic rhetoric of universally familiar mythological motifs.

Although literary psychology has been called reductive by those unsympathetic to its methods, properly used it is an approach that recognizes its inherent limitations. I do not intend, therefore, to produce a composite psychobiography of Unamuno; rather, I hope to illuminate his psychological constitution through an evaluation of his male protagonists. I refer to Unamuno's personal biography only when necessary to substantiate an interpretation of his psyche that textual analysis enables me to formulate. Jung's theory of aesthetics upholds a similar view: he believed that art explained the artist, and not the insufficiencies and conflicts of an artist's life that explained his art (15:102). However, since Unamuno's work is largely autobiographical,[8] it is safe to consider the archetypes that surface in his novels, and the repetition of psychological configurations found among his fictional characters, as analogues of the same, or similar, archetypes within the author's own unconscious.

Literary psychology shares with the theory of literary autobiography the point of view that an author reconstructs his self through the use of metaphor. For James Olney, as well as for Jung, a written work, whether empirical or fictional in nature, always reflects or re-creates its author's unique being.[9] Jung commented that, "Whether or not these stories are 'true' is not the problem. The only question is whether what I tell is *my* fable, *my* truth."[10] Along these same lines, Unamuno himself noted, "Toda novela, toda obra de ficción, todo poema, cuando es vivo es autobiográfico." Continuing this thought, he observed that even "Los grandes historiadores son también auto-biógrafos," and referring specifically to autobiography as a literary genre, Unamuno remarked that autobiographies "aun mintiendo revelan el alma de su autor" (8:732, All great historians are also auto-biographers; 1:782, And autobiographies, even when they lie, reveal the true souls of their authors).

In the context of the novels produced by the Spanish Generation of 1898—to which Unamuno belonged—Leon Livingstone observed that its members showed a marked tendency to create imaginary selves in their fiction. As for Unamuno himself, Livingstone noted, "Quiere decir que la novela—en efecto, toda literatura creadora—es autobiográfica. Y así lo hace constar don Miguel sin ambages" (Don Miguel states, without any circumlocutions, that the novel, and for that matter all creative literature, is autobiographical).[11] The implication being made here is that every writer chooses metaphors that he feels best express his quest for self-definition, or most successfully re-create him in his work. The contribution literary psychology makes to the study of letters lies in its goal to go beyond the surface of a given work to decode the myths and images provided by the text. This approach thus furnishes the reader with an intimate, as well as a critical view, of the personality concealed by authorial (fictional) disguise. In the specific case of Unamuno, literary psychology adds the reality of a psychological framework to his otherwise unidimensional characters who thereby acquire a complexity and texture less easily grasped by the philosophical and existential studies most prevalent in Unamuno scholarship.

Based on these findings, I propose that the actual struggle of Unamuno's *agonista* is necessarily linked to don Miguel's personal inability to complete a process of individuation. According to Jung, a maturing male takes the first step toward psychic independence by freeing himself from the anima fascination of his mother (9.1:71). This procedure is described metaphorically as a confrontation between the conscious, or male contents of the psyche, with its unconscious, or female, counterparts. In practice, the male "liberates" his anima from subordination to the dominant mother archetype by recognizing his unconscious, female nature in a woman from outside those of his immediate family circle. He must then successfully integrate the female characteristics that the anima represents into his own consciousness. It is only at this juncture that a man can achieve a "true capacity for relatedness to women."[12] Men such as the Unamuno protagonist, however, for whom the feminine is irrevocably identified with the bounteous qualities of the Great Mother, are not prime candidates for a total process of self-realization since their inability to distinguish the anima from mother leaves them in an infantile state of psychic dependence upon her.

If we are to explain the dominance of the mother archetype in Unamuno's life and work, we must take into account the two most traumatic events that occurred in his life prior to the beginning of his career as a creative artist. To reach conscious expression, an archetype must be awakened from its normally dormant state by a "challenging experience."[13] A variety of psychic traumata, especially the loss of a parent, is frequently responsible for stimulating the obsessive repetition of image and metaphor in an artist's work.[14] The death of don Miguel's father eliminated a masculine presence from the Unamuno household and brought his mother to the center of his life. For young Miguel, the mother assumed a decisive role, and in later life Unamuno became the typical man for whom women were always maternal in attitude, the mother and wife playing interchangeable roles. The matriarchal order that reigns in Unamuno's fictional world thus appears to be the familial organization that Unamuno came to accept as the norm in his own youth.

After his father's death, Unamuno's spiritual crisis of 1897 was perhaps the most important event relative to his psychic development. Carlos Blanco Aguinaga notes that the mature Unamuno was an "hombre que tomó conciencia de sí a raíz de esta crisis religiosa" (man who reached self-awareness through his religious crisis).[15] This religious upheaval wounded Unamuno's psyche and was instrumental in his subsequent, highly personal interpretations of death and the meaning of existence, his intense ontological preoccupations, and the development of the *nivola*, with its clashes of human wills and personalities. Especially significant to this crisis is the role played in it by Unamuno's wife, Concepción Lizárraga, and the "¡hijo mío!" (my child) that escaped her lips as she gathered the shaken Unamuno into her arms for comfort. This moment seems to have made such an impression on don Miguel that he re-created it in all his work subsequent to *Paz en la guerra*. The episode is doubly significant in that it also signals a definitive metamorphosis of the anima archetype into the more emotionally desirable "wife-mother": the closest approximation to the biological mother the incest prohibition would allow Unamuno to make.

Unamuno's obsession with personal immortality, instilled in him by the upheaval of 1897, was directly responsible for his cultivation of the mother-complex and the idealization of infancy in his work. Quite sensibly, the Unamuno protagonist, much like his creator, prefers to assume the role of a son to his wife-mother since this positions him favorably in relation to the female progenitor of life. Ironically, Unamuno's fear of permanent annihilation also endangered his protagonists' psychological health by consistently placing them within the confines of the maternal and uroboric circle. Feal Deibe noted, "al aceptar este dictado el hombre se condena a no poder amar a la mujer, asimilada a la madre, a causa de la barrera del incesto" (due to the incest prohibition, a man who thinks of women as assimilated to the mother is forever condemned to be incapable of loving a woman).[16]

Analytical psychology suggests that in the creative man the mother-imago is often dominant and tends to overwhelm the weaker anima archetype, thus accounting for the man's urge to death or madness.[17] Death, especially by way of suicide, is commonly symbolic of a willing return to the unconscious world of the Magna Mater. Referred to as "uroboric incest," this need to be in psychological proximity to the mother is nothing less than a regressive desire to return to the Great Womb in pursuit of rebirth and immortality.[18] In

Unamuno's work, the frequently repeated scene in which a male protagonist retreats from adulthood to childhood, and from there to infancy and death (the process of *des-nacer;* that of being "unborn"), serves a very practical purpose indeed: not only does it offer the male a peaceful existence in the realm of the unconscious but, at the same time, the generative aspect of the mother's womb extends to him the key to perpetual life.

When the process of individuation is left aborted by a man's excessive assimilation to the mother-imago, his instinctive urge to self-totality often finds expression in projected form. Jung believed that not only dreams, but any act of creative fantasy, could be compensatory to actual situations or attitudes found in the human psyche (5:310). Creative activity, therefore, has the potential to become an avenue through which the artistically gifted find "symbolic solutions for the tensions and dissociations" from which they may suffer.[19] The archetype of individuation that invariably surfaces in all of Unamuno's ostensibly existential and ontological novels seems to indicate that the author, in an attempt to purge himself of his unconscious demons, projected his own psychic dilemma onto his fictional characters. Don Miguel's creative work thus became a stage on which his infinite *yo ex-futuros* (potential, but unrealized selves), played out their hypothetical destinies, always carrying within them the indelible stamp of the author's unconscious personality. It has been suggested that "the legendary aspects of Unamuno's personality assume more human dimensions when his agony is associated with the struggle to become free of unconscious obsessions through literary discourse."[20] This supposition permits us to assume that the cathartic act of literary expression became Unamuno's attempt at self-analysis, the unconscious purpose of which was to solve, creatively, many a difficult psychological impasse. If such is the case, then every novel written by Unamuno reflects the state of his psyche at the time any given piece was committed to paper.[21]

It is not surprising that confessional genres appealed to Unamuno. "Me encantan las autobiografías, las confesiones, las memorias, los epistolarios," he wrote in the 1913 essay "Sobre mí mismo" (8:301). Years later, in *Cómo se hace una novela,* he observed that men who favor self-expression in diaries, confessions, and autobiographies do so because they try to find themselves through their own work (8:764). Due to their need to expose the self, these authors, continued Unamuno (and he could very well have been referring to himself), have a propensity to repeat themselves in each of their own works. This is a revealing observation, especially when considered in its psychological dimension, for it is through confession that the human being unburdens himself of any real, or imagined, sins, guilt, and personal secrets. Unamuno's literature is so controlled by his confessional and therapeutic needs that the autonomy of his fictional characters is repeatedly called into question: "Unamuno isolates aspects of his own personality and shapes them into fictional characters in order to understand and analyze himself. He does not pretend to enter another personality, nor to see things from a different perspective. Thus, the majority of his characters lack true autonomy."[22] This appraisal of Unamuno's fiction suggests that the characterization of his male protagonists is a mere reflection of the author's own attempts to analyze his personality at different stages of its development. I therefore consider the issues of *querer creer* (desire for religious belief), immortality, and the problem of personality as literary manifestations of an authentic psychological crisis which, due to its unresolved nature, accounts for the incessant repetition of the same thematic concerns throughout Unamuno's work.

Ironically it is don Miguel's continued struggle to liberate the self through literature that has been negatively perceived, and improperly understood, by those determined to prove that he cultivated his agony in order to provide unlimited source material for his literature.[23] Only when we understand the unflagging determination with which Unamuno's disturbance sought an outlet through creative activity can we begin to explain the monolithic nature of his work. His own analysis of the motivation behind his creative drive is of inestimable value in this regard: "Y no hay más remedio, entre otras razones, por lo que decía Nietzsche, porque hay ideas que nos estorban y sólo echándolas al público nos libertamos de ellas" (8:188; And we have no other recourse because, as Nietzsche used to say, there are ideas that haunt us, and only when we hurl them out at the public do we become free). It is significant that Unamuno was intrigued by the madmen Dr. Montarco and Don Quijote, identifying them as examples of the compulsive human need to create (1:1127–36). According to Jung, the type of personality that transforms its vision into its own life, and makes that life symbolic, "adapted . . . to the inner and internal meaning of events, but unadapted to present-day reality," is characterized as an "introverted intuitive" personality type. The introverted intuitive, continues Jung, can only profess or proclaim; his voice is one that "cries in the wilderness" (6:402). Like Nietzsche, Montarco, and Don Quijote, Unamuno always perceived himself as isolated and misunderstood. In the biographical sketch that precedes *Cómo se hace una novela,* Jean Cassou reinforced the quixotic aspect of Unamuno's personality, describing him in Jungian fashion as an *orador en el desierto* (8:717). Unamuno himself frequently identified with Don Quijote's solitary vocation, exclaiming in *Del sentimiento trágico de la vida:* "¿Cuál es, pues, la nueva misión de Don Quijote en este mundo? Clamar, clamar en el desierto" (7:301; What is, then, Don Quijote's new mission in this world? To cry, to cry out in the wilderness).[24]

But Unamuno's words did not fall on deaf ears. It remains for each succeeding generation of readers to appreciate, in its own way, the transcendental nature of the voluminous body of work produced by don Miguel. A Jungian evaluation of this literary corpus indicates that perhaps Unamuno's universal appeal lies in his ability to recreate the archetypal contents of collective mythology, and to give them life through metaphors that awaken the eternally numinous qualities of the human psyche. "Whoever speaks in primordial images," wrote Jung, "speaks with a thousand voices . . . he lifts the idea he is seeking to express out of the occasional and the transitory into the realm of the ever-lasting. . . . He transmutes our personal destiny into the destiny of mankind" (15:82). Unamuno left us, as few authors have done, profound insights into the human struggle for psychological wholeness. Therein lies his enduring contemporaneity.

1. *En torno al casticismo*
The Psychological Sources
of *Intrahistoria*

WILLIAM JAMES: A REEXAMINATION

The sea is the favorite symbol for the unconscious, the mother of all that lives.

(Jung, 9.1:177–78)

Most critical approaches to *En torno al casticismo* consider its five essays to be heavily influenced by Unamuno's involvement with positivism and post-Darwinian thought.[1] Only Pelayo H. Fernández studied the role nineteenth-century psychology may have played in the overall conception of *ETC*, devoting part of his short monograph *Miguel de Unamuno y William James: un paralelo pragmático* to what he saw as the influence of Jamesian psychology on Unamuno's essays. Based on don Miguel's statement that "del 80 al 92 leí enormemente . . . sobre todo de psicología (de psicología fisiológica, Wundt, James, Bain, Ribot, etc., a que he hecho oposiciones) . . ." (9:817), Fernández concludes, first, that Unamuno read James's *The Principles of Psychology* shortly after its publication in 1890 and, second, that although neither James nor his book is mentioned in *ETC*, Unamuno's "fondo de continuidad . . . tal y como lo expone en *En torno al casticismo*, es trasunto de la teoría del flujo de la conciencia jamesiana, según se encuentra en *The Principles of Psychology*" (substratum of continuity . . . such as Unamuno defines it in *ETC*, duplicates James's flow of consciousness theory found in *The Principles of Psychology*).[2]

To substantiate his argument, Fernández refers to seven occasions in which he alleges that Unamuno cites *The Principles of Psychology*.[3] Of the seven references, none is earlier than 1895, the date of publication of *ETC*; five mention James only in passing, making no reference at all to *The Principles*; the remaining two, while they allude to content found in James's book, make no direct allusion to the work itself and occur well after 1895. Material Unamuno may have acquired from having read James does not appear in his work until the 1901 essay "La España de hoy, vista por Rubén Darío." In addressing what he termed the "dissociated" Spanish mentality, Unamuno observes: "Cuesta descubrir en éste [el español] la famosa corriente y flujo continuo de James (the stream of consciousness); parece más bien un espejo que reproduce . . . las imágenes que ante él se suceden" (4:756; It is difficult to discern in the Spaniard James's famous stream of consciousness theory. The Spaniard seems to be a mirror faithfully reproducing . . . the images that pass, one succeeding the other, before him). The second citation from *The Principles* occurs in Unamuno's essay "Ciudad y campo" (1902), in which Unamuno extrapolates and translates into Spanish a lengthy passage from James's chapter on the genesis of the emotions (1:1038–39).[4]

Given the fact that the only two direct citations of material from William James appear in Unamuno's writing following the publication of *ETC*, it is difficult to understand why Fernández would conclude that *The Principles of Psychology* played an influential role in the five essays. Furthermore, although it is impossible to determine what Unamuno may have read by James between 1880 and 1892, it is highly unlikely that he would have read *The Principles* immediately after its 1890 publication as suggested by Fernández. James's book appears not to have been translated into Spanish until 1909, and although Unamuno did read English, he did not begin to study the language until sometime late in 1892 or early 1893.[5] Since we have no reason to doubt Unamuno's affirmation that he had read something of James before 1892 (9:817), I suggest that rather than having any direct contact with *The Principles of Psychology,* Unamuno might have read any number of James's essays translated into French and made available through French psychological journals.[6]

While Fernández correctly points out that James's "stream of consciousness" theory revolutionized the psychological community by rejecting heretofore accepted doctrines of the British associationist school, his claim that Unamuno made exclusive use of "stream of consciousness" theory in *ETC* is questionable. Although there are passages in the five essays that have a vague, Jamesian aura about them, it is the "psicología inglesa" that Unamuno actually quotes in *ETC* (1:813). That Unamuno was familiar with both physiological as well as British associationist psychology is beyond argument, proved not only by the content of don Miguel's letter to Federico Urales

(9:817), but also by the actual references Unamuno makes in *ETC* to associationist psychology and by the many works of associationist philosophy housed in his personal library.[7]

The significance of Alexander Bain (1818–1903), perhaps the most prominent of all associationists, was acknowledged by none other than William James himself, who, in modified form, adapted some of Bain's ideas concerning contiguity to his own notion of the continuous flow of mental activity. The cornerstone of Bain's theory was the premise that "actions, sensations or states of feeling occurring together or in close succession, tend to grow together or cohere in such a way that when one of them is afterward presented to the mind, the others are apt to be brought up."[8] This notion bears striking resemblance to Unamuno's theory that "cada impresión, cada idea lleva un nimbo, su atmósfera etérea: la impresión, de todo lo que la rodeaba; la idea, de las representaciones concretas de que brotó" (1:814; each impression, each idea, bears its own nimbus, its ethereal atmosphere: the impression, of all that surrounds it; the idea, all the concrete representations from which it springs).

Building on the notions of contiguity, similarity, and the resurgence of previous concurrences of action or sensation, Bain theorized that "thoughts follow in trains, and we can resolve many of the successions into general laws of succession."[9] Seeming to adopt the associationist ideas of "contiguity" and consciousness as an accumulation of discrete impressions, Unamuno, following Bain, theorized that "en la sucesión de impresiones discretas hay un fondo de continuidad, un nimbo que envuelve a lo precedente con lo subsiguiente; la vida de la mente es como un mar eterno sobre que ruedan y se suceden las olas" (1:813–14; in a series of discrete impressions there is a depth of continuity, a nimbus that envelops the preceding with that which follows. The life of the mind is like an eternal sea upon whose surface the waves rise and fall and succeed one another).

Bain's theory, while it allowed for the decay of an impression, simultaneously provided for the possibility that "after a suitable remission or interruption, the impression may be renewed in all its fulness."[10] This notion bears comparison to Unamuno's concept of *intrahistoria*. Formed of a compounding, or a "legado de los siglos" (1:793), *intrahistoria* was considered by Unamuno to be a living sediment of tradition and perception that could be recalled at will if properly stimulated. As did the associationists, Unamuno seems to have believed that "Toda serie discontinua persiste y se mantiene merced a un proceso continuo de que arranca; ésta es una forma más de la verdad de que el tiempo es forma de la eternidad" (1:806; The discontinuous series persists thanks to the unbroken depths from which it springs; this is yet another proof that time is a variant of eternity). One year after the publication of *ETC*, Unamuno was still repeating a basically associationist line of thought: "Es corriente doctrina de la psicología la de que no hay impresión alguna recibida que del todo se borre sino que se precipita al lecho de nuestro espíritu, yendo a engrosar en él el riquísimo sedimento que yace allí sepultado mas no muerto, por debajo de la conciencia, en el insondable campo de lo subconsciente [*sic*]" (9:48; It is currently accepted psychological theory that no received impression totally disappears, rather it plunges to the depths of our soul to enrich the sediment that lies there, buried but not dead, beneath consciousness, in the unfathomable depths of the subconscious).

Anticipating James, Alexander Bain also spoke of a stream of consciousness which, unlike the uninterrupted Jamesian flow, Bain described as a "series of ebullitions." The novelty of James's *The Principles of Psychology* was not so much its revision of associationist belief regarding the mechanics relative to thought processes, but its outright rejection of what the associationists saw as an intimate correspondence between mind and body, each mental act producing concurrent bodily response.[11] James, however, acknowledged the validity of the associationist theory of discrimination, agreeing with Bain that "things are discrete and discontinuous; they do pass before us in a chain or train. . . . But their . . . contrasts no more break the flow of the thought that thinks them than they break the time and the space in which they lie." In revising Bain, James suggested that "chain" and "train" did not describe thought "fitly." For him thought was "nothing jointed; it flows. A 'river' or a 'stream' are the metaphors by which it is most naturally described. In talking of it hereafter, let us call it the stream of thought, of consciousness, or of subjective life."[12]

Unamuno seems to have had no conflict with associationist theory since he credited the British school with discovering "el principio luminoso de que el acto más elemental de percepción, de discernimiento, como ellos dicen gráficamente, es la percepción de una diferencia y que conocer una cosa es distinguirla de las demás, conociéndola mejor cuanto de más y mejor se la distingue" (1:813; the enlightening principle that the most elementary function of perception or discernment, as they say graphically, is the perception of difference, and that to be familiar with something is to distinguish it from other things, getting to know it best the more and the better we differentiate it from others). Continuing this line of reasoning, Unamuno concluded that the perception of difference between particles of thought "sólo se reconoce sobre un fondo de semejanza" (1:813), against which discrete impressions assume dimensionality depending upon whether or not they are recalled to consciousness: "Los islotes que aparecen en la conciencia y se separan o aproximan más, uniéndose a las veces, a medida que el nivel de ella baja o sube, se enlazan allá en el fondo del mar mental, en un suelo continuo" (1:814; The islets that appear in consciousness and that draw farther from or nearer to one another, sometimes joining together as the level of consciousness rises or falls, these islets link together in the continuous depths of a mental sea). If, at the time he drafted the essays of *ETC*, Unamuno had any familiarity with James's stream of consciousness theory, it would have appeared in passages such as the one above in which Unamuno attempts to synthesize the associationist idea of discrete fragments of thought with a uniform, possibly Jamesian, continuous background.

Within James's cautious approval of certain aspects of associationist doctrine, only the "repulsive" and "hideous glib jargon" of J. F. Herbart (1776–1841) was rejected without further consideration.[13] Unamuno was also familiar with Herbart's work (cf. 1:1068–69), although what he knew is, again, open to speculation.[14] There are, however, moments when *intrahistoria* begins to resemble Herbart's notion of the "threshold of perception." Unamuno compared his *tradición eterna* to the depths of the sea, the waves on its surface being representative of the fleeting *presente momento histórico* (1:792). Unamuno also established a dialogic relationship between *historia* and *intrahistoria*, describing the latter as a living sediment of the past constantly filtering out from the ephemeral present moment that which is of lasting value. The dialogic relationship between the external and the internal aspects of history, together with this filtering process, recalls Herbart's description of the threshold of perception as a surface on which a changing multitude of perceptions and representations was in constant conflict. There were stronger and weaker representations, the weaker ones being pushed down under the threshold of perception to "constitute a kind of chorus that accompanies the drama being played on the conscious stage." This last speculation is reminiscent of Unamuno's intrahistoric sediment, which he considered a metaphorical pillar of accumulated tradition sustaining the boiling cauldron of history being made on the surface above (1:793).[15]

Unamuno grew to admire James, referring to the American psychologist in 1907 as "el prestigiosísimo profesor de Harvard . . . el más sutil psicólogo acaso" (3:353). It is tempting to suggest that had Unamuno been aware of the scathing indictment of Herbart's work James made in *The Principles of Psychology*, perhaps certain passages of *ETC* may have sounded less Herbartian in character.

En torno al casticismo shows not only the influence of associationist philosophy and psychology, but also that of physiological psychology whose proponents were primarily interested in the laboratory techniques of measuring the time elapsed between mental stimulation and physiological response. In discussing the dissociated Spanish mind, Unamuno remarked: "Diríase que es en él [el español] largo lo que llaman los psicofisiólogos el tiempo de reacción, que necesita de bastante rato para darse cuenta de una impresión o una idea" (1:812; One could say that in the Spaniard, what psychophysiologists call reaction time is rather lengthy; the Spaniard needs quite a while to become aware of an impression or an idea). According to Unamuno, the mental impairment found among individual Spaniards was reflected on a much larger, national scale. Since Spain was a macrocosmic amalgam of the individual characteristics of her inhabitants, it was logical to suppose that she, too, would suffer the same abnormalities of body and spirit: "Como a los individuos de que se forma, distingue a nuestra sociedad un enorme tiempo de reacción psíquica, es tarda en recibir una impresión, a despecho de una aparente impresionabilidad que no pasa de ser irritabilidad epidérmica" (1:859–60; Like the individuals who comprise Spain, our society is characterized by its lengthy reaction time; in spite of a superficial impressionability, which is really nothing more than an irritation of the epidermis, the Spaniard is difficult to stimulate). Unamuno concluded *ETC* with a plea that the Spanish abandon their customary way of thinking in a "serie discreta" (1:815), and learn to develop their thoughts in a more synthetic fashion.

After considering the supporting material Fernández adduces to uphold his assessment of Jamesian influence in *ETC*, I believe that assessment is not entirely convincing, and that the judgments drawn from that material are perhaps excessively categorical. As for as any officially recognized psychological doctrine making an appearance in Unamuno's work, only the influence of associationist and physiological psychology can be documented. Unamuno may or may not have read *The Principles of Psychology* before he wrote the five essays of *ETC*, but it is quite possible for him to have inferred on his own an idea of continuity similar to James's, since they most likely shared some of the same limited source materials on which research in the nascent field of psychology was first based. This was the case with some ingenious anticipations Unamuno made, also in *ETC*, of concepts C. G. Jung was to elaborate early in the twentieth century.

UNAMUNO AND JUNG: CONVERGENCES AND COMMON SOURCES

In his pioneering book on the Generation of 1898, Pedro Laín Entralgo was the first to offer the opinion "No creo que sea violento establecer una relación inmediata entre la 'intrahistoria' de Unamuno y la tesis del 'inconsciente sobrepersonal o colectivo' de Jung" (I don't think it out of place to point out a relationship between Unamuno's intrahistory and Jung's thesis of the collective or suprapersonal unconscious). Since then, Carlos Blanco Aguinaga compared *intrahistoria* to the idea of an "unconscious" in Unamuno's work and, more recently, Francisco Fernández Turienzo again made a connection between *intrahistoria* and Jung: "En todo caso, hemos tropezado con la 'intrahistoria,' con el sentido universal de lo 'castizo,' que será luego lo 'inconsciente colectivo' (Jung)" (In any case, we have come upon "intrahistory," the notion of a universal tradition that will later become Jung's collective unconscious).[16] None of these suggestive observations, however, has been the object of substantive critical inquiry. I propose that an understanding of the points of contact between *intrahistoria* and the collective unconscious is crucial, not only because it places *ETC* in the larger context of nineteenth-century European social psychology, but also because such an understanding is indispensable to readings of *Paz en la guerra* and Unamuno's last, great novel, *San Manuel Bueno, mártir.*

Unamuno and Jung came from similar family backgrounds, but, more importantly, they were nurtured by the same late nineteenth-century European *Zeitgeist.* The adolescent and young adult years of both men were those in which positivism reigned nearly unchallenged: anything that could not be proved by the laws of science, or by the accumulation of data, was discounted as irrelevant. No mysterious "unknowable" existed since, according to Herbert Spencer, what was unknown today would become known through the advances of science tomorrow. Evolutionistic determinism ruled the social sciences while realism and naturalism pervaded the world of letters. Within this intellectual climate, Unamuno and Jung elected to pursue very similar courses of study: in 1888 Unamuno competed for a chair of psychology and ethics (4:18-19), while Jung entered medical school in 1895 and later chose to specialize in psychiatry. This shared interest in human mental life was perhaps the single most important factor in establishing a common ground for both men.

Although Unamuno was unsuccessful in obtaining an academic position in the field of psychology, his interest in the subject clearly began while he was still a university student, and it continued beyond his failed attempt to enter the field professionally (cf. 9:817).[17] Physiological psychology dominated the fledgling science in its developmental stages. Although the creators of the new depth psychology were to move away from the strictly laboratory techniques prevalent in physiological psychology, its literature was the first available not only to Unamuno, but also to Freud, only eight years Unamuno's senior, and to Jung, eleven years Unamuno's junior. It is a curious phenomenon, then, that given Unamuno's interest in psychology, he scarcely mentions the work of Freud in his own, and Jung appears not to have attracted his notice at all.[18] Any coincidence between Unamuno and Jung must therefore be attributed to causes other than direct intellectual contact.

While Unamuno and Jung were clearly the products of the age of positivism, their adult development may be considered a reaction to the dehumanizing aspects of its overly rational and materialistic ideology. Since they were both raised in religious family environments, Unamuno and Jung seem to have maintained ties to the world of the emotions, the spirit, and the unknown despite the influence of their formal education. Perhaps it was this childhood heritage that inculcated in both of them a natural predisposition to the neo-Romantic current that at times (1860-1914) ran parallel to *fin-de-siècle* positivism.[19] The rift between the mind and the heart that later defined Unamuno as a *persona* is actually rooted in this early disparity between his external environment and the interior world; the result of don Miguel's essentially existential philosophy confronted by his romantic sensibility.

Following a youthful enthusiasm for the scientific orientation of the day, Jung and Unamuno moved away from what they regarded as the depersonalized scientism of the age. In 1891 Unamuno counted among "los más profundos de hoy" men who were "bien nutrido[s] de ciencias positivas, química, física, historia natural, etc., etc.," and he included in this category Taine, Spencer, and Wundt. By 1895, however, at the height of his involvement with German socialism, Unamuno revealed that his *correligionarios* had begun calling him a "mystic."[20] In 1898 Unamuno was already distancing himself from positivism and socialist Germany, remarking, "Sigo aferrado a la Alemania romántica, la de Uhland";[21] by 1902 he had clearly turned his back on the positivist ethos, observing that "hay que predicar de continuo contra esa barbarie de la supremacía de los conocimientos de aplicación" (1:1017; it is necessary to preach continually against this barbaric supremacy of the applied sciences).

Jung experienced a similar conflict between the outside world and his own, spiritual leanings. While still a student, immersed in the laboratory environment of medical school, Jung found the time to deliver to a select university club a lecture titled "Reflections on the Attitudes to Christianity, with Special Reference to Albrecht Ritschl."[22] Jung left medical school convinced of the existence of an unconscious mind and wanting to distance himself from the materialism of the physiological psychology prevalent in his day.[23] As a young psychiatrist he became aware of the inadequacy of psychological literature that could describe and classify various forms of mental illness, but was unable to provide adequate guidelines for its treatment. In his clinical experience Jung noticed an inexplicable recurrence of mythological motifs in the dreams and fantasies of many patients, and his search for an explanation of this phenomenon led Jung to consult a wide variety of material, including the work of the Romantic Philosophers of Nature and that of their successors, the German Volksgeist theorists. Jung's "deviance" from Freud's exclusively materialistic and biologically oriented sexual theories was ultimately responsible for the break between them. Since Freud considered metaphysical inquiry superfluous and mythology a danger, he became, as Unamuno's socialist colleagues had become earlier, suspicious of Jung's "mysticism."[24]

As in the case of Jung, Unamuno was familiar with German Volksgeist theory and had an extensive knowledge of Romantic philosophy, perhaps drawn to it by his own romantic nature. It is therefore not surprising that historians of psychology agree that some of Jung's most important sources are to be found in the Romantics, while Hispanists concur that the background of *intrahistoria* is also "almost entirely romantic."[25] Given the peculiar blend of their academic preparation, contrasted with their innately spiritual natures, it is easy to understand why Unamuno and Jung might have found the "psychology" of the Romantic philosophers, and the research interests of the Volksgeist theorists, more congenial than the ideas of their immediate predecessors.

Although *ETC* undeniably reflects the influence of positivist approaches to history, sociology, and geography, the five essays also attest to Unamuno's concurrent interest in social, or ethnopsychology. In essence, *ETC* turns on two axes. The first is a positivist/historical analysis in which climate and geography determine national character, an opinion Unamuno supplemented with theories drawn from physiological psychology (cf. 1:813–14). The second is an ethnopsychological approach to the problem of Spain through which Unamuno set out to explore the peculiar Spanish Volksgeist. However, J. W. Butt's conclusion that Unamuno "borrowed the notion of Volksgeist almost unaltered from the best-known German linguists and psychologists" seems to warrant some amplification.[26]

Prior to the recognition of Volksgeist theory as a "science of man," the German Romantics engaged in the study of other cultures and their folklore, traditions, and popular literature.[27] Hegel, read extensively by Unamuno and Jung, is often credited with coining the term *Volksgeist* in reference to mores, laws, and constitutions as forming the inner life, or spirit, of a people.[28] The views Hegel elaborates in *Vorlesungen über die Philosophie der Geschichte* postulate the totality of a spirit of the people (*Gesamtheit*), which includes their history and is conceived as a dynamic past composed of the actions of a nation's forefathers, living on in the memory of the present generation. Volksgeist forms part of the *Gesamtheit* and can be inferred from the customs, art, and religious practices of a people.[29] Unamuno approximates this Hegelian notion when he describes the "public spirit" as something "más hondo y más permanente; es la resultante de la totalidad de la vida del pueblo, con su inmenso lecho de tendencias subconcientes [*sic*], con el riquísimo fondo en que palpita el silencioso sedimento de los siglos hundidos en la tradición" (9:49; deeper and more permanent; it is the product of the entire life of a people, an immense bed of subconscious tendencies in whose depth beats the silent sediment of centuries, imbued with tradition).[30]

Similar to the dialectic Hegel envisioned between the past and the present, and the dialogic relationship Unamuno establishes between *historia* and *intrahistoria*, Jung perceived a comparable affiliation between the conscious and the unconscious. He seems to have elaborated an idea analogous to Hegel's proposal that each succeeding civilization not only inherits its past, but with the aid of that heritage, is able to go beyond the achievements of the preceding generation: "In so far as no man is born totally new, but continually repeats the stage of development last reached by the species, he contains unconsciously

. . . the entire psychic structure developed . . . by his ancestors. . . .
That is what gives the unconscious its characteristic 'historical' aspect, but it is at the same time the sine qua non for shaping the future" (Jung, 9.2:279–80).

Hegel, nevertheless, was not the first to employ the term *Volksgeist*. Ideas developed by the "great instigator of the Romantic movement," Johann Gottfried Herder (1744–1803), bear an astonishing
resemblance to those of the later Volksgeist theorists and, ultimately,
to those of Unamuno and Jung. Herder spoke of civilizations as "organic wholes" constituted by a totality of individuals, its "lesser
parts." Although Jung does not appear to have made any reference to
Herder at all in his own studies, the probability he had some knowledge of the philosopher/historian's work is rather high since one of
Jung's most important sources acknowledges Herder as his spiritual
mentor.[31] Unamuno, however, was familiar enough with Herder's
work to be able to include him among the "grandes clásicos germanos," Goethe, Schiller, Lessing, and Heine (among his favorite
authors), whose "latinized" style of German he preferred to the her-
metic form of "esos insoportables escritores germanos germanizantes"
(4:533).[32]

Anticipating Hegel, Herder saw a dialectical relationship between
tradition and progress, a notion also fundamental to Unamuno's proposed solution for the Spanish crisis. According to the views Unamuno defends in *ETC*, the Spanish problem could be overcome if
Spain were able to achieve a synthesis between tradition (*intrahistoria*) and progress (*europeización*). As Unamuno would do later,
Herder perceived historical events as "outward" forms, while suggesting that an "inner" force sustained external, sociopolitical activity.[33] This appears to be a reasonable correlative of Unamuno's claim
that "todo lo que cuentan a diario los periódicos, la historia toda del
'presente momento histórico,' no es sino la superficie del mar" (1:793;
everything the newspapers write about daily, that is, the "present
historical moment," represents nothing but the surface of the ocean).
More important to Unamuno was the deep sea of tradition and precedent that sustained the "olas de la historia" (waves of history).[34]

In Herder's sociology, the guardians of national tradition were the
common people, or Volk, and much like his successors, the ethnopsychologists, Herder saw the native language of a group as the sustaining element of its political association.[35] The common folk in
Herder's view were not an insignificant mass, but the source of a
nation's culture. He concluded that in order to initiate change within

any political structure, one had to begin the reform from "below"; that is, by first understanding and recognizing the importance of the individuals composing the nation's Volk.[36] Herder's ideas are highly reminiscent of Unamuno's sociology, which presents the silent, archetypal Spanish *pueblo* as the standard-bearer of *intrahistoria*. In Unamuno's view, Spain's problem was partially attributable to her scorn of the *pueblo:* "no se le ama, no se le estudia, y como no se le estudia, no se le conoce para amarle" (1:868; we have no affection for the masses, we do not study them, and because they are ignored, we do not know the people well enough to care about them). He concluded that only "chapuzándonos en pueblo, regeneraremos esta estepa moral" (1:869; only by submerging ourselves in the life of our common people, will we be able to regenerate our spiritual desert). At fault in this matter were what Unamuno termed "las clases históricas," the political and social leadership of Spain that had stifled the intrahistoric life of the nation by closing off her contacts with the collective spirit of the world beyond the Pyrenees (1:867).

Anticipating Jung's psychology, which focuses on bringing unconscious life to the light of consciousness, Unamuno recommended that Spanish leaders seek out their eternal tradition: "La tradición eterna es lo que deben buscar los videntes de todo pueblo, para llevarse a la luz, haciendo conciente [*sic*] en ellos lo que en el pueblo es inconciente, para guiarle así mejor" (1:794; If they are to guide a people effectively, the leaders of any nation must search for their eternal tradition, enlightening themselves and bringing to consciousness that which in the people remains at the unconscious level).[37] Integrating the unconscious, collective spirit to consciousness was apparently an important concept in Unamuno's world view. As Jung was to conclude more than a decade later, Unamuno intuited that bringing the unconscious to active participation in conscious life was of paramount importance to achieving the fullness of self: "In the darkest layers of our unconscious dwells the collective spirit (Kollectiv-Seele) . . . we must illuminate it with the light of our consciousness, bringing it to life to assist our individuality towards full social realisation."[38]

Almost from their inception, Volksgeist studies were connected to the development of a psychology of the people, as well as to an understanding of their cultural history. J. G. Herder seems to have been the first to establish a link between historical methodology and the advances being made in philosophical psychology, arguing that to understand the "spirit of the age," a historian needed insight into human motivation.[39] Unamuno employs a similar approach in *ETC*. In his opinion, Spanish history could only be rendered intelligible if accompanied by an understanding of Spanish national psychology. As did the Romantics, Unamuno believed that philological study was the best way to gain access to the core of any national psyche. By the 1880s the idea of an "unconscious," both as an individual as well as a collective phenomenon, seemed to be rather common currency.[40] Ironically it was positivism that contributed to a resurgence of interest in the study of national spirit, a notion first encountered in the Romantic canon. As the age of scientism and the machine progressed, it dispersed traditional communities and, with them, a style of life, custom, and folklore. This prompted an international movement for the study and preservation of folkways, popular language, and regional traditions. In Spain there was renewed interest in the *Romancero* and oral tradition; Joaquín Costa, a figure much admired by Unamuno, went as far as to propose a new economic program for Spain based on her oral traditions, giving his book the unwieldy title *Introducción a un tratado de política sacado textualmente de los refranes, romanceros y gestas de la Península. En torno al casticismo* is Unamuno's response to this type of interdisciplinary study, which he acknowledged as a "movimiento científico internacional [que] ha despertado el estudio de los dialectos, de las costumbres, y de las tradiciones locales" (1:853, note 1).

The idea of national "Volksgeist" was popularized by the anthropologist Theodor Waitz (1813–1866) and his students, the mythologist Heymann Steinthal (1823–1899), and the ethnolinguist Moritz Lazarus (1824–1899). Together they were the first to engage in the study of comparative mythology, folklore, philology, and religions, their intellectual pursuits culminating in 1860 with the publication of *Zeitschrift für Völkerpsychologie und Sprachwissenschaft.*[41] Although Unamuno refers to Waitz, Steinthal, and Lazarus quite frequently in his work both before and after the publication of *ETC*, it is impossible to determine which of their many studies he may have read. Unamuno's personal library does not contain any of their work, and no direct citation of specific titles appears in his essays.[42]

Since the Germans were primarily responsible for developing philology as a science, it would not have been unlikely for Unamuno, who presented a doctoral dissertation on the Basque language, to have come across the linguistic theories of Theodor Waitz somewhere in the course of his university studies. Through Waitz he may have had his attention drawn to Steinthal and Lazarus. After Unamuno obtained his degree, his interest in philology continued, and later coincided with his study of psychology. As is evident in Unamuno's correspondence with Pedro Múgica, these dual research interests were viewed as complementary intellectual pursuits. If Unamuno did not come upon Waitz in his philological work, he would certainly have discovered not only Waitz, but also Steinthal and Lazarus, in the physiological psychology texts he was reading to prepare for an academic competition in psychology.[43]

Mention of Volksgeist theory first appears in Unamuno's 1887 lecture "El espíritu de la raza vasca," in which Waitz, Steinthal, and Lazarus are cited as the originators of Völkerpsychologie, "lo que llaman los psicólogos alemanes . . . Allgeist, el espíritu total, que recuerda en cierto modo la razón impersonal, la misma en todos" (4:154; what the German psychologists call . . . Allgeist, the "whole" spirit, reminiscent to a certain degree of the universal mind shared by all mankind).[44] References to the three ethnopsychologists are especially frequent in the synthesis Unamuno attempts to derive from his knowledge of psychology and his ongoing research in philology. This effort is evident in Unamuno's theory that psychology is a "campo fecundísimo de enseñanzas filológicas." Since language manifests the spontaneous thought of a people, it follows logically that popular speech would reflect a particular national psychology. Unamuno credits "los creadores de la Völkerpsychologie" with endowing philology with this important significance.[45]

Theodor Waitz seems to have provided Unamuno with a foundation upon which to base his theories of psycho-linguistic affiliation. Waitz considered the peculiarities of language to be transmitted by unconscious imitation. He likewise maintained that despite differences among the many languages of the world, the fact that Man had created any language at all, proved the psychic unity of mankind. Ironically, while language united peoples it also separated them, since it was responsible for endowing an individual language group with its own psychical idiosyncracies.[46] In his correspondence with Pedro Múgica, Unamuno made similar observations regarding language and its connection to national psychologies: "Concretándome a la filología esta ciencia ha de servir como auxiliar para darnos luz sobre historia y la psicología . . . y ésta, la psicología, psicología del hombre y de los pueblos, tiene que ser la base de la pedagogía, de la política, de todas las disciplinas fecundas y civilizadoras" (Confining myself to philology, this science must serve as a way of shedding light upon history and the psychology of mankind and nations . . . it must be the foundation of pedagogy, of politics, and all productive and civilizing disciplines).[47] One year prior to beginning work on the five essays of *ETC*, Unamuno noted that linguistics was an invaluable tool for psychological research, and affirmed that it was one of the most important sources available to students of "allgeist, del espíritu colectivo, del alma de los pueblos, y del desarrollo superior psíquico del hombre" (1:879–80). Finally in *ETC*, Unamuno suggests that because language harbors the collective spirit of the group that speaks it, it must be considered a "receptacle" for the intrahistoric tradition of each particular language group: "La lengua es el receptáculo de la experiencia de un pueblo y el sedimento de su pensar; en los hondos repliegues de sus metáforas . . . ha ido dejando sus huellas el espíritu colectivo del pueblo" (1:801; Language is a repository for a nation's experience and the sum of its ideas; the collective spirit of a people leaves its mark in the deep folds of its metaphors).[48]

Volksgeist methodology involved the identification of national spirit through the study of comparative folklore, vernacular speech, and the popular poetry of politically associated groups. Cultures and civilizations were understood as "wholes," and tradition as the guiding norm of the evolution of men and their political organization.[49] Heymann Steinthal, a disciple of Theodor Waitz, developed the theory of a "group mind," proposing that the integration of individual minds could, under certain conditions, function in a unified manner. His brother-in-law, Moritz Lazarus, whose work was known to Unamuno but apparently not to Jung, concluded that when imitated by large groups of people, shared behavioral patterns could foster a recognition of similarity, or group cohesiveness, and subsequently lead to political association and statehood. According to Lazarus, a spirit of the people, or *Volksseele*, is endemic to the social constitution of any state. Much as the national spirit is determined by the individual psyches composing the nation, so is the individual himself shaped by the *Volksseele* of which he partakes.[50] The extent to which German Volksgeist theory permeates Unamuno's thinking is evident throughout *ETC*:

> Cuando se afirma que en el espíritu colectivo de un pueblo, en el Volksgeist, hay algo más que la suma de los caracteres comunes a los espíritus individuales que lo integran . . . se afirma la existencia de un nimbo colectivo, de una hondura del alma común, en que viven y obran todos los sentimientos . . . que hay una verdadera subconciencia popular. El espíritu colectivo, si es vivo, lo es por inclusión de todo el contenido anímico de cada uno de sus miembros. (1:867)
>
> (When it is stated that in the collective spirit of a nation, in its Volksgeist, there is something more than the sum total of the characteristics shared

by the individual souls of which it is composed . . . one affirms the
existence of a collective nimbus, a depth of common spirit . . . one confirms that there is a true, popular subconscious. The collective spirit, if it
is viable, proves to be so because it includes the psychic contents of each
one of its members.)

Steinthal and Lazarus provide a link between the Romantic, J. G.
Herder, and one of Jung's principle sources, Adolf Bastian (1826–
1905). Bastian resolved to put psychology on firmly scientific ground
by intimately connecting it with ethnology and creating a new branch
of the social sciences, known later as "ethnopsychology."[51] A great
deal of Bastian's thinking, however, is based on ideas first espoused
by Herder and developed by Steinthal and Lazarus. Like Herder,
Bastian adopted the notion that popular language was the best manifestation of folk spirit.[52] Herder's view of national character also
seems to be the foundation for Bastian's "Idea of the People" and the
"elemental ideas" (*elementargedanken*), which he thought explained
the universal nature of the human psyche and the uniformity of mythological motif.[53] Bastian posited the "elementary ideas" to be a kind
of common substratum of collective representation that accounted
for the psychic unity of mankind. Metamorphoses of these elementary ideas, determined by the specific cultural orientation of associated groups, he called "folk ideas." According to Bastian, folk ideas
could form the basis of a social psychology because their expression
in the mythology and religious teachings of different ethnic groups
reflected their mental life. Described metaphorically, the *elementargedanken* were a "monotonous substratum. . . . These few elementary ideas exist . . . under the artificial veneer of every civilization."[54]
Although references to Bastian seem to be absent from Unamuno's
work, don Miguel would have come across Bastian's name in Théodule Ribot's *La psychologie allemande contemporaine*, which mentions
the German anthropologist as one of the founders of Völkerpsychologie (67, n. 1). Bastian's monotonous substratum of elementary ideas
quite resembles *intrahistoria*, "este fondo del mar debajo de la historia, es donde vive la verdadera tradición" (1:794).

Jung, however, openly acknowledged his debt to Bastian, noting
that "the theory of preconscious primordial ideas is by no means my
invention. With special reference to psychology we find this theory
in the works of Adolf Bastian and then in Nietzsche" (11:50–51).[55]
The universal and atemporal substratum of the human psyche that
Jung called the "collective unconscious" corresponds to Bastian's
monotonous substratum of elementary ideas. Jung's archetypes of

the collective unconscious, or articulated representations of collective thought, modified by, and adapted to, individual expression, are nothing less than Bastian's "folk ideas." In developing his theory of the collective unconscious, Jung also found much supporting material and guidance in the "philosophers of the unconscious," Carl Gustav Carus, Eduard von Hartmann, Schelling, Schopenhauer, Nietzsche, and the Protestant theologian Schleiermacher, all of whose views, according to Jung, focus on "the obvious uniformity of the unconscious" (Jung, 5 [1956]:176). With the exception of Carus, the work of all the writers to have influenced Jung was equally familiar to Unamuno.[56]

Historians of psychology generally agree that depth psychology would be unintelligible without the context of Schopenhauer and Nietzsche, and that the teaching of Jung in particular is enhanced when related to Schelling's "Philosophy of Nature."[57] To understand the dichotomies that permeate analytical psychology, and the dialogic relationships that lie beneath much of Unamuno's work, one must turn again to the Romantics. As both Jung and Unamuno were to do, J. G. Herder intuited man's dual nature and used the term *Doppelgeschöpf* to describe the two opposite worlds contained in every man. Herder postulated that this duality was responsible for the inner struggle in men whose task it was to reduce the incompatibilities at the source of the conflict. Anticipating Jung, Herder also used the term *individuation* to mean a "conscious becoming."[58] In the teaching of Jung, the most important goal of human life is the process of individuation, or the recognition and integration of the unconscious contents of the psyche to consciousness. Psychic totality is to be achieved by eliminating as many of an individual's inner polarities as possible and by moving away from ego-centeredness toward the wholeness of self (Jung, 5:408, 9.2:42).

Duality was an integral part of the Romantic *Weltanschauung*, playing an especially prominent role in the Philosophy of Nature, which considered the world in terms of pairs of antagonistic yet complementary opposites, ascribing particular importance to the male/female dichotomy. Prior to Jung's theory concerning the anima, a subordinate female personality in men, and the animus, an inferior male personality in women, Novalis went as far as to posit man's drive to perfect himself through his beloved, and conversely, to help the beloved reach perfection through relatedness to her lover.[59] As early as 1887, Unamuno echoed the Romantic concept of male/female polarity in a metaphorical description of his ideal vision of community development: "como el hombre busca en la mujer y en el hombre la mujer lo que les falta, formando el verdadero individuo humano que decía Michelet, vendrían unas razas a completar las otras" (4:155; just as man seeks to find in woman, and woman finds in man, that which they both lack, forming the complete human being as Michelet used to say, the different races could come to enhance one another).[60]

That Unamuno perceived a polarity between interiority and exteriority in all aspects of life is evident in his description of childhood memories as being contained, alive, within the developed adult consciousness: "tiene más aliento y eficacia la santa idea de nuestra infancia enterrada en nuestra conciencia que no la que actualmente se agita turbulenta en ella y parece dominarle" (1892; 8:154). Unamuno's sense of the dichotomy between the unconscious, inner world of *intrahistoria* and the conscious, external milieu of daily events, seems to presage the essence of what was to become one kernel of discord between Freud and Jung. Whereas Freud proposed that the human subconscious contained nothing but material rejected or repressed by the individual mind, Jung preferred to use the term *unconscious*, arguing that it consisted of two entirely unrelated levels. What Jung called the "personal unconscious" is comparable to Freud's "subconscious": a realm of forgotten perceptions, complexes, and memories acquired by an individual and meaningful only to him (Jung, 17:116). Jung, however, inferred a deeper layer of the human mind which he called the "collective unconscious of psychic representation" thought to be shared by the entire human race (6:443).

Unamuno, very much like Jung, preferred to use the term *intra-conciente* or *inconciente* [sic]. One year prior to publishing the essays of *ETC*, he observed that by studying his own language, man would become aware of "lo inconciente en nosotros," that is, of the common, unconscious bond that he shared with all men (1:880). As defined in *ETC*, *intra-conciente* has no resemblance at all to Freud's subconscious of repressed contents: "Le llamo así [intra-conciente], y no inconciente o subconciente, por parecerme estos términos inexactos. Lo que se suele llamar inconciente es de ordinario el contenido de lo conciente, sus entrañas, está más bien dentro que debajo de él" (1:814, n. 1; I've called it the "intraconscious," and not the unconscious or subconscious, because these terms seem to me imprecise. What one generally calls the unconscious is ordinarily the content of consciousness, its very marrow; it is inside consciousness rather than beneath it). However much Unamuno rejected the term *unconscious*, he nevertheless anticipated its Jungian definition.[61] Like Jung's "unconscious," Unamuno's *intra-conciente* refers to a vital part of the human mind, a river of mental life running not below the threshold of consciousness but within it, sustaining consciousness as the viscera sustain the external, human body.

Unamuno and Jung appear to have also shared the view that human psychic life, perhaps history itself, is of a cyclical nature. Jung conceived the collective unconscious as an "inherited brain which is the product of our ancestral life. It consists of the structural deposits or equivalents of psychic activities which were repeated innumerable times in the life of our ancestors" (17:177). Even prior to the publication of *ETC*, the past had already assumed an important dimension in Unamuno's thought: "El pasado ha recobrado nuevo interés como germen y razón de ser del presente, la tradición como base de todo progreso" (1894; 1:879; The past has regained a new interest as the origin and reason for being of the present, tradition as the foundation of all progress). As Jung was to do with the collective unconscious, Unamuno presented *intrahistoria* as a repository for ancestral patterns of apperception and behavior: "Estos hombres [los del pueblo] tienen un alma viva y en ella el alma de sus antepasados, adormecida tal vez, soterrada bajo capas sobrepuestas, pero viva siempre" (1:815; The common man has a living soul, and in it is harbored the soul of all his ancestors, perhaps it is numb, buried beneath superimposed layers, but it is always alive).

Jung thought the collective unconscious to be an "ancestral heritage of possibilities . . . common to all men" (8:152). These possibilities of representation he called the "archetypes," or primordial images, which find expression in the familiar symbols of mythological motif (Jung, 6:443).[62] The catholicity germane to an idea of the unconscious shared collectively by mankind is likewise present in Unamuno's reference to an "espíritu universal, [el] hombre que duerme en todos nosotros" (1:791; universal spirit, the Man who dozes in all of us), and in his supposition that "en la intrahistoria vive con la masa difusa y desdeñada el principio de honda continuidad internacional y de cosmopolitismo, el protoplasma universal humano" (1:869; in intrahistory, together with the diffuse and scorned masses, exists the principle of a cosmopolitan and international continuity, a universal human protoplasm). Just how close Unamuno came to inferring something comparable to Jung's belief that the archetypes reveal themselves in universally recognized mythological motifs is evident in the essay "Sobre el cultivo de la demótica," where Unamuno draws attention to the "profunda vida de los pueblos, leyendas o dichos que son tal vez el último resto de potentes mitologías enterradas en el augusto silencio de los siglos dormidos" (1896; 9:56; complex life of the common folk, their legends or proverbs that perhaps represent the last vestiges of powerful mythologies buried in the deep silence of bygone epochs).

Jung suggested that the archetypes, much like the instincts, were transmitted by heredity, had never been in consciousness, and were not individually acquired (8:133; 11:50). Rather they constituted "a common psychic substrate of a supra-personal nature which is present in every one of us" (9.1:3-4). Unamuno, too, saw tradition as playing an important role in the transmission of *intrahistoria*:

> Tradición, de *tradere*, equivale a "entrega," es lo que pasa de uno a otro, *trans*, un concepto hermano de los de transmisión, traslado, traspaso. Pero lo que pasa queda, porque hay algo que sirve de sustento al perpetuo flujo de las cosas. (1:792)

> (Tradition, from *tradere*, means "to pass on"; it is that which is handed over from one person to another, *trans*, a concept related to those of transmission, transferral, translation. But that which passes on also endures because there is something which sustains the perpetual flow of things.)

For Unamuno *intrahistoria* is synonymous with the *pueblo*, "raíz de la continuidad humana . . . sustancia que nos une con nuestros remotos antepasados y nuestros lejanos contemporáneos" (1:898). Unamuno's inclusion of the future as a beneficiary of past experience approximates Jung's view of the collective unconscious as an acquired human birthright that is passed on from one generation to another.

Unamuno represented *intrahistoria* metaphorically as the sea, its unchanging depths symbolic of the continuity of tradition, the sediment of time and history: "Las olas de la historia, con su rumor y espuma ruedan sobre un mar continuo, hondo, inmensamente más hondo que la capa que ondula sobre un mar silencioso y a cuyo último fondo nunca llega el sol" (1:793; The waves of history, with their murmur and foam roll upon an eternal, deep sea, appreciably deeper than the superficial layer which ripples on top of the silent ocean to whose depths the sun never penetrates). He saw tradition not only as the sustenance of history but also as a tangible expression of the abstract concept "lo inconciente en la historia," which became an unmistakable equivalent of the "unconscious" in Unamuno's thinking. Elsewhere in his work, Unamuno identifies the continuity implied by the idea of a "tradition" with the female sex: "La mujer es la base de la tradición en las sociedades, es la calma en la agitación, es el reposo en las luchas" (8:787; Woman is the foundation of tradition in organized societies, she provides calm in times of turbulence, peace in times of conflict). At the same time Unamuno allies the female (mother) with the sea. He is fond of metaphors such as *madre mar* or *mar materna* and of describing the sea as a mother who lulls her children to sleep with the rhythmic sound of her waves ("A pesca de metáforas," 7:901–3).

From this series of analogous relationships, a circular pattern emerges: *intrahistoria*, compared to the depths of the sea, is also referred to as "tradition," itself described as a concrete revelation of the unconscious element in history. Tradition is furthermore related to the female who, like *intrahistoria*, is not only the sustenance of progress but also a link to the sea. Thus it may be ventured that Unamuno imagines the unconscious to be connected to the sea and, by extension, to the female, or mother.[63] In analytical psychology, the sea, or any large body of water, is symbolic of maternal depths, or the unconscious in its positive and negative aspects (Jung, 5:218, 389). The sea is a place of generation as well as that of death, and is represented iconically by the rise of the sun from its waters at dawn, and its fall into the sea at dusk. The association Unamuno establishes between *intrahistoria* (the unconscious), the sea, the female, and tradition is exactly the same anthropomorphic connection Jung would make between the collective unconscious and its representation by the Mother and the maternal depths of the sea.

As remarkable as is the coincidence of metaphorical expression between Unamuno and Jung, the spiritual affinity they shared is nothing less than uncanny. Like Unamuno, Jung came from an extremely religious family environment, most of the male relatives on both sides of the family being either Protestant ministers or theologians. Again like Unamuno, Jung lost touch with his faith upon beginning a life of greater "historical consciousness" at the university. Steeped in the materialistic positivism of their intellectual background, both young men began to question their faith, eventually moving away from unqualified belief in Christian dogma. Of these years Jung wrote, "The farther away I was from the Church, the better I felt."[64]

The seeds of religious doubt, however, were sown in both youths during their preparation for the first communion/confirmation. Of his experience Unamuno noted: "De mi primera comunión recuerdo muy poco. . . . Tanto y tanto se nos prepara para ella, tanto se le habla al niño de delicias y consuelos que no necesita porque no se halla desconsolado . . . tanto se le quiere sugestionar, que cuando llega al acto, el niño, poco sugestionable en realidad, se queda frío" (8:128; I remember very little about my first communion. . . . We were prepared for it so intensely, taught so much about its delights and consolations which, in fact, a child does not require since he is never disconsolate . . . he is so mesmerized by it all, that when the moment arrives, the child, scarcely prepared for this type of suggestion, remains unmoved). Jung was prepared for confirmation and communion by his father, a Protestant pastor. This was a man, Jung realized years later, profoundly troubled because he had never allowed himself to "think" about the meaning of religious teaching, for fear that if he did, he would lose his faith entirely. As a young man, Jung became painfully aware that his father's tremendous suffering, much like that of Unamuno's San Manuel Bueno, was the result of feeling torn between personal doubt and the apparent "belief without understanding" he felt obliged to maintain for the sake of his parishioners.[65] Jung later speculated that while having been prepared for confirmation by his father, he might have unconsciously assimilated some of the older man's religious misgivings. Although he recalled preparing for the first communion rather earnestly and "had hoped for an experience of grace and illumination . . . nothing had happened. God had been absent," and Jung remembers feeling himself cut off from the faith of his fathers.[66]

As a young man Jung always felt unable to communicate with his own father, isolated from him by an unbreachable spiritual gulf. As did Unamuno, who was left fatherless before reaching his sixth birthday, Jung grew close to his mother, drawn by her intuitive sensibilities. In both cases, the absence of a flesh-and-blood father as a significant presence in the lives of Jung and Unamuno is relative to their progressive questioning of Logos—the Word of God. Perceived as an unknowable entity, the very existence of God, the Divine Father, is placed in doubt by both men.[67] As an adult Jung observed that people who claim to have an unquestioning (that is, unthinking) belief in their faith, are also those who continually expose themselves to doubt. Truly thinking people, he argued, welcome doubt since it, ironically, serves as the surest way to a more profound kind of belief (11:110). Jung's conclusion recalls Unamuno's condemnation of the *fe del carbonero* (blind faith), his position in *Del sentimiento trágico de la vida* that doubt was the basis of true faith, and his decision not to "poner paz entre mi corazón y mi cabeza, entre mi fe y mi razón; quiero más bien que se peleen entre sí (7:180; strive for peace between my heart and my head, between my faith and my mind; I would rather they be at odds with each other).

Jung and Unamuno shared the feeling that the dogma of life after death was an unsubstantiated myth. Jung was puzzled by the paradox of a supposedly benevolent Divinity who created a "life of contradictions in which one creature devoured another and life meant simply being born to die." Although Jung claimed to be "religious" in the broadest sense of the word, his reservations, like those of Unamuno, were prompted by doubts such as: "But it is not so certain as all that!" or "What about that thing under the ground?"[68] As is well known, the irreversibility of bodily death also caused Unamuno no small amount of anguish: "Mi terror ha sido el aniquilamiento, la anulación, la nada más allá de la tumba" (8:793). Unamuno found great irony in hearing his fellow men offer conjectures as to the horrors of death: the lack of air and movement they might experience, or the darkness and worm-eaten cadavers with whom they might have to share a crypt. Unamuno considered such projections mere absurdities since they did not take into account the fact that death precluded any continuation of life forms. For Unamuno, the greatest horror posed by death was the cessation of conscious activity: "Es terrible estado de conciencia en que pensamos que no hay tal estado, el pensar que no pensamos da un vértigo de que ya la razón no cura" (8:830; It's a terrible state of consciousness when we realize that consciousness will not last forever; to ponder that one day we will not be conscious produces a frenzy from which the intellect never recovers).

Jung resolved his dilemma with what came to be a favorite aphorism: "I cannot believe in what I do not know, and what I know I need not believe in."[69] Jung's solution evokes Unamuno's rewording of the catechistic inquiry "¿Qué cosa es fe? —Creer lo que no vimos" (What is faith? To believe in that which is unseen). Like Jung, Unamuno was unable to believe in that for which no tangible proof could be supplied. And what he did not understand of Church teaching, Unamuno would apparently not accept at face value. Therefore he reworded the traditional response to the query "¿Qué cosa es fe?" to read: "¡Creer lo que no vimos, no!, sino crear lo que no vemos" (1:962; To believe in that which is unseen, no!, but to create that which we do not see). Clearly Unamuno chose not to cast his lot with *gnosis*, or the acceptance of "consecrated" knowledge, but with *pistis*, the re-creation of those aspects of the faith he could not "see" (that is, comprehend), to suit his personal needs.[70]

Not only are there suggestive coincidences in the spiritual views held by Unamuno and Jung, but the two also seem to have shared certain personality traits. Despite a reportedly introverted childhood and adolescence, both Jung and Unamuno developed into aggressive young men. The anonymous letters of "M," which document Unamuno's early years in Salamanca, portray a fascinating yet argumentative and opinionated personality that dominated any social or intellectual gathering. In much the same fashion, once enrolled at the university, Jung developed into an aggressive young man, aware of his intellectual gifts, and one who dominated student discussions "to the point of generating dislike and opposition among fellow students." It was during his university years that Jung earned for himself the nickname *Walze:* steamroller.[71] Like Unamuno, Jung "gave the impression of feeling himself superior to others, needed companions who would listen to him . . . was oversensitive to the criticism of others, although he was not always tactful himself."[72]

Outside the personal realm, Unamuno and Jung coincide once again. Unamuno was fond of pointing out that fictional characters supersede the reality of their creators. At the moment that Augusto Pérez (*N*) is informed of his pending demise, he reminds Unamuno: "Vamos a cuentas: ¿no ha sido usted el que no una, sino varias veces, ha dicho que Don Quijote y Sancho son, no ya tan reales, sino más reales que Cervantes?"(2:667; Let's settle accounts here: didn't you say, not once, but quite a few times, that Don Quijote and Sancho are not only as real, but more real, than Cervantes?). We are reminded, again in *Niebla*, that Hamlet was "uno de los que inventaron a Shakespeare" (2:664; one of those who invented Shakespeare). Jung held that while an artist worked, his project, flowing from the depths of the unconscious, possessed and guided his psychic life. Therefore, surmised Jung, it was not Goethe, for example, who had created Faust, but Faust—the unconscious personified—who "created" Goethe (15:103).

Goethe himself provided a metaphor that both Jung and Unamuno adopted to express psychological extraversion and introversion. Jung considered Goethe's image of the diastolic and systolic activity of the heart to be a brilliant intuition of the contrasting movements of human psychic energy: an extraverted reaching out to seize the moment coupled with the reflex action of detachment and withdrawal of energy from the exterior world (Jung, 6:4–5). In *Del sentimiento trágico de la vida*, Unamuno also speaks of experiencing "la diástole del alma y me empapo en vida ambiente, y creo en mi porvenir; pero al punto la voz del misterio me susurra ¡dejarás de ser!, me roza con el ala el Angel de la Muerte, y la sístole del alma me inunda las entrañas espirituales en sangre de divinidad" (7:133; "the diastole of my soul and am bathed in the flood of life that flows around me, and I believe in my own future. But [immediately the voice of mystery whispers]: 'You will cease to be!,' [and the] wing of the Angel of Death brushes against me, and the systole of my soul inundates the depths of my spirit with the blood of divinity" [K-N, 4:45–46]). Carlos Blanco aptly interprets Unamuno's *diástole* to signify an opening up of consciousness to the outside, while *sístole* marks a turning inward, together with a recognition of one's limitations within the external world.[73]

The coincidence of intellectual expression and spiritual vision between Jung and Unamuno remains to be explained. In reference to *ETC*, can we agree with Fernández Turienzo that "hemos tropezado con . . . [lo] que será luego lo 'inconsciente colectivo' " (we have discovered in Unamuno something that Jung would later call the "collective unconscious")? Although some of the concepts Unamuno elaborates in the five essays of *ETC* approximate those C. G. Jung would develop early in the twentieth century, *intrahistoria* is not altogether a comprehensive anticipation of Jung's "collective unconscious."[74] Both *intrahistoria* and the collective unconscious are, however, the products of a similar response on the part of two men to the same bibliographical sources and to a shared experience of the same historical moment. In short, Unamuno and Jung arrived at similar ideas because they shared a similar philosophical outlook. In fact, Unamuno himself explained that it was possible for contemporaries, working in different corners of the globe, and having no knowledge of the other's work, to generate analogous results. Responding to his belated discovery of Pirandello, whose work was compared to his own by Italian critics, an astounded Unamuno suggested:

> Es un fenómeno curioso y que se ha dado muchas veces en la historia de la literatura, del arte, de la ciencia o de la filosofía, el que dos espíritus, sin conocerse ni conocer sus sendas obras . . . hayan perseguido un mismo camino y hayan tramado análogas concepciones o llegado a los mismos resultados. Diríase que es algo que flotaba en el ambiente. O mejor dicho algo que late en las profundidades de la historia y busca quien lo revele. (8:501)

> (It is a curious phenomenon, and one which has occurred many times in the history of literature, art, science, and philosophy: the fact that two persons, without knowing each other or their respective ideas . . . have

followed the same path and have developed similar notions, or arrived at the same conclusions. We could attribute this kind of occurrence to something which floats in the intellectual environment. Or better yet, to something which throbs in the depths of history, awaiting the one who might bring it to light.)

It is in the instinctive repetition of tradition and psychic structures as data contained in the unconscious of mankind, and in the proposal that *intrahistoria* is the sustenance of history and the future, that Unamuno's ideas herald those of Jung. Both Unamuno and Jung availed themselves of the psychological intuitions of the Romantic philosophers, and of the work of the Volksgeist theorists who were responsible for elaborating not a few of the Romantics' ideas on collective spirit, and for putting them on an acceptably "scientific" footing. Although the sources they both used were at times identical, Jung's findings tend toward the psychological, while those of Unamuno are primarily sociological in orientation. Jung, however, was an innovator while Unamuno was not. A felicitous association of the comparative mythology, religion, and folklore learned from the methods of the ethnopsychologists, combined with Jung's own, strictly medical preparation, enabled the Swiss psychiatrist to create an entirely novel approach to individual psychology. *En torno al casticismo*, on the other hand, is the result of fact and intuition Unamuno gleaned from two separate but compatible courses of personal inquiry. The social scientist in Unamuno derived *intrahistoria* from positivist approaches to history, sociology, geography, and physiological psychology: Taine, Comte, Spencer, Wundt, Bain, Ribot, perhaps William James. The metaphysical aspects of *intrahistoria* are based on the doctrines of Herder, and those of Waitz, Steinthal, and Lazarus, heirs of the Romantic spirit. Unamuno simply applied the results of his reading to the Spanish circumstance, and named it *intrahistoria*.

However, if Unamuno was unsuccessful in making an original contribution to Spanish sociology, what he managed to accomplish for himself was of great importance. In pointing to *intrahistoria* as a vital legacy that would live on within future generations of men and women, Unamuno may have partially solved his uniquely personal dilemma of attaining spiritual immortality. With a view to ensuring its longevity, Unamuno took special care to endow *intrahistoria* with quasi-biological properties:

El pueblo, el hondo pueblo, el que vive bajo la historia, es la masa común a todas las castas, es su materia protoplásmica; lo diferenciante y excluyente son las clases e instituciones históricas. Y éstas sólo se remozan zambulléndose en aquél. (1:867)[75]

(The mass, the anonymous common man who exists beneath historical events, is the common denominator, the protoplasmic matter of all peoples; what differentiates men among each other is social class and historical institutions. And social institutions are reinvigorated only if they maintain close ties to the life of the common people.)

According to this scheme, Unamuno would himself become part of the eternal, dynamic sediment of tradition that the future would incorporate into its own spirit and social organization.

The dichotomy Unamuno establishes between history and intrahistory, time and eternity in *ETC*, is recast as fiction in his first novel, *Paz en la guerra*. The sea-and-wave metaphor of the five essays is replaced in the novel by the duality of peace and war, but the relationship Unamuno envisioned between time and eternity is maintained without change:

Así como la tradición es la sustancia de la historia, la eternidad lo es del tiempo, la historia es la forma de la tradición como el tiempo la de la eternidad. (*ETC*, 1:794)

(Just as tradition is the sustenance of history, eternity is that of time; history is a form of tradition just as time is that of eternity.)

. . . paz en la guerra misma y bajo la guerra inacabable, sustentándola y coronándola. Es la guerra a la paz lo que a la eternidad el tiempo: su forma pasajera. (*PG*, 2:300)

(. . . there is peace in war itself, peace beneath war, sustaining it and crowning it. War is to peace what time is to eternity: its transitory form.)

In *Paz en la guerra*, the dialogue between history and intrahistory, time and eternity, plays itself out against the backdrop of an industrial Bilbao under siege by the Carlists who are implicitly identified with the common man (Volk) of the Basque countryside, with tradition, and with Mother Nature.

Intrahistoria reaches its final avatar in *San Manuel Bueno, mártir.* While the "hondo pueblo, el que vive bajo la historia," had only a figurative meaning in *ETC*, it assumes a literal representation in the sunken village of Valverde de Lucerna. The lake, whose waters carry a maternal significance, and in whose depths life continues undisturbed by the fluctuating currents of time and history, becomes an anthropomorphic symbol of *intrahistoria*, tradition, and the unconscious. In the communal womb of the lake the past is restored and immortalized into a vibrant inheritance destined to become part of the collective spirit and life experience of the present, and future generations.

2. *Paz en la guerra*
The Emerging Self

¡Ay amigo! He ahí mis dos grandes anhelos. El anhelo de acción y el anhelo de reposo. Llevo dentro de mí . . . dos hombres, uno activo y otro contemplativo, uno guerrero y otro pacífico, uno enamorado de la agitación y otro del sosiego. (Unamuno, 3:373)

(Dear friend! I have here my two greatest longings. A longing for action and a longing for repose. I bear two men within me . . . one active, the other contemplative; one a warrior, the other a pacifist; one enamored of turbulence, the other of tranquility.)

In "Notas sobre el determinismo en la novela" (1898), perhaps Unamuno's first statement of any length concerning literary theory, he suggests that the most valuable contribution made to letters by naturalism was its "cuidado de la documentación" (9:772). He adds that the historical novel was an important exponent of naturalism in literature, and concludes that "lo que respecto a una época no nos dicen secos anales y escuetos documentos diplomáticos, nos enseña su literatura: la vida cotidiana, intrahistórica" (9:772; what cut-and-dried annals and diplomatic records do not tell us about the daily, intrahistoric life of an era, literature will).

Several years later, Unamuno published two important essays, "De vuelta" and "Escritor ovíparo" (1902), in which he set forth his ideas regarding the "viviparous" and "oviparous" methods of writing (7:206–10). Finally, in 1904, he made his most definitive statement on the mechanics of writing in the essay "A lo que salga" (7:1194–1204). He defined the oviparous manner of work as one of a methodical accumulation of notes, data, outlines, drafts, and revisions, and compared this procedure to the brooding of a hen on her eggs. To illustrate his point, Unamuno described the meticulous care he took in gathering material for his first novel, *Paz en la guerra*:

> Hace ya años, estando en Madrid, se me ocurrió la idea de hacer un cuento con el suceso de la muerte en el campo carlista de un sujeto de quien me dieron noticia. . . . Sobre esta base compuse un cuento y lo compuse tachando, añadiendo, sustituyendo y alterando detalles y noticias. Una vez escrito el cuento, se me ocurrió hacer una novela corta (8:208–9) . . .

> (Many years ago, while I was in Madrid, I heard about the death of a young Carlist soldier, and it occurred to me to write a story based on the event. . . . I wrote this story adding things, then eliminating them, substituting others, changing details, and adapting information. Once the story was written, I considered expanding it to a short novel . . .)

According to Unamuno, the task of the historical novel was to fuse, rather than to juxtapose, fiction and history, science and art. "A tales principios pretendí ajustar, en la medida de mis fuerzas, mi novela *Paz en la guerra*. . . . Quise fundir . . . lo histórico y lo novelesco, contar una historia por dentro y encajar una ficción en un exterior rigurosamente documentado" (9:772–73; I wanted my novel *Peace in War* to conform to these principles as much as possible. . . . I wanted to meld . . . history with fiction, giving an intimate view of history at the same time that I situated the fictional within a rigorously documented historical framework).[1]

Paz en la guerra is Unamuno's first, and only truly oviparous work. His intent to "anovelar la historia" or "historiar la novela" (9:773) places history and intrahistory in a dichotomous relationship, at the same time that it sets the two sociological aspects that *intrahistoria* represents at opposite poles. The novel is steeped in chiastic and dialogic alliances that presage, thematically and aesthetically, the Cervantine mirror-games of a great deal of Unamuno's subsequent work.[2] *Paz en la guerra* is also Unamuno's most autobiographical novel in the documentary sense of the term:

> Aquí, en este libro—que es el que fui—, encerré más de doce años de trabajo . . . aquí está el eco, y acaso el perfume, de los más hondos recuerdos de mi vida y de la vida del pueblo en que nací y me crié; aquí está la revelación que me fue la historia y con ella el arte. (2:91)

> (Here, in this book—the book of who I was—, I invested more than twelve years of work. Here I gathered in the flowers and the fruits of my

experience of childhood and adolescence. It contains the echo and perhaps the perfume of the most profound memories of my life and of the life of the town where I was born and raised. It contains the revelation of what history—and art—meant for me. [K-N, 1:5])

Paradoxically, however, while the context of *Paz en la guerra* is oriented outward, toward specific personal and historical events, its content is turned inward, to *intrahistoria*. Unamuno chose two protagonists, Ignacio Iturriondo and Pachico Zabalbide, as his alter egos. Each functions as an exponent of one aspect of Unamuno's theory of *intrahistoria*. The sociohistorical aspect of intrahistory is couched in the metaphor "time and eternity": the economic center, Castile (the urban *cainitas*), is aligned against the feudal Carlist provinces (the agriculturally oriented *abelitas*). Beneath the abstract ideals of the dynastic disputes that ostensibly generated the Carlist Wars, Unamuno sees the recurring clash of two Spains and two economic systems forever in opposition. Passages such as the following abound:

> Los hijos de los hidalgüelos . . . dirigían de nuevo a sus labradores mesnaderos contra los villanos, contra los hijos del comercio. Resucitaba allí la apagada voz de los siglos muertos de viejos rencores. (2:166–67)[3]

> (The sons of ancient nobility . . . now directed their armed peasant followers once again to harry the townsfolk, the sons of commerce. The stilled voice of dead centuries of ancient feuds was here brought back to life. [K-N, 1:42])

Although the Carlists precipitated a historical conflagration, Unamuno uses them as his symbol of *intrahistoria*. As the recipients of Catholic values and politically conservative thought patterns, they are custodians of the unconscious repetition of habit and custom exemplary of intrahistory. Herein lies another paradox. While Ignacio, a young Carlist volunteer, is associated with the eternally universal human values flowing beneath the "olas de la historia," ironically it is he who actively participates in the armed conflict and, through it, is able to achieve consciousness of historical reality. The psychosociological feature of *intrahistoria* is accorded to Pachico, the complementary other half of Ignacio's personality. Normally associated with the conscious world, Pachico chooses to withdraw from history into his own intimate war of psychic individuation. The external, physical conflict of the Third Carlist War thus becomes a metaphorical backdrop against which the internal, metaphysical struggle for individuation takes place.

Most interesting about Ignacio and Pachico is Unamuno's juxtaposition of the two characters in chiastic opposition. Ignacio, representing intrahistory, progressively sheds his intellectual lethargy through an involvement in historical events, while Pachico, symbolic of a historical consciousness, gradually submerges himself in philosophical ruminations. This chiasmus also serves to underscore Unamuno's predilection for paradox, and contains in incipient form the favorite Unamuno theme that each man carries within himself a personality opposed to his "true" nature—an archetype that Jung was to call the "shadow." Inner duality, the seed of the problem of personality that culminates in the novel *San Manuel Bueno, mártir,* is most overt in Pachico. Forming part of his character is the undercurrent of conflict between intellect and faith, as well as ontological and existential issues quite similar to the ones that began to torment Unamuno during the twelve years' gestation of this novel. It must be remembered that *Paz en la guerra* received its final redaction exactly during the years preceding Unamuno's religious crisis of 1897.[4] Consequently, while Pachico reflects the psychic trajectory of Unamuno's young adult years, Ignacio represents an Unamuno that may have been, one enjoying life as an anonymous, intrahistoric entity.[5]

Ignacio and his family, staunch supporters of the Carlist cause, live immersed in a primordial kind of world where tradition and community ideology are transmitted from father to son. Unamuno described this type of biological continuity as a "lazo espiritual entre las generaciones de la aldea; . . . habíanse sucedido, cual sobre permanente fondo, los lentos procesos de la vida interior de los abuelos de los abuelos, y se sucederían los de los nietos de los nietos" (2:273; "spiritual link between all the generations of his village; against the eternal background of its vision of calm, the slow processes of the inner lives of the grandparents of grandparents had unfolded, just as would happen with the grandsons of grandsons" [K-N, 1:334]). *Sedimento,* a word Unamuno first introduced to describe *intrahistoria* in *ETC,* reappears in *Paz en la guerra.* The popular folktales Ignacio enjoys reading "eran el sedimento poético de los siglos, que . . . viven . . . en la fantasía, siempre verde, del pueblo" (2:107; "were the poetic sediment of the centuries . . . they now lived on . . . in the evergreen fantasy of the populace" [K-N, 1:32]). The organic nature that Unamuno associated with intrahistory in the five sociological essays of *ETC* is again used in *PG* to portray the Carlist movement as "todo aquel movimiento popular, surgido del seno del pueblo, de la masa amorfa . . . de su fondo protoplasmático" (2:167; "that whole popu-

lar movement surging out of the depths of the people, out of the form-
less and protoplasmic mass from which nations are made" [K-N,
1:142]). The entire Basque people are characterized by a collectively
childlike mentality in which the individual ego is subordinate to the
tribe, the family, and a group plurality. As in Jung's collective unconscious, Unamuno's *intrahistoria* has its roots in the instincts and inherited manners of apperception. Describing Carlist ideology, Unamuno observed:

> Tirábanles con fuerza los prístinos instintos de errante vida predatoria,
> instintos que resurgían potentes en ellos desde el indestructible poso del
> alma en que llevaban el alma de las almas de sus más remotos abuelos.
> (2:168)

> (They were impelled by the primitive instincts of the wandering preda-
> tory life, instincts which welled up in them from the immutable source of
> inner being where dwells the soul of the souls of the remotest ancestors.
> [K-N, 1:144-45])

The sense of distance from the present, and almost biological contact with the past that dominates Unamuno's *San Manuel Bueno,
mártir,* is already present in *Paz en la guerra.* The excruciatingly slow
pace of the Carlist *marchas y contramarchas* during which nothing is
ever gained, as well as the mists, mountains, and greenness of the
landscape, remove the Carlists from any sense of contact with daily
reality. Ignacio's first conception of war is a romanticized vision of
the "siete años épicos" of his father's generation. Indeed, the war
fantasies in which Ignacio likes to immerse himself are peopled by
archetypal figures into whose midst Unamuno often inserts a contemporary Carlist hero, thus achieving a surprisingly humorous effect through serendipitous juxtaposition:

> . . . y en la misma nube confusa . . . los de Carlomagno acuchillando con
> sus doce pares, turbantes, cotas y mallas de acero; el gigantazo Fiera-
> brás, torre de huesos; Oliveros de Castilla y Artús de Algarbe, el Cid Ruy
> Díaz . . . y Cabrera con su flotante capa blanca. Todo esto en confuso
> pelotón, sin él darse de ello cuenta clara, llenándole el alma del rumor
> silencioso de un mundo en que viviera antes de haber nacido . . . (2:162)

> (. . . and a series of confused images, all in a tangle, a misty cloud of
> evocations, of Charlemagne with his twelve peers cleaving their way
> through turbanned coats of mail; the giant Fierabrás, a tower of bones;
> Oliveros of Castile and Arthur of Algarve, the Cid . . . and Cabrera with
> his wildly flapping white cape. All the images crowded upon each other
> in confusion, without his being clearly aware of it all, and his soul filled

with a silent sound which evoked a world in which he had lived before he was born . . . [K-N, 1:133])

The archaic nature of Carlism ultimately proves to be its demise: reliance on the instincts, guidance from the dated experience of aged generals, and a shared conservative ideology are not sufficient military hardware with which to win a war. Flowing beneath the history being made in Madrid, the Carlist insurgence is an intrahistoric current that no one seems to take seriously. Even the Carlist leadership consistently takes a nonchalant attitude toward the administration of its interests. As in the work of his literary favorite, Cervantes, Unamuno seems to indicate in this "political" novel that the modern world cannot function coherently when its foundations are structured along archaic lines. The Carlist army is described as a "banda," a "hueste medieval," a "tragicomedia"; its leaders as an "hombre de otros tiempos," and "el pobre viejo de Oriamendi."[6]

Similar to Jung's association of the collective unconscious with tradition, nature, and the primordial aspect of life, Unamuno identifies *intrahistoria* with the stable qualities of the unconscious and the feminine.[7] In *Paz en la guerra* the Great Mother is represented by the communal nature of Carlism and the maternal qualities associated with Catholicism, intrahistory, and tradition. In Jungian psychology the Great Mother personifies the unconscious and is first represented to the male ego by his own mother (5:330). The adolescent male generally begins to emerge from an undifferentiated, symbiotic identification with his mother through a recognition of the "other" and of sexual polarity.[8] Transference of the anima archetype from the mother to a nonrelated female usually occurs when the male falls in love with his "first girl." Love acts as the primary agent of differentiation in that it forces both male and female to recognize their individuality, and each sex to affirm the characteristics of the other.[9] The initial move toward independence from the mother is completed when the anima archetype is extricated from dominance by the mother-imago.

As Ignacio matures from youth to manhood, we observe in him the initial process of ego coalescence. As an adolescent and youth he demonstrates an infantile stage of ego development, described in psychology as undifferentiated containment in the mother's womb.[10] Ignacio first becomes aware of sexual otherness during instruction for the First Communion, projecting the anima archetype upon his neighbor Rafaela: "Ignacio se quedaba mirando, sin saber, por qué, a Rafaela, la hermana de Juanito, que tiraba de sus vestidos para cubrirse bien las canillas" (2:103; "Ignacio, without knowing why, gazed long on Rafaela, Juanito's sister, who kept tugging at her skirt, to cover her shins" [K-N, 1:26]).[11] As Ignacio enters puberty and youth, he no longer perceives Rafaela as the "girl-next-door," but as a young woman who causes him to blush and to feel the typical confusions of adolescence. When Ignacio goes off to war, he projects himself into a fantasy life with his young neighbor: there are scenes of domestic bliss, and of Rafaela greeting him during an imaginary, triumphal entry into Bilbao. What is interesting about this "relationship" is that from its inception it exists only in Ignacio's imagination. In reality Rafaela never reciprocates his attentions, and finally marries Enrique, "el gallito de la calle" (the bantam cock of the street).[12] Sexuality, in fact, never enters into the anima Ignacio projects onto Rafaela, a pattern that will be followed by Ignacio's fictional successors, Apolodoro Carrascal (*AP*) and Augusto Pérez (*N*), who keep sexuality quite apart from their love interests.

Like Apolodoro and Augusto, Ignacio proceeds from an awareness of a specific female to a fascination with women in general. This leads to repeated visits to brothels, being sent off to war to "curb his appetites," and to his subsequent liaison with a "rubia de los ojos bovinos" (blonde with bovine eyes), who becomes the recipient of Ignacio's purely sexual projections. What is notable about this woman is her anonymity: she has no name, only her cowlike eyes and an earthy sensuality. This "moza de los ojos bovinos" also sets the precedent for Unamuno's fascination with womens' eyes as symbols of peace and refuge for the agonic hero. Ignacio is drawn to "¡aquellos ojazos de vaca, en que se reflejaba la calma de la montaña!" (2:145; those cowlike eyes that reflect the peace of the mountainside).

Just as Unamuno establishes a dichotomous relationship between his two masculine characters, Rafaela and "la rubia" (the blonde) are two sundered halves of what, under normal circumstances, should have been portrayed as one woman. The wholeness of a female partner is determined by a male's ability to relate to her sexually as well as spiritually. In the case of Unamuno's protagonists, the ability to find and to accept both characteristics in a single female seems impossible. If we accept Jung's premise that what is expressed through fantasy may more than likely be endemic to the mind that generated it (5:310), then there is something to be said here about Unamuno's separation of sex and motherhood. In his fiction, as well as in his personal life, *maternidad virginal* (virginal maternity) is a favorite adjective, and the wife is habitually portrayed as an *esposa-madre* (wife-mother). It is especially suggestive that highly sexual women in

Unamuno's work are presented as negative variants of the feminine archetype: Helena of *Abel Sánchez*, Raquel of *Dos madres* (*Two Mothers*), and to the extent that she is unsympathetic to Ramiro's sexual and psychological needs, Tula of *La tía Tula* (*Aunt Tula*) are all women unconcerned with the development of male consciousness and individuality.

In addition to his discovery of women, Ignacio's self-awareness is reinforced by the invasion of history into his drowsy consciousness. Liberated of the consciousness-dulling *intrahistoria* in which he was born and raised, the soldier Ignacio quickly becomes disillusioned with the irrationality of Carlist war tactics. This awareness takes place at first on a purely instinctive level: "Y entonces comprendió oscuramente, en las honduras de su espíritu, sin conciencia clara de tal comprensión, la vacuidad de las ideas clasificables, lo hueco de la palabrería de toda propaganda" (2:159; "And then it struck him . . . even if only dimly in the depths of his spirit, all the emptiness of classified ideas, the hollowness behind the verbiage [of all propaganda]" [K-N, 1:127]). As Ignacio divests himself of his mythical veneration of the war, he is able to perceive its reality for what it is: "una riña de comadres," an "escapatoria de niños grandes"; and he observes the "encubierta farsa del asedio de Bilbao" (2:182–212). Male comradeship, and the historical consciousness acquired by Ignacio during the war, inevitably lead to an awareness of the self, and his newly strengthened ego confers upon him an identity apart from the collective norm. Ignacio perceives the differences in his companions' personalities, chooses friendships according to his needs, and develops new judgmental and discriminatory capabilities that enable him to think independently. Although his contacts now with the metaphysically inclined Pachico Zabalbide are sporadic, Ignacio no longer scoffs at his friend's ideas and, on a more primitive level, himself begins a similar ontological questioning.

Ignacio's final transformation occurs while he is on leave from the army due to illness. Illness and its attendant delirium are frequently symbolic of a hero's death and metaphorical voyage into darkness from which he is reborn, ready to assume the responsibilities of manhood. In his semiconscious state, Ignacio alternately imagines being attended by the "rubia de los ojos bovinos," by Rafaela, and finally by his mother, "que entrando . . . disipaba los ensueños vagos, acabando de despertarle" (2:188; who, upon entering his room . . . dispelled his vague dreams, awakening him completely). Although he recovers from his sickness cleansed and strengthened, the contents of Ignacio's dreams indicate that the anima archetype of his unconscious is still held in check by the more dominant mother-imago. It is at this vital crossroad in Ignacio's development that Unamuno chooses to rid himself of his intrahistoric *yo ex-futuro* (ex-future self). Ignacio's is an interesting death: although *des-nacer* (to unbirth oneself) does not yet exist in Unamuno's lexicon, the expiring youth views his life in reverse, toward infancy, until finally *la madre tierra* (mother earth) receives his blood like a sponge. The actual moment of death is one in which time and eternity stand still, and for a moment merge together: "Junto a él resonaba el fragor del combate, mientras las olas del tiempo se rompían en la eternidad" (2:251; "Close by the roar of combat resounded, while the waves of time broke against eternity" [K-N, 1:294]). Death has had a long association with the idea of a return to the mother whose womb is described as both cradle and tomb, a shelter for the unborn, and a vessel that receives the dead.[13] Ignacio's death thus represents a return to Mother Earth, and to the collective unconscious of which she is a universal symbol.[14] At this juncture of the novel it becomes clear that Unamuno has made a rather significant choice: Pachico, firmly established in the masculine world of ratiocination, action, and conscious extraversion, survives, while *intrahistoria* expires by way of a bullet to the heart.[15]

Given the fact that Ignacio and Pachico are, to a great extent, rather accurate representations of two different facets of young Unamuno, the novelist's decision to identify with the historically inclined alter ego carries much psychological weight. In his study of the double in literature, Otto Rank notes that the murder of one's alter ego is essentially a suicide since the double represents a part of the protagonist's own psyche. The character who murders his alter ego does so in an attempt to "save himself for his self."[16] "Self-immolation" of this type occurs in many Unamuno novels, culminating in U. Jugo de la Raza's temptation to drown himself in the Seine, and in Manuel Bueno's attraction to the lake of Valverde for the same reason. Suicide, especially by drowning, is symbolic of the desire to reunite a divided ego by connecting the living self with the banished "other" reflected in a body of water. It is also worth noting that it is in *Cómo se hace una novela* and *San Manuel Bueno, mártir* that Unamuno questions with greatest intensity whether the politically committed, extraverted self he decided to "save for himself" in *Paz en la guerra* was actually the wisest choice he could have made. Although it is Pachico rather than Ignacio who is destined to survive, he does not live up to the expectations he represents. Following him is a long line of masculine characters who either commit suicide or die under very suspicious circumstances. This family tree is epitomized by the priest Manuel Bueno, who advocates anything but inciting his people to a consciousness of the world around them.

Of all Unamuno's masculine characters, Pachico Zabalbide is also the most overtly autobiographical. It is well known that Unamuno used his own experiences as a university student in Madrid—his loss of faith, and his return to it in the hope of recovering childhood innocence—as the model for this character.[17] But beyond the most obvious biographical coincidences, Unamuno scholarship has consistently avoided any discussion of the inferiority complexes that the adolescent Pachico and Unamuno appear to share. Pachico begins life as a bookish, highly sensitive young boy, who suffers from poor health and is given to inexplicable bouts of emotion. We are told his schoolmates thought him odd, and that he began puberty "enclenque y canijo, presa de una renovación interior . . . de una especial cobardía que le hacía replegarse en sí y desplegar su voluntad hacia dentro. . . . Entró en la virilidad pasando por un período de misticismo infantil y de voracidad intelectual. Sentía fuertes deseos de ser santo" (2:126; "weak and sickly, prey to a consuming inner turmoil and to a certain timidity which turned him in on himself. . . . He came to manhood after passing through a youthful stage of mysticism and intellectual voracity. He wanted badly to be a saint" [K-N, 1:67]).

The bookishness and insecurity one glimpses in Pachico are echoed by Unamuno's childhood memories in *Recuerdos de niñez y mocedad*. He remembers himself as a *devoralibros* (bookworm) and notes that "con el ardor de mi inteligencia crecía la debilidad de mi cuerpo" (8:136). He recalls his adolescence as "aquellos días en que me empañaba en llorar sin motivo" (8:143). Like the timid Pachico, Unamuno writes: "era yo de chico tan callado cuanto suelto de lengua soy ahora" (8:105). It is public knowledge that the young Unamuno, too, experienced a phase of mysticism, participated actively in a religious brotherhood, and even interpreted a scriptural passage to mean that he should seek the priesthood (8:143–46). The adolescent Unamuno whom we glimpse through Pachico, and in Unamuno's own memoirs, is one who seems to have been an introverted, physically slight, and lonely boy.[18]

Feelings of inferiority are often consonant with an introverted personality (Jung, 6:93). An inferiority complex may be triggered by any number of events occurring during the formative years of childhood: poverty, shame inflicted by teachers or schoolmates, or a sense of physiological inadequacy. Quite frequently an inferiority complex is unconsciously suppressed in favor of a more aggressive personality that seeks notoriety at all costs in a desperate attempt to affirm its sense of self.[19] By the time Pachico enters the university he is a young man who "hablaba mucho . . . molestando a muchos su conversación por fatigosa y pedantesca, pues quería llevar la batuta en ella, volviendo tercamente a su hilo cuando se lo cortaban" (2:128; "talked a great deal, and his conversation annoyed many people; it was pedantic and tiresome. He always tried to dominate discussions, and if he were cut off he would stubbornly return to his point" [K-N, 1:72]).[20]

A series of all-but-forgotten, anonymous letters written about professor Unamuno in the early 1900s contributes a great deal to our understanding of the similarity between Pachico and don Miguel. In a letter dated November 9, 1901, the author, "M", remarks: "me encontré con Unamuno predicando . . . los demás hacíamos papel de oyentes" (I came upon Unamuno, preaching . . . and those of us around him, playing the role of a captive audience). In another letter, dated May 14, 1902, the anonymous author notes, "Lo encuentro un poco pedante" (I find him a little bit pedantic).[21] Regarding his fictional character Pachico Zabalbide, Unamuno offered the following, similar commentary: "Éranle las conversaciones pretextos de monólogos. . . . Preocupábase mucho, por su parte, del concepto en que se le tuviera . . . con honda preocupación de cómo se reflejaba en las mentes ajenas" (2:129; "Any conversation was a pretext for a monologue. . . . For his part, he was much concerned with what other people thought of him, felt wounded when he was judged harshly, and strove to be liked and understood by everyone" [K-N, 1:72]). In reference to Unamuno, the anonymous "M" made a parallel observation: "Me gusta oírle hablar, por el entusiasmo con que se expresa, sobre todo cuando estamos solos, porque cuando hay más gente se pone jactancioso y hueco y lo echa a perder" (I like to hear him talk because of the enthusiasm with which he expresses himself, above all when we are alone, for when there are other people about, he sounds like a hollow braggart and loses it all). "M" also takes note of the "fin deliberado, según dice, que se ha propuesto haciéndose aparecer excéntrico y loco, que es el darse a conocer, el dar que hablar, el volver locos a los demás, para que así . . . poder hacerse oír y que no pase desapercibido" (the conscious intent, as he likes to say, of appearing eccentric and rash in order to draw attention to himself, to give people something to talk about, to drive others mad, thus ensuring that he will be seen and heard). These vignettes recorded by "M" not only leave us with an objective view of don Miguel before he became well-known, but also afford a rare glimpse of the incipient schism between Unamuno the private person, and Unamuno the notoriety-seeking *persona*.[22]

Several factors were involved in Unamuno's cultivated singularity. His desire to immortalize himself through a public image must be taken as much into account as his desire to achieve immortality through literary fame. Unamuno's psychological need for recognition was always coupled with a resentment directed toward a mediocre Spanish public that don Miguel felt did not appreciate his talent, and to which he referred as "este pueblo que ni sabe comprenderme, ni puede levantarme sobre sus cabezas" (9:838). Very early in his career Unamuno rebelled against all attempts to associate him with any form of sectarianism, preferring to maintain a fierce ideological independence in defiance of any intent to "classify" him or his ideology. This attitude resulted in a peculiarly Unamunian aesthetics of paradox, contradiction, and ill-perceived though it was, a sense of irresponsible spontaneity that confounded friends and enemies alike. Unamuno thought any type of group cohesiveness or "belonging" an impediment to his *yo* (ego), although he also recognized the egotistical motivation behind such an attitude: "Nunca he podido ser un sectario, siempre he combatido todo dogmatismo, alegando libertad, pero en realidad por soberbia, por no formar fila ni reconocer superior ni disciplinarme" (8:780; I have never believed in sectarianism and I have always fought against all forms of dogmatism, alleging freedom of choice, but in reality this is due to my pride; I do not want to fall into line or to recognize anyone's superiority, or even to control myself). The psychiatrist Manuel Cabaleiro Goas studied Goethe's Werther, Dostoyevsky's Mischkin, and Unamuno's Joaquín Monegro as exponents of their creators' hypertrophic egos. Goas maintains that in all three cases the inherent inferiority complexes of the authors in question are masked by their excessively valued egos, which permitted neither the self, nor its fictional representative, to accept the opinion or intellectual parity of others, unless, of course, the "other" was of such incontrovertible superiority that he could not be left unacknowledged. Such was the case, Goas suggests, of Unamuno's unqualified respect for Kierkegaard.[23]

The introvert who feels he must compensate for his inferiority tends to manufacture a *persona* meant to camouflage what he understands to be his "authentic" but inferior self. An undertaking of this sort disrupts the natural integration of light and dark sides of the personality so crucial to a successful process of individuation. José Luis Abellán suggests that Unamuno developed a neurosis precisely because of the ensuing tensions between his public *persona* and his autochthonous self.[24] Abellán's intuition is confirmed by Jung's clinical assessments of the neurotic personality: "Identifications with a social role are a fruitful source of neuroses," he concludes (7:194). Jung further determined that attempts to replace one's self with an artificial personality lead to discrepancy between one's conscious attitude and the trends of the unconscious. When repression into the unconscious occurs, "this life turns against us . . . as happens in neurosis" (Jung, 9.1:288). Only upon recognition and assimilation of the repressed contents of the unconscious can a dissociation between the private and the public selves be resolved (Jung, 6:20). Thus Pachico's consciously initiated metamorphosis is unquestionably a presage of the gargantuan egos and schizophrenic personalities that occur in Unamuno's mature work, most notably in the novels *Nada menos que todo un hombre* and *Cómo se hace una novela*. Pachico is, perhaps, also an anticipation of the familiar Promethean ego that Unamuno would create for himself and impose on those around him.

The ontological insecurity with which Pachico struggles throughout most of *Paz en la guerra* was likewise shared by Unamuno. For him the process began with an unconscious intuition of religious doubt, and proceeded to the rationalization of faith, and its subsequent loss. Like Unamuno, Pachico "empeñábase en racionalizar su fe"; he trembles at times "como un azogado y sin saber por qué" (2:126). While Pachico exalts his imagination "con la lectura de Chateaubriand y de los demás divagadores del catolicismo romántico" (2:126), Unamuno, too, remembered his own youth in similar fashion: "Y me dio una congoja que no sabía de dónde arrancaba y me puse a llorar sin saber por qué. Fue la primera vez que me ha sucedido esto, y fue el campo el que en silencio me susurró al corazón el misterio de la vida. Empezaba yo entonces a bañarme en un romanticismo de que luego diré" (8:163; I felt inexplicable distress and began to cry without knowing why. It was the first time that happened to me; perhaps because the silent countryside revealed the mystery of life to my heart. It was then that I began to immerse myself in the romanticism which I will relate at another time).

For both Pachico and Unamuno ontological vulnerability was compounded by the loss of faith. Pachico suffers from "el terrible misterio del tiempo. . . . Tener que pasar del ayer al mañana sin poder vivir a la vez en toda la serie del tiempo!," and he feels a "terror loco a la nada" (2:128; the terrible mystery of time. . . . To have to pass from yesterday to tomorrow without being able to live the entire series of time simultaneously!; a wild terror of nothingness).[25] In the *Diario íntimo*, dating from his years of religious crisis (1897–1902), Unamuno describes his own, parallel fear of death: "de aquí ese terror a la muerte. Llegué a persuadirme de que muerto yo se acababa el mundo" (8:791; hence this fear of death. I persuaded myself that once I was dead, the world would come to an end). Exacerbated by the loss of faith, ontological insecurity clearly served to reinforce an already existing need to impose the self in both Pachico and Unamuno.[26] So overwhelming did this need for self-determination become that Unamuno eventually sought a position equal, perhaps even superior, to the will of a possibly nonexistent God:

> Y el secreto de la vida humana . . . es el ansia de más vida, es el furioso e insaciable anhelo de ser todo lo demás sin dejar de ser nosotros mismos, de adueñarnos del universo . . . es, en una palabra, el apetito de divinidad, el hambre de Dios. (3:884)[27]

> (And the secret of human life . . . is the desire for more life, it is a tremendous and insatiable longing to be everything at once without relinquishing our own selves, of possessing the universe . . . it is, in a word, an appetite for divinity, a hunger for God.)

The elaborately structured, agonizing personality to which the crisis of 1897 gave birth may have additionally served Unamuno's purposes in diverting attention away from the latent inferiority complex that characterized his primary self. Not only did Unamuno attempt to hide his sense of inferiority from others, but by repressing his "inferior" self into the unconscious, he even attempted to remove the undesirable "other" from his own psyche.[28] The following entry from the *Diario*, although it relates specifically to Unamuno's religious "conversion," is also indicative of his general psychic condition during the years of acute crisis:

> La comedia de la vida. Obstinación en hundirse en el sueño y representar el papel sin ver la realidad. Y llega al punto de representar a solas, y seguir la comedia en la soledad, y ser cómico para sí mismo. (8:781–82)

> (The comedy of life. An obstinate desire to lose oneself in fantasy and to play a role without seeing the truth. And a man can reach the point of play-acting for his own benefit, going on with the comedy even while alone, becoming an actor before his own consciousness.)

As a child who suffered from physical weakness, physiological slightness, and a hypersensitivity usually associated with femininity, it is not surprising that Unamuno, like his hero Pachico, would have sought to promote, at least superficially, personal characteristics thought to confer masculinity: aggression, action, and the agony of perpetual suffering. This anticipates the legendary Unamuno who would write to Clarín: "¿Por qué he de creerme superior a los demás hasta en mi capacidad para la tribulación y la lucha? Estoy enfermo y enfermo de 'yoismo'" (Why do I believe myself superior to others even in my capacity for suffering and struggle? I am ill with "egoitis").[29] The apparent shell of strength and self-confidence Unamuno preferred to show the world seems to have been fabricated in order to hide a "timid child" with an "infantile need" of positive reinforcement from the outside, a man whose enormous ego disguised his fear and envy of others' achievement.[30]

The fundamental difference between Unamuno and his fictional protagonist is that Pachico accepts the sincerity of his religious conversion while questioning the very authenticity of the doubt which preceded it:

> ¿Qué eran aquellas pretendidas angustias de la crisis íntima, cuando se calmaban, como por ensalmo al ponerse él a comer, por ejemplo? Mera sugestión, ilusión pura, comedia de la duda.
>
> Por fin la paz interior se había hecho en él, y disueltos los contrarios ejércitos de sus ideas, vivían las de uno y otro en su conciencia, como hermanas. (2:265)
>
> (But what did those supposed crises of intimate anguish come to, after all, when they died down, as if by magic, when, to take one instance, he sat down to eat? He had been playing out a doubt, pure illusion, a matter of being too suggestible!
>
> At last he achieved inner peace. The contending armies of ideas melted away, and now his ideas lived together like brothers in his consciousness. [K-N, 1:321])

Unamuno concludes that, "Pachico ha sacado provecho de la guerra" (Pachico has benefited from the war). The Civil War, which Pachico tried to evade, is now appreciated for its metaphysical significance, and the battlefield becomes a symbol of the conflictive psyche. Contemplating his crisis retrospectively, Pachico describes the tension of his inner dualities in bellicose metaphor:

> . . . recorría en su conciencia los combates de ideas . . . disciplinadas en columnas de argumentos dialécticos; sometidas a la táctica formal de la

lógica . . . habían llenado las ideas su mente con batallas, marchas, contramarchas, encuentros, emboscadas y sorpresas. (2:265)[31]

(. . . he remembered . . . the battle of ideas which had raged in his mind. . . . His ideas had been clad in the uniforms of their concrete expression, and they stayed under military discipline—columns of dialectical arguments guided by reason and obedient to the formal tactics of logic. His mind brimmed with these ideas and their marches and counter-marches and skirmishes and surprise attacks. [K-N, 1:320–21])

With the resolution of his interior combat, Pachico finally encounters peace. The childhood devotions that he practices recall to him the "mundo neblinoso que vive en las oscuras entrañas de la inconciencia, en los hondos senos, adonde no llega el rumor del oleaje de las ideas, sus ondas superficiales" (2:266; "the misty world which lies in the deep and dark places of the unconscious, where the noise of rushing ideas, their superficial waves, can never reach" [K-N, 1:322]). The sea and wave metaphor that in *ETC* expressed Unamuno's idea of the duality between *historia* and *intrahistoria* makes its appearance in *Paz en la guerra* as the war and peace dichotomy. On the mountaintop Pachico decides that only "en el seno de la paz verdadera y honda es donde . . . se comprende y justifica la guerra. . . . No fuera de ésta, sino dentro de ella, en su seno mismo, hay que buscar la paz; paz en la guerra misma" (2:301; "only in the refuge of true and profound peace is war understood and justified. . . . [Peace must be sought] not outside war, but within it, in its very heart . . . peace in war itself" [K-N, 1:383]).

In this first novel Unamuno quotes on several occasions Jesus's words as recorded in Matthew 10:34: "Nuestro Señor Jesucristo no vino a meter en la tierra paz, sino espada y fuego, lo dijo El mismo; vino a poner disensión y guerra, y a dividir los de cada casa" (2:288, 255; "Our Lord Jesus Christ came not to bring peace, but a sword and fire. He said so Himself. He came to sow dissension and war and to divide every house against itself" [K-N, 1:361]). Unamuno uses this quotation to refer to the dual significance of war in his novel. On one level he suggests that peace cannot be properly valued without an experience of war, its opposite; on the figurative level, however, Unamuno uses war as a metaphor to describe the internal battle a man must wage before overcoming his fear of death and the temporal existence of the self. He seems to intuit that the requisite for psychic peace is found only in the reconciliation of time and eternity; of mortality and the will to immortality.

Jung was equally fond of quoting the same passage from Matthew (5:311). In the study of archetypes, Christ represented for Jung the archetype of the self, a whole in which opposites are successfully united (5:368; 6:460).[32] According to Jung, Christ's words as recorded by Matthew should be interpreted as referring to the inner struggle for individuation that Jesus bequeathed to mankind as a most valuable inheritance. In Jung's view, if man was to imitate Christ, he had to cut off his family associations, especially with the mother, as he struggled to differentiate himself from the collective unconscious that she represents (6:449). Much later in his career, Unamuno returned once again to Matthew (10:34–37), where his vision of individuation as separation from the collective coincides even more with that of Jung: "Para seguir a Cristo hay que dejar padre y madre, y hermanos, y esposa e hijos" (*AC*, 7:308, 341). The common ground, then, between Unamuno's and Jung's explanations of this passage from Matthew is that Christ's message is taken to mean that only by engaging in a struggle within the self can a man affirm his existence and avoid slipping into the complacency of unconsciousness. That Unamuno had a similar intuition along these lines is evident in a passage from "El Cristo de Velázquez" (The Christ of Velázquez), where Unamuno refers to the *guerra creadora* (creative warfare) Jesus had willed to men, and observes: "Sólo en tu guerra espiritual nos cabe / tomar la paz" (2:428; Only in your spiritual war can we find peace). Both Jung and Unamuno interpret the words of Christ as a warning that the peace of individuation can be purchased only at the price of an uncompromising battle within the self.

Individuation is essentially a dialogic process whereby a man engages in the struggle to overcome and to reconcile (but never to fuse) his internal dichotomies. It is from this dialectical tension that the psyche and the self derive their vitality.[33] *Paz en la guerra* is commonly accepted as the novel that most overtly reflects Hegel's influence in Unamuno's thought.[34] As was his custom, however, Unamuno reinterprets Hegel to accommodate his own world view. Despite his contention that "aprendí de mi maestro Hegel a buscar el fondo en que los contrarios se armonizan" (9:818), for Unamuno thesis and antithesis never culminate in synthesis. He preferred to leave his ideas, and his male protagonists, in a perpetually antithetical dynamics, since achieving any kind of synthesis would be tantamount to allowing oneself to be "classified," fixed in time and space. Definition as one thing or another meant, for Unamuno, a sure sentence of death: " 'No logro definirle a usted,' me dijo una vez un teólogo. Y le contesté: 'Afortunadamente para mí, pues si usted u otro lograra definirme, es que me habría muerto yo ya' " (8:502; A theologian once said to me: "I can't quite define you." And I answered: "Lucky for me, because if you, or anyone else, were to succeed in classifying me, it would be because I had already died.")

Although unsuccessful, Ignacio Iturriondo's struggle for a historical consciousness represents an initial attempt at individuation before he succumbs to Mother Earth. It remains to be determined whether Pachico's inner duality is favorably resolved. In the last scene of *Paz en la guerra*, Pachico's intrahistoric self experiences a pantheistic vision of the Godhead through a mystical union with Nature. The archetypal Great Mother is frequently represented by Mother Nature, and, according to Jung, a blending with her, "whether pantheistic or aesthetic, is a reblending with the mother, who was our first object, with whom we were truly and wholly one" (5:324, 327). In his fusion with Nature, Pachico experiences such alienation from reality that he feels completely absorbed by the environment:

> Despiértasele entonces la comunión entre el mundo que le rodea y el que encierra en su propio seno; llegan a la fusión ambos, el inmenso panorama y él, que libertado de la conciencia del lugar y del tiempo, lo contempla, se hacen uno y el mismo, . . . extinguido todo el deseo . . . goza de paz verdadera, de una como vida de la muerte. (2:300)

> ([In him a communion awakened between the outside and inside worlds: he was one with nature's panorama]. Free from the consciousness of time and space, he contemplates them in their fusion . . . all desire extinguished . . . he enjoys true peace, as if in the life of death. [K-N, 1:382])

The scene is reminiscent of Ignacio's *des-nacer* (unbirthing): Pachico is momentarily reduced to an infantile stage of unconscious existence in Mother Nature through whose womb he attains a mystical experience of God. There is another Pachico, however, one who descends the mountain vowing to "provocar en los demás el descontento, primer motor de todo progreso y de todo bien" (2:301; "arouse in [others] the discontent which is the prime mover of all progress and all good" [K-N, 1:383]). This appearance of pending intellectual and spiritual synthesis makes Pachico unique among Unamuno's heroes, for within him lies the secret of potential wholeness. The promise, however, remains unfulfilled, and a Pachico-like character never again surfaces in Unamuno's novels. Much like Unamuno himself, Pachico is left a double-edged sword, vacillating between idealizing

an unconscious, intrahistoric existence and praising the "lucha inacabable contra la inextinguible ignorancia humana" (2:300; unend-
ing struggle against inextinguishable human ignorance).[35]

Paz en la guerra is replete with allusions to man's archetypal urge
to wholeness. Nevertheless individuation, physical in the case of Ignacio, metaphysical in the case of Pachico, is not definitive. In both
instances, complete separation of the self from the collective unconscious is sacrificed to pantheism on the immense altar of the goddess
Mother Nature from whom man is born, and to whom he returns in
death. Of the two *yo ex-futuros* manifest in Pachico, the *despertador de
conciencias* (arouser of consciousnesses) will capitulate in the future
before the likes of Manuel Bueno, a matriarchal priest who promotes
the administration of religious "opium" in order to keep his flock in
a state of innocence.

Despite Unamuno's inability to carry through to its ultimate consequences the message of individuation contained in *Paz en la guerra*,
the archetypal urge to selfhood had surfaced in his work well before
the publication of his first novel. In the 1887 lecture "El espíritu de la
raza vasca," Unamuno seems to demonstrate an intuition of the masculine urge to individuation, as well as to have recognized the presence of a female anima in the male psyche: "como el hombre busca en
la mujer y en el hombre la mujer lo que les falta, formando el verdadero individuo humano que decía Michelet, vendrían unas razas a
completar a otras" (4:155).[36] As late as 1923, Unamuno still addressed the issue of a female presence in the male psyche: "Mucho
más fácil para un hombre representar a una mujer. Y es que el hombre lleva a la mujer dentro" (7:1490; It is much easier for a man to
play a woman, and it is because man bears woman within him). This
notion is comparable to Jung's postulating that "in the unconscious
of every man there is hidden a feminine personality, and in that of
every woman a masculine personality"—the anima and animus archetypes of paramount importance to analytical psychology (9.1:284).

Unamuno's intuition regarding the basic human need to integrate
the male and female elements of the personality never reached practical application. He never perceived his wife as anything but an
esposa-madre, while he himself consistently refused to stabilize his
personality, creating psychological counterparts in the *nivola* with its
cast of splintered male characters. Unamuno manifests symptoms of
the common schizophrenic complaint that the "self has been stolen,"
and Michelet's exclamation "¡Mi yo, que me arrancan mi yo!" is a
much-quoted litany throughout Unamuno's work.[37] However, a self

that cannot be readily defined is not easily stolen. This perhaps explains why Unamuno constantly undertook defenses such as contradiction, paradox, and the cry "¡Qué no me clasifiquen!" to guard against the danger of losing his self. In his fiction the same notion is best voiced by Fulgencio Entrambosmares's advice to Apolodoro (*AP*): "Que no te clasifiquen, haz como el zorro que con el jopo borra sus huellas; despístales" (2:361; Take care you're not classified, be like the fox who uses its tail to erase his tracks; lead people astray). Given by one fictional personage to another, this advice is one of the most frequently repeated in Unamuno's repertoire, undoubtedly because the author himself subscribed to its contents.

At the ends of their lives, Unamuno's *agonistas* (strugglers) are only able to find peace and security in the womb of the Great Mother. This idea is expressed particularly well in Unamuno's sonnet "Pasado y porvenir" (Past and Future), where the cloister of the earth's womb is spoken of as a great uroboros in which the past and future meld together:

> . . . el dulce abrullo
> de nuestra madre Tierra, ya cansada
> de parir hombres que a su seno oscuro
> en su entraña se funden y doliente
> breza a sus muertos mientras al no maduro
> fruto de su dolor rinde la frente.
> (6:400–401)

(. . . the sweet lowing of our Mother Earth, weary of giving birth to men who return to the murky depths of her breast, aching she cradles her dead, while to the still green fruit of her painful labor, she bows her head in submission.)

To reach this desired, paradisal state of existence, the union of mother and son becomes inevitable. In Unamuno's novels this is usually accomplished by a protagonist's retreat to the wife-mother's arms while she, in turn, calls him "hijo mío" (my child), an act symbolic of a regression of the libido (psychic energy) to an intrauterine, prenatal condition (Jung, 5:419–20).[38] Analytical psychology suggests that the ego which cannot differentiate itself from the mother is particularly vulnerable to self-surrender in uroboric incest of this type. In this light it becomes clear why, for Unamuno, the regression to childhood, to the act of "un-birthing" oneself, plays such a meaningful role. Here again Unamuno's poetry provides much supportive material:

¡Dormirme en el olvido del recuerdo,
en el recuerdo del olvido,
que en el claustro maternal me pierdo
y que en él desnazco perdido!

(6:633)

(To sleep in the oblivion of memory,
in the memory of oblivion,
I lose myself in the maternal cloister
and lost in its depths, I am unbirthed!)

Confirming Unamuno's poetic inference, analytical psychology posits that infancy represents both the preconscious and the postconscious stages of life. The preconscious state alludes to earliest childhood, while the postconscious essence foreshadows life after death (Jung, 9.1:178). That Unamuno thought along these lines is confirmed by the essay "Una entrevista con Augusto Pérez," in which the protagonist of *Niebla* returns from beyond the grave to inform Unamuno: "el mundo de ultratumba es el mismo que el de antes de la cuna" (8:362; the world beyond the grave is the same as the one which precedes the cradle). In other words, both *des-morir* (to undie) and *des-nacer* (to unbirth) amount to the same potential for future life, a rather consoling thought for someone as preoccupied by the finality of death as was don Miguel.

Unamuno's fascination with the New Testament story of Nicodemus, the Pharisee (John 3:2-3), also probably stems from his obsession with recovering the innocence of childhood.[39] According to Jung, also intrigued by the same biblical source, Jesus sends the Pharisee a confusing message that Nicodemus interprets literally rather than allegorically. Speaking of man's spiritual rebirth, Christ uses the female symbols of water and spirit to portray the individuation process. Nicodemus, however, understands the words of Jesus to mean a literal return to the mother's womb. Mobilized by an instinctive response to the incest prohibition, Nicodemus rebels against Jesus's "insinuation" and is unable to comprehend the symbolic value of the parable. For Jung, Nicodemus represents man's simultaneous desire for, and resistance to, uroboric incest (5:226-27, 133). The interpretation Unamuno offers of Nicodemus is similar to Jung's, and it is expressed quite succinctly in the little-known essay "Autoridad y poder, o el divino maestro y el fariseo" (November 21, 1931):

. . . el divino Maestro le dijo: "En verdad te digo que si alguien no naciese de nuevo no puede ver el reino de Dios." Y el fariseo le preguntó cómo puede renacer sin volver al seno materno, y Jesus respondió: "En verdad te digo que si no naciese uno de agua y de espíritu no puede entrar en el reino de Dios." (9:1221)

(. . . the Divine Master said unto him: "Verily I say unto thee, if man is not born again, he cannot enter the kingdom of God." And the Pharisee asked Him how it was that man could be reborn without entering into his mother's womb. And Jesus responded: "Verily I say unto thee that if man is not born of water and spirit, he cannot enter the kingdom of God.")

Unamuno concludes the passage noting that "el pobre fariseo tardó en comprender lo de renacer de agua y de espíritu" (the poor Pharisee was long in understanding this matter of rebirth through water and spirit).

In Jung's view, the fundamental importance of the Christian Church is the support system it extends to man in helping him achieve a fully integrated self, and in teaching him to resist the temptation to live peacefully within the "realm of the mothers." There is an essential difference, however, in the way both Jung and Unamuno view the denouement of this biblical episode. While in analytical psychology only man's ability to overcome the mother guarantees him a full process of individuation, Unamuno seems to imply that Nicodemus accepts the literal significance of Jesus's words, perceiving that a return to the mother's womb is his only guarantee of eternal life. When the male capitulates to the attraction of the unconscious in this way, it is to a devouring mother who disallows him liberation of the anima archetype, thus preventing the resolution of his inner polarities and leading to personality fragmentation and neurosis. Jung noted that the fear of becoming conscious, that is, of individuation, is characteristic of neurotics, and that the "neurotic who cannot leave his mother, has good reason for doing so: ultimately it is the fear of death which holds him there" (5:27).[40] For Unamuno, the tragic sense of life consisted of the will to be, to exist, and, finally, not to cease to exist. Unable to reconcile his mortality and his disbelief in the resurrection, Unamuno looks to the Great Mother as a solution for his personal dilemma. Without exception, his male protagonists will follow the pattern established by Pachico Zabalbide, finding refuge in the unconscious, chthonic aspects of *intrahistoria* whose principle metaphors, the woman and the sea, anticipate the very same symbols Jung would employ to describe the collective unconscious.

Paz en la guerra is the first variation of the major themes, aesthetic expressions, and ideologies that will dominate all of Unamuno's creative endeavor. One factor, however, remains constant in his work, quietly flowing beneath the surface of every novel: this is Unamuno's personal myth, or metaphor, which implies that only an essentially romantic dissolution of the individual in the collectivity of the Mother guarantees a perpetually cyclical return to life.

3. *Niebla*
A Struggle for Individuation

Yo soy hijo de viuda. En mi casa no hubo hombre, y sobre todo no hubo matrimonio. Y no sabe usted todo lo que esto creo yo que significa.[1]

(I am the son of a widow. There was no man in my home, and, above all, there was no marriage. I don't believe you have any idea what significance that has).

Niebla (1914) brings to a close the first stage of Unamuno's development as a novelist. It is significant that Unamuno's third novel appeared when he was fifty years old, precisely the age when individuation in a male should normally have been brought to completion (Jung, 17:v). Although on a much more complex level than Unamuno's previous two novels, *Niebla* also describes the awakening of male personality to consciousness through the growth and insight acquired by the protagonist in response to his circumstantial experience. In all three novels, love is the catalyst that sets in motion a series of actions and reactions, all of which contribute to the self-knowledge and psychic formation of the young men involved. Perhaps the closest fictional equivalent to the kind of self-discovery implicit in the individuation process is the educative and formative building of a personality at the core of any *Bildungsroman*. In the hands of Unamuno, however, the familiar paradigm suffers a unique inversion, and the conclusion one comes to expect in a typical *Bildungsroman* assumes an idiosyncratic, often ironic dimension, normally foreign to works of this type.[2]

Unamuno's second and third novels present youthful protagonists as fledgling *agonistas* engaged in a struggle to consolidate their sense of self. Although *Amor y pedagogía* (1902), his second novel, is theatrical and often grotesque, at times resembling Valle-Inclán's *esper-*

61

pento in technique, it serves as a rudimentary introduction to the ontological problems of free will and self-determination that Unamuno would develop more extensively in *Vida de Don Quijote y Sancho* (1905), *Del sentimiento trágico de la vida* (1912), and, most completely, in *Niebla*. The latter work is distinguished from the others in that it is Unamuno's first *nivola*, or novel written in the viviparous style.[3] In "A lo que salga" (1904), Unamuno defined the viviparous mode of writing as one in which the author would put pen to paper and begin "por la primera línea, y, sin volver atrás ni rehacer ya lo hecho, lo [escribe] todo en definitiva hasta la última línea" (1:1196). Don Miguel notes that although until recently he practiced the oviparous style of writing, of late he determined to attempt the "procedimiento vivíparo, y me pongo a escribir . . . a lo que salga, aunque guiado, ¡claro está!, por una idea inicial, de la que habrán de irse desarrollando las sucesivas" (1:1197).

As early as "Notas sobre el determinismo en la novela" (1898), Unamuno took issue with the predetermination of characters' lives and actions in naturalist novels. He felt that "los actos de cada uno . . . dependen de un plan predeterminado en vez de resultarnos esa determinación de los actos mismos" (9:771). Unamuno also demonstrated a particular aversion to psychological determinism, which he felt excluded "lo irracional, factor importantísimo de la vida real" (9:771). But he also had to admit, however grudgingly that "es difícil que el público educado a gustar ficciones cuidadosamente trabajadas sobre documentos de la realidad, se avenga en adelante a la ficción desenfrenada" (9:773). Nevertheless, by 1914, Unamuno was prepared to challenge the reading public with a new form of novelistic typology. *Niebla*, indeed, seems to be a novel in which spontaneity rules over any kind of preordained internal organization. To borrow a turn of phrase from Antonio Machado, Augusto Pérez "se hace el camino al andar." Certainly his unexpected encounter with Eugenia, when he had actually resolved to follow the footsteps of the first dog that crossed his path, is a humorous debunking of the determinism prevalent in the naturalist canon.

In actuality, the spontaneity of *viviparismo* is open to discussion. *Niebla* is very much the product of an author secure in his technical abilities and aesthetic vision. Its tightly knit structure and careful development belie Unamuno's theory that the *nivola* is written "casi a vuela pluma . . . casi sin idea previa" (8:206). The theory of the *nivola* seems to have been gestating in Unamuno's mind long before Víctor Goti articulated it in *Niebla* (2:615–16). In his exposition of the new genre's typology, Víctor "borrows" rather liberally from Unamuno's essays "De vuelta," "Escritor ovíparo," and "A lo que salga," written some ten years previously. Worth noting is the similarity between Víctor's discussion of his wife's taste for an abundance of dialogue in a novel and Unamuno's description, in "A lo que salga," of a young lady's predilection for the same:

> Sí, cuando en una [novela] que se lee se encuentra con largas descripciones, sermones o relatos, los salta diciendo: "¡Paja!, ¡paja!, ¡paja!." Para ella sólo el diálogo no es paja. (*Niebla*, 2:615)

> ¡Paja! . . . , ¡paja!," decía una señorita que conocí yo algo y que gustaba mucho de leer novelas. Cuando en éstas venían páginas sin los guiones y los regloncillos cortos de los diálogos, las saltaba y se iba a los diálogos. ("A lo que salga," 1:1200)

> (That's true. Whenever she reads a novel full of endless description, tirades, or anecdotes, she shouts: "Padding! Padding! Nothing but padding!" The only part that isn't padding is dialogue. [K-N, 6:129])

> (A young lady friend of mine who liked to read novels used to say, "Padding! Padding!," when she came across pages in a novel without the characteristic dashes and quotation marks of dialogue. She would skip all these, and go on to the next dialogue. [K-N, 1:1200])

In the same discussion in which Víctor reveals to Augusto that he plans to write a novel, Augusto disagrees with his friend's observation that although his characters will seem to be autonomous, they are, in fact, only puppets that he manipulates at will:

> Sí, que empezarás creyendo que los llevas tú, de tu mano, y es fácil que acabes convenciéndote de que son ellos que te llevan. Es muy frecuente que un autor acabe por ser juguete de sus ficciones. (2:616)

> (Well, you start by thinking you're leading the characters around with your own hand, when you suddenly discover that you're being led around by them instead. Often enough, it's the author who becomes the toy of his own creations. [K-N, 6:130])

This conversation between Víctor and Augusto serves to prepare the ground for the confrontation between Augusto and Unamuno at the end of the novel, flagrantly contradicting the ostensible spontaneity of this episode, which was clearly planned well in advance of its occurrence.[4] The great paradox of "Víctor's" theory concerning the viviparous, or anti-determinist novel, lies in the fact that while Unamuno had intended to create a novel challenging the constraints of naturalism, he was, in reality, writing a book that did, indeed, have a *plan previo* (predetermined plan). Although *Niebla* originates within the premise of *desenfreno* (unruliness), it gradually runs counter to the aesthetic of "ponerse uno a escribir una cosa sin saber adónde ha de ir a parar, descubriendo terreno según marcha, y cambiando de rumbo a medida que cambian las vistas" (1:1195; beginning to write something without having a clear idea of where it's going to lead, discovering new ground as one goes along, and changing direction as the landscape changes). Not only does Unamuno deny freedom of action to his "autonomous" characters, but he simultaneously impugns his own independence, all the while protesting the injustice of such an existential predicament.

Augusto Pérez is, without a doubt, an older, more psychologically integral version of his fictional predecessors. He somewhat resembles Apolodoro Carrascal (*AP*) in that he, too, is deprived of a psychologically acceptable father. Consequently both youths develop unusually strong attachments to their mothers, and later seek out women similar to mother either in appearance or in character. As *Niebla* unfolds, one is apprised of Sra. Pérez's recent death.[5] Elimination of the mother as a major influence in a young man's life should theoretically leave the door open for the self-discovery coincidental to severing ties with the mother-imago and to a rejection of ego containment in the "unconscious mist" of which she is a symbol.[6] Although the groundwork is laid for Augusto's emergence as an independent entity, his difficulty in developing a personality goes beyond his attachment to Doña Soledad, to the untimely death of his father. The adult Augusto evokes a childhood memory of a rather vivid scene of what seems to have been his father's death from a tubercular hemorrhage. Many years later, what remains of the father is a "sombra mítica que se le perdía en lo más lejano" (2:571; a mythical shadow lost in the distance). The father's shadow, however, looms much larger over Augusto than he consciously realizes. Sra. Pérez constantly remembers the dead husband/father to Augusto as a hero, a "sombra mítica" indeed. Fathers of flesh and blood are difficult enough for an adolescent male to cope with, but a dead one whose virtues are extolled while the faults are most probably left ignored, creates a much greater psychological handicap and sense of inadequacy in the child.

What has left an indelible impression on Augusto is the "aquel ¡hijo! de su madre, que desgarró la casa; aquel ¡hijo! que no se sabía si dirigido al padre moribundo o a él, a Augusto, empedernido de incomprensión ante el misterio de la muerte" (2:571; "'My child!', a cry torn from his mother and rending the house, a cry which was directed indeterminately either at the dying [father] or at the child—it was impossible to tell. Augusto . . . had been petrified into incomprehension before the mystery of death" [K-N, 6:51]). The child's confusion is justified. To whom is the "¡hijo!" addressed: to the dying father, or to the soon-to-be orphaned son? And, if father was also the mother's son, does that now mean Augusto has the right to usurp the dead father and to become his mother's new "son/husband"; that is, can he exercise a father's prerogative and engender himself in mother? Augusto's psychological confusion is further complicated since he is never fully emancipated of his father's presence. Upon making Eugenia's acquaintance, Augusto notes the emptiness of his home, offering the comment that it is really nothing but a *cenicero* (ashtray). The ashtray is again brought up in relation to the father: "Allí estaba siempre el cenicero con la ceniza del último puro que apuró su padre. Y allí en la pared, el retrato de ambos, del padre y de la madre . . . hecho el día mismo en que se casaron" (2:572; They had kept an ashtray with the ashes of father's last cigar. And on the wall, a photograph of both father and mother . . . taken on their wedding day). Augusto's home is never entirely free of his father's physical presence, who observes, and threatens, his young rival from the photograph on the wall. The metonymic cigar, the ashtray, and the portrait taken on father's wedding day all reinforce his "derechos de señor" (seignorial rights) over mother, while also thwarting his son's desire to possess her. Under these circumstances it is no wonder that Augusto would harbor ambivalent feelings about his relationship to Sra. Pérez, who throughout her life apparently did not discourage the formation of a symbiotic bond between herself and her son. This ambivalence, as shall be discussed later, is carried forward by Augusto into his relationship with other women.

From a psychological point of view, a male child's yearning to replace his father makes good common sense. Post-Freudian psychology refers to the "Oedipal project" as one in which the male child renounces passive susceptibility to obliteration and resorts to conquering death through incestuous union with his mother, thus assuring himself immortality by becoming the creator and sustainer of his own life.[7] In a larger, more mythological context, the "Oedipal project" is fundamentally a sophisticated playing out of the primitive belief, prevalent in matriarchal fertility cults, that a young god's death in autumn signified his return to Mother Earth. Through an incestuous union with Her, the young god begot himself, thereby ensuring his own resurrection in the spring. Unamuno's interest in Wordsworth's "Ode: Intimations of Immortality," whose epigraph begins "The Child is father of the Man," perhaps stems from a similar interest on Unamuno's part in seeking assurances of personal immortality through self-creation, a theme he pursued at great length in all his creative work.[8] Perhaps it is also an unconscious response to the incest taboo that led Unamuno to create fictional wives in whom maternal qualities are dominant, and then to transform these wife-mothers into virgin-mothers, thereby avoiding the implication of a consummated relationship between mother and son.[9]

Unamuno's personal history is particularly relevant to any discussion of the psychological subtext in *Niebla*. Don Miguel lost his father before he reached his sixth birthday and, like Augusto Pérez, remembered him only from the portraits that hung on the walls of his mother's home.[10] According to Emilio Salcedo, Unamuno grew up "sometido a un régimen afectivo y familiar de orden matriarcal . . . [en que] la influencia de la madre es decisiva."[11] So strong was the maternal influence in Unamuno's life, he once confessed to Clarín, that concern for his mother's opinion played an important role in deterring him from the publication of material that she might have found objectionable.[12] Luis Granjel suggests that for a man in whose life the mother plays a dominant role, the love of all women will become maternal in nature.[13] This, too, can be documented in Unamuno's life through biographical as well as literary evidence. Unamuno's adolescent attachment to Concepción Lizárraga, who later became his wife, signals an early transferral of the mother-imago to what, under normal conditions, should have evolved to an independent anima archetype. Concha, however, did not replace his mother; rather she became a mother substitute and eventually the model for the *esposa-madre* of Unamuno's fiction.[14] Recalling the first months of his marriage, Unamuno wrote, "allí soñé, en sus brazos, tanto o más que nupciales, maternales, mi nueva vida, una vida de celda matrimonial, nupcial y monástica a la vez" (8:271). Woman, for Unamuno, was synonymous with Mother, and the son's role that his male protagonists prefer to assume before their wife-mothers was clearly operative in the author's personal life as well. It is quite likely that the absence of strong masculine figures in don Miguel's work reflects the lack of paternal influence in his life at a moment when, as an adolescent, Unamuno was most in need of a masculine role model for the construction of his adult personality.

The relationship between Unamuno and his mother has not been studied extensively. Of all the fictional mothers in his work, Sra. Pérez's relationship to Augusto may perhaps be the most suggestive in terms of biographical parallels. Certainly she is the most dominant and instrumental in the formation of her son as an individual. Behind her apparent façade of birdlike delicacy, hides a shrewd and overpowering woman who "nurtures" her son to the point of robbing him of any sense of self. Her astute repetition of "tengo que vivir para ti, para ti, para ti solo" (I must live for your sake, for you, for you alone) places Augusto in a prison-cell of eternal gratitude and psychological dependence: the *niebla* (mist) of which he is not cognizant until after his mother's death.

After her husband passes away, the energies Sra. Pérez would normally have divided between husband and son are focused entirely upon Augusto. She reviews his lessons with him in the evening; in fact, her peculiar aversion to her son's physiology textbook may be a manifestation of Sra. Pérez's unconscious desire to delay recognition of sexual polarity between herself and Augusto for as long as possible. So entirely symbiotic does the relationship become, that the mother leaves on her dinner plate the same food Augusto chooses not to taste at the evening meal. Only after her death does Augusto realize just how much direction his mother had given to his life: "Pues el caso es que he estado aburriéndome sin saberlo . . . desde que murió mi santa madre" (2:568). In her overprotectiveness, Sra. Pérez is a classic, negative variant of the Great Mother archetype who possesses her son by cultivating his inability to exist apart from her mothering.[15] At the same time that she suggests Augusto find a suitable marriage partner, Sra. Pérez becomes melancholy when her son tests his wings. In addition to promoting psychological dependence, she now begins to foster a guilt complex in Augusto: "Yo para ti, yo para ti -solía decirle-, y tú ¡quién sabe para qué otra!" (2:572; "I exist for you, only for you," she would say, "and who knows what woman you exist for!"). Such a behavioral pattern is characteristic of archetypal, incestuous mother/son relationships illustrated by the mythological pairings of Cybele and Attis, Ishtar and Tammuz, Astarte and Adonis, in which the mother deprives her son not only of a father, but also of the company of other women.[16] Essentially what Sra. Pérez does is to replace her "husband/son" with a "son/husband," yet she does not permit Augusto to function completely as a replacement. He is thus not only condemned to an external fixation on his mother, but is equally stymied by his absent father through the watchful presence of the ubiquitous ashtray:

Cuando Augusto se hizo bachiller le tomó en brazos. . . . Después le
hizo sentarse sobre sus rodillas . . . y así le tuvo, en silencio, mirando al
cenicero de su difunto. (2:572)

(When Augusto graduated from high school, his mother embraced
him. . . . Afterward she made him sit on her lap . . . and held him there,
in silence, while she gazed off, engrossed in the memories evoked by her
dead husband's ashtray.)

Before a youth feels himself strong enough to provoke a confrontation between himself and mother—that is, to wage a battle of deliverance from her—he lives submerged in a state of undifferentiated
identity within the uroboric circle (Jung, 6:449–50). Had Sra. Pérez
not passed away so opportunely, Augusto might never have reached
this second phase of masculine development. But, once she is gone,
Augusto typically discovers the world "when he comes out of the
mists of containment in the mother."[17] The first step in separating
from the collectivity of the uroboros, and in achieving personal wholeness, is a male's recognition of contrasexuality, symbolized by the
anima archetype.[18] Through an awareness of his anima, a man is able
to apprehend the general nature of women. This is exactly what
transpires when Augusto "meets" Eugenia. As his friend Víctor Goti
points out, Augusto always carried within himself a slumbering potential for relatedness to women, which Eugenia happens to awaken
and make concrete. From the awareness of a specific woman, observes
Víctor, Augusto proceeds to an awareness of women in general: "Has
pasado, pues, de lo abstracto a lo concreto y de lo concreto a lo ge-
nérico, de la mujer a una mujer y de una mujer a las mujeres" (2:588;
"You've gone, then, from the abstract to the concrete and from the
concrete to the generic, from woman to one woman and from one
woman to all women" [K-N, 6:81–82]).

Love, then, is the catalyst that clears away the mists of unconsciousness and offers Augusto a basis for existence. "¡Amo, ergo
sum!" he exults triumphantly. "Gracias al amor siento el alma de
bulto, la toco" (2:578; "Thanks to love I can feel my own soul take on
shape, respond to my touch" [K-N, 6:64]). This comic inversion of
the Cartesian principle for the basis of human cognition illustrates
rather nicely Jung's theory that first love is a necessary ingredient for
individuation and self-awareness. This kind of reaction was also true
in the case of Ignacio Iturriondo (PG) who, through the self-consciousness fostered by love, was able to develop a more critical view
of the Carlist War; the same holds true in the case of Apolodoro Ca-

rrascal (*AP*) and his recognition of his father as a pitiable caricature. In *Niebla*, love brings to Augusto Pérez an awareness of his opaque, mother-bound personality. Similar to Apolodoro's evaluation of love as "el interno ordenador del caos externo," love transforms Augusto from a "paseante de la vida" (wanderer through life) to a man with a goal in life: "Ya tengo una conquista que llevar a cabo" (I now have a conquest to carry out), he repeats over and over, almost as if to confirm his newly found sense of self (2:563, 564, 585).

Meeting the right woman can be, for a man of Augusto's upbringing, the only chance for salvation. Unfortunately, on the unconscious level, Augusto's perception of the anima archetype is so identified with a dominant mother-imago that he cannot "cut the Gordian knot."[19] Lamed by maternal solicitude, Augusto cannot bring himself to sacrifice his mother completely; rather he follows a neurotic temptation to replace her with an iron-willed, albeit younger, version of the original. Shortly after his first encounter with Eugenia, Augusto recognizes that a woman is precisely what he had been looking for, a godsend to fill the gap left by his mother, someone who would give his life a sense of order once again. "La vida es una nebulosa," observes Augusto. "Ahora surge de ella Eugenia. . . . Ah, caigo en la cuenta de que hace tiempo que la andaba buscando" (2:561; "Life is a nebula. And now suddenly Eugenia emerges from the mist. . . . Ah, now I see it all: I have been looking for her for a long time" [K-N, 6:34]). For Augusto, Eugenia is a "bendición de Dios" (blessing from God) since she gives his life the sense of direction that he lacks: "sé adónde voy y que tengo adónde ir" (2:562; I know where I'm going and that I have somewhere to go). Perceptive enough to acknowledge his lack of personality, Augusto has the misfortune to choose the wrong woman for all the right reasons: "¡Sí esta recia independencia de carácter, a mí que no lo tengo, es lo que más me entusiasma! ¡Sí es ésta, ésta y no otra la mujer que yo necesito!" (2:581–82; Yes, this healthy independence of character, which I don't have, is what I find most attractive! It is she, she and no other woman, that I need!).

For the purposes of a psychological analysis, it is crucial to remember that the anima archetype is a man's projection of his personal knowledge of the feminine as he has encountered it among the actual women of his past experience. The penchant Unamuno's heroes have for women who resemble their mothers has been duly noted as a fictional manifestation of the author's own mother-complex.[20] Unamuno, whose knowledge of women was based on his familiarity with, and acceptance of the matriarchal household, frequently creates weak male characters with an unusual dependence upon strong female counterparts. Augusto Pérez's choice falls on a woman whose very name suggests masculinity. He is disconcerted, although never quite realizing why, by Eugenia's surname: Domingo del Arco. The strong vowels of *domingo* allude to the Spanish verb *dominar* (to dominate), while *arco* is suggestive of a triumphal arch, imparting to Eugenia the qualities of a "machi-hembra . . . o madre fálica" (virile female or phallic mother).[21] Augusto's predecessor, Apolodoro Carrascal (*AP*), is reminded by his "demonio familiar" (guardian demon) of Clarita's resemblance to his mother. Clarita's eyes exert a particular magnetism, and Apolodoro likes to imagine he is curled up there in a fetal position (2:239). Eugenia presents a more subtle variation on the same theme. Her eyes mesmerize Augusto, and hopefully the "estrellas mellizas en la niebla" (twin stars in the mist) will guide him out of his psychological fog. Eugenia's resemblance to Sra. Pérez, however, is more characterological than physical: both women are equally strong, cunning, and manipulative females.

For the time being, however, Augusto enjoys the effects of his progressive transformation, not yet detecting in Eugenia any of the negative qualities of the Terrible Mother. He describes the incipient effects of love as a "lluvia bienhechora en que se deshace y concreta la niebla de la existencia" (2:578; "blessed rain which dissipates and condenses the mist of daily existence" [K-N, 6:64]). The fertilizing effect of water upon the earth has long been associated with the female.[22] In Augusto's case, love's "blessed rain" predisposes him to a positive reception of the feminine sex. He experiences a zest and energy he has never felt before, intuiting in Eugenia life-giving qualities: "Sentíase otro Augusto y como si aquella visita y la revelación en ella de la mujer fuerte . . . le hubiera arado las entrañas del alma. . . . Pisaba con más fuerza, respiraba con más libertad" (2:586; "Augusto felt like a different man. [His visit revealed] the valiant nature of the girl he pursued . . . he felt as if his spirit had been newly ploughed . . . his step was firmer, he breathed more freely" [K-N, 6:77]). Augusto manifests all the classic symptoms of *Bildung*, or the experience of self-formation implied in every individuation process. Believing himself free of subjugation to mother, he responds successfully to a potentially conflictive situation involving another male. The fact that Eugenia has a fiancé at first causes Augusto so much distress that his initial reaction is to call out to heaven for his mother's assistance (2:570-72). On the other hand, the existence of a hostile male makes Eugenia that much more inaccessible, and therefore increasingly desirable. Augusto is able to plan strategy for self-defense and conquest. It is only later that his insufficient preparation for experiments with women places him in a sadomasochistic relationship at the hands of the object of his affection.

The love triangle of *Niebla* is anticipated by the Federico-Clarita-Apolodoro threesome of *Amor y pedagogía*. However, in *Niebla*, the sadomasochism is much more overt: "¡Pégame Eugenia, pégame; insúltame, escúpeme, haz de mí lo que quieras!" (2:598; "Hit me Eugenia, hit me, insult me, spit on me, do whatever you like!") shouts Augusto when the lady chooses to interpret his buying her mortgage as an attempt to "buy her body." Paradoxically, experiences of sadistic psychological or physical pain confer an intensity of "self-feeling" on the one who receives the abuse, tending to displace what is perceived as personal emptiness or vagueness.[23] Augusto's attraction to Eugenia, although she showers him with cruelty and scorn, therefore actually contributes toward strengthening his existentially tenuous sense of self. Jung characterizes women such as Eugenia as those possessed of an overdeveloped Eros that arouses moral conflict in men, particularly in those whose life has been stifled by maternal solicitude (9.1:95). Women of this type represent the negative anima figure, known in literature as the femme fatale. Augusto seems to be rendered utterly helpless by Eugenia's magnetism, to the point that when he resolves to end their relationship, he cannot make the final break and remains absorbed in Eugenia's mysterious aura. Because Augusto's only previous relationship to a woman was the quasi-symbiotic existence he had led as an extension of his mother, he cannot relate to Eugenia on any but a submissive level, as an inferior son rather than an adult lover.

Psychological disaster is bound to occur when a male is unable to free his love object from identification with the mother-imago. This crippling dependency on the mother substitute impedes a man's self-affirmation, leaving him in a "nonexistent" state tantamount to castration and death. It is important to recognize that Augusto so much desires a mother substitute in his lover that he is unable to project any sexual desire upon her at all. Eugenia appeals to his imagination, he says, to his head, rather than to his heart (2:643), and when she finally accepts his proposal of marriage, Augusto manifests a resigned fatalism rather than elation: "Y tengo que casarme, no tengo más remedio que casarme . . . si no, jamás voy a salir del sueño!"

(2:657; "And I have to get married. There's no other way. Otherwise I'd never awake from this dream!" [K-N, 6:202]).

After Eugenia rejects the gift of her mortgage, Augusto instinctively takes refuge in the hospitable shelter of a church whose murky interior he describes as an "hogar de siglos" (centuries-old hearth). The Church, and other objects arousing feelings of awe or devotion—the sea, nature, and mountains—are all mother symbols whose underlying significance refers to the womb of the collective unconscious (Jung, 5:345; 10:35). "Mother Church" is generally associated with the Great and Good Mother; a refuge for humanity in times of distress, the Church extends to mankind a feeling of containment in the "whole" that cannot be duplicated in the harsh world outside the womb. It is highly significant, then, that Augusto retreats to a church whose dark, womblike interior elicits from him the observation of its ageless viability as "hearth." The symbolism of Church as Mother finds lengthy elaboration in Unamuno's 1906 poem "La catedral de Barcelona" (The Barcelona Cathedral), in which the cathedral is described in terms of all the symbols Jungian psychology relates to the uroboric qualities of the Great Mother:

Ven, mortal afligido, entra en mi pecho,
entra en mi pecho y bajaré hasta el tuyo;
modelarán tu corazón mis manos
—manos de sombra en luz, manos de madre—
Cuerpo soy de piedad, en mi regazo
duermen besos de amor, . . .

. . . .
Recuerda aquí su hogar al forastero,

. . . .
todos son uno en mí, la muchedumbre
en mi remanso es agua eterna y pura.

. . . .
Venid a mí, que todos en mí caben,
entre mis brazos todos sois hermanos,
tienda del cielo soy acá en la tierra,
del cielo, patria universal del hombre.

(6:195-97)[24]

(Come, afflicted mortal, come unto my breast,
enter my breast and I will descend to yours;
my hands, hands of shadow in light, a mother's hands,
will shape your heart.
I offer you compassion, in my lap

doze kisses of love . . .
. . . .
In me the wanderer recalls his hearth,
. . . .
all in me are one,
a haven of pure and eternal waters.
. . . .
Come unto to me, there is room for all,
in my arms all of you are brothers,
a heavenly refuge here on earth,
the universal homeland of all mankind.)

The connection in *Niebla* of Mother and Church is doubly significant because it is in the church that Augusto recalls his life with mother: "repasó su vida toda de hijo, cuando formaba parte de su madre y vivía a su amparo . . . . Luego recordó o resoñó el encuentro de Orfeo" (2:598; "he dreamt of his life with her, under her care and protection. . . . He next thought of his finding Orfeo" [K-N, 6:99]). In the church Augusto also comes upon his friend Avito Carrascal (*AP*), who reinforces the symbolic association of church, wife, and mother by revealing to Augusto that his own wife, Marina, adopted him as a son after their Apolodoro committed suicide. He advises Augusto to marry as quickly as possible if he wishes to have a mother once again (2:600).

Just such a notion must have been present subliminally in Augusto's unconscious all the while, but its articulation and confirmation by another male gives him much to ponder. Shortly thereafter, Víctor Goti echoes, although with a sarcastic intent, Avito Carrascal's advice. To Víctor's urging that he marry quickly, Augusto half-consciously responds: "Y ¡quién sabe! . . . acaso casándome volveré a tener madre" (2:604; "Yes, and who knows, [perhaps if I marry] I might find a mother for myself again, too" [K-N, 6:109]). The ensuing conversation between Víctor and Augusto revolves around the unexpected pregnancy of Víctor's wife. Here it is Augusto who encourages Víctor to approach his problem with a more positive attitude: "Acaso ahora, Víctor, empieces a tener en tu mujer una madre, una madre tuya" (2:604; "Perhaps now, Víctor, you will find that your wife is also a mother to you" [K-N, 6:109]). Once more we return to the possibility that engendering a child in a mother-substitute enables a man to re-create himself, that is, to become his own father. To Víctor's remark that a child will not bring any mother at all into his life, only a loss of sleep, Augusto counters with the enigmatic comment that rather than losing nights, his friend will stand to gain many more, again making an allusion to the immortality that children assure their parents.

While alive, Augusto's mother played the role of confidante to her son and at times functioned as his alter ego. She even anticipated that her death might leave Augusto without a trusted *lazarillo* (blindman's guide): "Lo que temo, hijo mío -solía decirle su madre-, es cuando te encuentres con la primera espina en el camino de tu vida" (2:572; "What I fear, my son," his mother used to say, "is the moment when you might encounter the first thorn on life's way"). The first, and only, thorn to scratch Augusto is Eugenia. Left alone, he is confident that his mother, who could solve complicated mathematical problems, would be able to find a solution to his emotional quandary. It is at this moment of sheer need for Sra. Pérez's sensible guidance that Augusto finds his puppy, Orfeo, who becomes "el confidente de sus soliloquios" (2:573). From this moment on Orfeo assumes the role of a living alter ego, always mentioned contiguously with his predecessor, Sra. Pérez.[25]

As a symbol, Orpheus has a multivalent significance. Son of Apollo and the muse Calliope, Orpheus was a gifted musician who sang and played the lyre, taming the beasts and guiding the Argonauts to safety by lulling the dragon who guarded the Golden Fleece to sleep.[26] For Jung, Orpheus represented the archetype of the "Wise Old Man," a symbol of intuition and a willingness to help the mythological hero in a hopeless or desperate situation (9.1:37, 212–22). By substituting for Sra. Pérez, Orfeo takes on her role of guide and mediator between Augusto and the rest of the world. The self is also frequently represented by a helpful animal, a symbol of the instinctual foundation of the psyche. The fact that Augusto's new acquaintance is a dog, man's most faithful companion, becomes that much more significant when he is baptized "Orfeo," since Orpheus was also a mythological figure who embodied the principles of devotion and piety.[27] Furthermore, a mythological dog, Cerberus, was the guardian of the underworld—that is, of the unconscious. Orfeo is thus a personification of Augusto's psyche, and the conversations that take place between them are, in fact, "monodialogues" between Augusto and his personal unconscious, represented theriomorphically by the dog. Orpheus, the mythological figure, was most likely modeled on a historical personage, a singer and prophet martyred by the Thracian maenads who, because Orpheus neglected their company, tore him to pieces.[28] The martyrdom suffered by the Orphean prototype, known as *sparagmos*,

the tearing apart of a sacrificial body, is paradigmatic of Christ's cru-
cifixion. The cannibalism surrounding this kind of destruction is relevant to Augusto's entrapment between the laundress Rosario and
Eugenia, both of whom use the man for their own ends, ultimately
pulling him to pieces: "Entre una y otra," muses Augusto, "me van a
volver loco de atar . . . ; yo ya no soy yo" (2:629; "Between the one
and the other they're going to drive me out of my mind . . . I'm no
longer myself. I've lost my I, my ego" [K-N, 6:152]).

Rosario and Eugenia attract Augusto with their eyes. Eugenia's
burning eyes fascinate Augusto so much that for a long while he is
unable to recall what she looks like; twice he does not recognize her
on the street (2:562, 566). In the mythology surrounding Isis, the
heavenly cow of the moon eye, the goddess received in her eye the
seed that begot Horus. The human eye physically resembles the female genitalia and in the Isis myth evidently functions as such (Jung,
5:268). Ignacio Iturriondo's sexual fascination in *Paz en la guerra*
with the "rubia de los ojos bovinos" (blonde with bovine eyes) has
been discussed in the preceding chapter. The hero of Unamuno's second novel, *Amor y pedagogía*, not only sleeps in a fetal position at
night, but likes to observe his reflection in Clarita's eyes "chiquitito,
patas arriba, acurrucadito en las redonditas niñas de sus ojos vir-
ginales" (reduced to a miniature, upside down, curled up in the
roundness of her virginal eyes). The male image reflected in a female
"pupila" represents the man who becomes a child once again by
entering the mother's womb through its symbolic equivalent, the
female eye. Understood in this context, it is easy to appreciate the
vital role Unamuno gives to womens' eyes as symbols of the womb to
which a man withdraws for self-renewal.[29] For Unamuno the eyes,
laps, and arms of the *esposa-madre*, as well as the depths of the sea
that he associates with her, are symbolic of the unconscious toward
which a male instinctively retreats for peace and regeneration.

Augusto begs Rosario to open her eyes wide so that he can better
see himself reflected there: "Abrelos. Así, así, cada vez más. Déjame
que me vea en ellos, tan chiquitito. . . . Sólo así llegaré a conocerme
. . . viéndome en ojos de mujer" (2:645–46; "Don't shut your eyes,
Rosario. . . . Open them. That's the way . . . more, more. Let me
see myself—so tiny—in them. . . . Only then will I get to know myself. . . . Seeing myself reflected in a woman's eyes" [K-N, 6:183]).
Augusto's intuition that he will only know himself through the reflection he sees in a woman's eyes is psychologically correct since the
eyes are also mirrors, objective reflections of the observer's psyche.

At one point earlier in the novel, Augusto casually mentions that one of the things that strikes greatest fear into him is to look at his own reflection in a mirror, "acaso por dudar de mi propia existencia e imaginarme viéndome como otro yo, que soy un sueño, un ente de ficción," a presage of the horrible truth he must face at the end of the novel (2:634; perhaps because I begin to doubt my own existence and imagine myself to be an "other," a dream character, a fictional being). Loss of one's reflection in the eyes of another is symbolic of a dismemberment of the self and a consequent loss of personal identity.[30] While Augusto is attracted to womens' eyes for their symbolic value as the mother's womb, his desire not to lose his reflection in Rosario's eyes marks a simultaneous fear of being engulfed by the all-embracing Feminine. A poem Augusto composes for Eugenia reveals the entire story of his unintegrated soul, separated from the materiality of his body, and the function Eugenia's eyes possess as symbols of unification:

> . . . yacía mi cuerpo solitario
> sin alma . . .
> Nacidos para arar juntos la vida
> no vivían; porque él era materia
> tan sólo y ella nada más que espíritu
> buscando completarse, ¡dulce Eugenia!
> Mas brotaron tus ojos como fuentes
> de viva luz encima de mi senda,
> y prendieron a mi alma y la trajeron
> del vago cielo a la dudosa tierra,
> metiéronla en mi cuerpo.
>
> (2:653)

> (. . . and my solitary body remained
> soulless . . .
> Though born to travail side by side,
> life did not materialize this way
> for he was matter pure and simple
> and she a spiritual creature through and through,
> constantly striving for completion: my sweet Eugenia!
> But from your sparkling fountains of eyes
> a brilliant light lit up my path,
> and took hold of my soul and carried it
> back from a hazy heaven to a dubious earth,
> planting it [firmly] in my body.
>
> [K-N, 6:195])

It is not long afterward that Eugenia cruelly deceives Augusto. Analytical psychology postulates that the actual process of individuation, "the conscious coming to terms with oneself," begins with a wound to the personality and the suffering that it entails.[31] The *escarnio*, the *burla* (affront, mockery), of which Augusto is a victim at the hands of Mauricio and Eugenia is just such a wound to the psyche, giving Augusto a final push into self-consciousness. He confesses to Víctor that the pain and humiliation he suffers have made him "give birth" to another self, and from the cocoon of the child there emerges a mature man: "¡Es que me ha hecho padre, Víctor! Con esto creo haber nacido de veras" ("I've become a father, Víctor! I feel as if I've been born for the first time"). To which Víctor replies: "Pero si te has hecho padre de ti mismo es que te has hecho hijo de ti mismo también" (2:662; "But if you've become your own father, then you've also become your own son" [K-N, 6:212]). Again Unamuno circles Wordsworth's proposal that "The child is father of the man," but he extends the idea further to suggest that in becoming his own father, a man is likewise capable of becoming his own son.

Not every self-transformation, however, can be termed a process of individuation. This was already proved to be the case when Ignacio Iturriondo and Apolodoro Carrascal were obliterated before the final changes of individuation took effect. The same situation is repeated in the case of Augusto Pérez who, disillusioned by his failed love affair, resolves to commit suicide. Self-immolation is an act of desperation, a seeking out of psychological regression to the unconscious through an artificially precipitated death.[32] The idea of death, especially by suicide, haunted Unamuno just as much in his personal life as it did the lives of his male characters, a great many of whom die by their own hand. In the context of *Niebla*, Augusto's "suicide" does not stand alone: Eugenia's father committed suicide (2:575), and Augusto comes upon the ingenious idea of discussing his resolution to die with Unamuno, whose articles on suicide had recently caught his attention.[33]

Although the transformative process of individuation sets in motion a series of changes in Augusto's personality, the abrupt end of his life is not unusual in men who find it impossible to resist the magnetism of the mother-imago. Given Unamuno's personal development and ontological insecurity, the tragic outcome of Augusto's life is inevitable. Erich Neumann observes that the first stage of individuation is marked by "strugglers," whose fear of the Great Mother is the first sign of their desire for emancipation.[34] Unamuno's choice of the term *agonista,* whose Greek etymology refers to struggle or anguish, is thus quite appropriate for all his male protagonists. Augusto Pérez rebels against his fictional "mother," Unamuno, when informed of his preordained death. For the first time since Eugenia's elopement, Augusto's appetite for life is renewed, and he puts up a valiant struggle against dissolution in the mist from which he had just begun to emerge: "Ahora que usted quiere matarme, quiero yo vivir, vivir, vivir" (2:669; Now that you wish to kill me, I want to live, to live, to live).

Unamuno's authorial interventions in *Niebla* present interesting psychological revelations. The final outcome of the novel implies that the thwarted processes of individuation experienced by Unamuno's *agonistas* reflect a similar truncation in the author's own psychological development. This is corroborated by the autobiographical nature of Unamuno's work, particularly by his admission that he wrote only about that which he knew best, himself: "Yo, como los demás que han vivido y viven de escribir -y escriben para vivir- no he dicho más que una sola cosa, me he dicho a mí" (8:426; Like all those who live to write—and write to live—I have talked about only one thing; I have talked about myself). *Niebla* thus represents the longest extant Unamunian *monodiálogo,* one in which Augusto Pérez functions as a shadow archetype, rejected not because of its typically negative associations, but simply because Augusto figures as a "positive shadow," or one that is feared because it represents the "unknown."[35] The archetype of individuation clearly tempts Unamuno at the same time that it inspires in him a terror of complete removal from the sphere of maternal influence. Unamuno therefore banishes the urge to individuation from consciousness by projecting the archetype out of himself onto Augusto, a fictional personage whose life is ultimately snuffed out when he proves to be excessively autonomous, perhaps even psychologically threatening.

Paul Olson suggested that a return to the mother's womb through death "implies the possibility of adding the mother to the chronological sequence of women in Augusto's life."[36] This is typical not only of Augusto but also of many Unamunian protagonists. Whether Augusto "commits suicide" or is killed by Unamuno, is not as important to a psychological analysis of *Niebla,* as is the fact that once again a masculine attempt at self-realization is routed by a debacle before the Great Mother who overwhelms the hero, and defeats him in his battle for deliverance from the undifferentiated mists of the female matrix. Orfeo has the final word on the significance of his master's death, concluding that Augusto returned to the "niebla en que él al fin se deshizo, a la niebla de que brotó y a que revertió" (2:681; "mist into which he was at last dissolved, the mist out of which he emerged and into which he disappeared" [K-N, 6:246]).

While at first glance the female archetype operative in Unamuno's fiction gives the impression of being a benevolent, nurturing mother, she quickly proves herself to be one whose stranglehold the male is incapable of breaking. In her engulfing and devouring characteristics, the feminine archetype dominant in Unamuno's psyche, as expressed by his literature, is the Terrible Mother whose magnetism the Male Child finds irresistible. A man whose psyche is dominated by a negative feminine archetype often exists as a mere projection, a dream of the mother, which she takes back to herself at will (Jung, 5:258). Thus Augusto, whose dreamlike state of being is commented upon frequently throughout *Niebla*, has never had a life apart from Unamuno, the "mother" who gave him birth and just as capriciously takes it away.

In his essay "Una entrevista con Augusto Pérez," published one year after *Niebla*, Unamuno reiterates that "no le había dejado suicidarse a Augusto Pérez, haciéndole en cambio que muriera por mi albedrío de autor" (8:364; I had not permitted Augusto to commit suicide, but killed him thanks to my authorial free will). By suppressing Augusto's rebellion, Unamuno assumes the adjudicative attributes not only of God but also of the Great Mother, "the source of the water of life as she is also man's only security against death" (Jung, 5:296). In challenging God, and by replacing His death-dealing and life-giving capabilities with those of the Mother, Unamuno implies that it is not God, after all, who assures one's immortality, but the cyclical aspect of female nature that guarantees a perpetual circle of birth, death, and rebirth. Unamuno's tendency to compare artistic creation to motherhood lends additional credibility to the idea that he always had a subliminal desire to take on a maternal role.[37] Augusto's last cry—"¡madre mía! . . . Eugenia . . . Rosario . . . Unamuno" (2:675)—is, in fact, a progression from biological mother to mother substitutes and finally to Unamuno, himself the creator of Augusto's life.

Structurally *Niebla* also consists of a series of duplications of relationships between fathers and sons, godlike and inferior entities. The lowest totem in this hierarchy is Orfeo, "porque su amo era para él como un dios" (2:679; because he regarded his master as a god). Orfeo is succeeded by Augusto and Víctor, together with their fathers and sons, while above, much like Valle-Inclán manipulating his puppet characters, is Unamuno, "el dios de estos dos pobres diablos nivolescos" (2:650; the god of these two wretched "nivolesque" devils). In turn, Unamuno himself is dependent upon his God to continuously dream him into existence. As Víctor Goti suspects, life is a projection of God's dreams, and if man wishes to continue to exist, he must humor God with sleep-inducing hymns and prayers (2:616).[38] Unamuno's last entry in his *Diario íntimo* is particularly evocative as it is both arrogant and desperate in its view of man's relationship to God:

> Yo, proyectado al infinito, y tú, que al infinito te proyectas, nos encontramos; nuestras vidas paralelas en el infinito se encuentran y mi yo infinito es tu yo, es el Yo colectivo, el Yo universo, el Universo personalizado, es Dios. Y yo, ¿no soy padre mío? ¿No soy mi hijo? (January 15, 1902; 8:880)

> (I, projected into infinity, and you, who toward infinity project yourself, we encounter each other; our parallel lives find each other and my infinite I is your I, it is the collective I, the universal I, it is the Universe personified, it is God. And I, am I not my own father? Am I not my own son?)

Unamuno's notion that free will was largely a matter of self-deception surfaced previously in the tragicomic novel *Amor y pedagogía,* where among the humbug of Fulgencio Entrambosmares's aphorisms, the reader first encounters Unamuno's suggestion that life is nothing more than a puppet show: "Representamos cada uno nuestro papel, nos tiran de los hilos cuando creemos obrar . . . el Apuntador nos guía; el gran Tramoyista maquina todo esto" (2:339; Each one of us plays his role, and when we believe we are acting of our own accord, someone else is really pulling at our strings . . . the Prompter guides us, the great Scene Shifter conjures all of this). The same insinuation is developed further in *Vida de Don Quijote y Sancho* where Unamuno discusses man's existential dilemma again in terms of God's dreamlike projections: "¡La vida es sueño! . . . ¿será que nos estás soñando? . . . Y si así fuese, ¿qué será del Universo todo, qué será de nosotros, qué será de mí cuando Tú, Dios de mi vida, despiertes? ¡Suéñanos Señor!" (3:251; "Life is dream! . . . May it perhaps be that you are dreaming us? . . . And if such is the case, what will become of the Universe, what will become of us, what will become of me, when you, God of my life, awaken? Dream us, Lord!" [K-N, 3:319]).

Prior to its appearance in *Niebla*, the issue as to whether it is man who creates God, or God who creates man, who then re-creates God, surfaced not only in *Del sentimiento trágico de la vida* (7:201), but as early as Unamuno's 1906 poem "Salmo I":

> ¿Tú, Señor, nos hiciste
> para que a Ti te hagamos
> o es que te hacemos
> para que Tú nos hagas?
> (6:218)

> (Is it, Lord, that You created us
> so that we may re-create You
> or is it that we create You
> so that You may re-create us?).

Unamuno finds consolation in suggesting that God is just as dependent on mankind as mankind is dependent upon Him. In *Niebla*, Unamuno projects his ontological insecurity onto his fictional alter ego, Augusto Pérez, and onto his relationship with Augusto, the same challenge he would have liked to pose to God. The debate that ensues between creator and creation in Salamanca is thus a wish-fulfilling dialogue between Unamuno and God: as Augusto demands emancipation from his maker, so Unamuno, too, demands freedom from God's will, all the while insisting, through his denial of autonomy to Augusto, on the fallacy of the concepts of free will and self-determination. [39]

The ultimate deception of *Niebla* is that having survived Eugenia's elopement with Mauricio, having resisted the temptation to commit suicide, and having emerged from psychological trauma prepared to resume a normal life, Augusto is told that he exists only as a fictional projection of Miguel de Unamuno's imagination. There is, however, another deception in the novel to which scant attention has been paid. *Niebla* constitutes a new literary typology: ". . . nivola! Así nadie tendrá derecho a decir que deroga las leyes de su género" (2:616; ". . . nivola! Then no one can say I'm violating the rules of the novel form" [K-N, 6:130]). By "reinventing" the novel, Unamuno thereby gains the artistic freedom that allows him to manipulate the customary reader/author relationship. At the same time that Unamuno uses the reader's willing suspension of disbelief to lull him into accepting Augusto's viability as a self-determining entity, he ends the "novel" by violating the very literary convention he had initially espoused. Unamuno not only robs Augusto of his human "reality," but he just as easily plays the reader for a fool for having accepted generic convention in the first place. Unamuno further deepens a sense of confusion in the reader when, through his *portavoz* (mouthpiece), Víctor Goti, he incites in us the same kind of ontological doubt experienced by Augusto. Unamuno undermines our feeling of security and ontological superiority by suggesting that the reader should also "dudar, siquiera fuese un fugitivo momento, de su propia realidad de bulto y se crea a su vez no más que un personaje nivolesco, como nosotros" (2:664; begin to doubt his own flesh-and-blood existence, if only for a fleeting moment, and come to believe that he, too, might be nothing more than a "nivolistic" character like ourselves). Once more a game of fiction springs from the pages of this novel and, in violation of all literary boundaries, assaults the reader's ontological complacency.

While Unamuno implies that immortality can be attained only through fame, and in his particular case, through his literature, he also suggests that the work of art is itself perishable. It is Augusto Pérez who threatens Unamuno with just this possibility:

> Pues bien mi señor creador don Miguel, también usted se morirá . . . y se volverá a la nada de que salió . . . ! ¡Dios dejará de soñarle! . . . Se morirán todos los que lean mi historia . . . sin quedar uno! . . . Se morirán todos. . . . Porque, usted, mi creador don Miguel, no es usted más que otro ente nivolesco, y entes nivolescos sus lectores. (2:670)

> (Very well, my lord creator, Don Miguel . . . you will die too! . . . And you'll return to the nothingness from which you came! God will cease to dream you! You will die, and so will all those who read my story . . . every single one, without a single exception! . . . Because you, my creator, my dear Don Miguel, are nothing more than just another "nivolistic" creature, and the same holds true for your readers. [K-N, 6:226])

This astute observation by Unamuno regarding the artist's psychological motivation to create has been amply discussed by Otto Rank in *Art and the Artist*. In Rank's view, an artist attempts to transform death into life through the creative act, but what he actually practices is self-deception. The finished work does not go on living: "It is dead, both as regards the material . . . and also spiritually and psychologically, in that it no longer has any significance for its creator, once he has produced it."[40] Unamuno would have agreed with Rank. In *Cómo se hace una novela*, his solution for superseding the "deadness" of a finished work of literature is to have it remain inconclusive:

Y ahora, ¿para qué acabar la novela de Jugo? . . . Lo acabado, lo perfecto es la muerte, y la vida no puede morirse. El lector que busque novelas acabadas no merece ser mi lector; él está ya acabado antes de haberme leído. (8:753)

(And now, why put an end to the novel of Jugo? . . . What comes to an end, is finished, is perfect, is death, and life cannot die. The reader in search of finished novels does not merit being my reader; he himself is finished before having read me. [K-N, 6:454])

Unamuno attempts to overcome the mortality of his supposedly immortal characters by attributing to them mythopoeic qualities: through a kind of eternal return, some of them continually reappear in his other work. Fulgencio Entrambosmares makes several appearances in the *Monodiálogos*, as does Augusto Pérez; Avito Carrascal resurfaces in *Niebla* only to contradict the implication Unamuno made earlier in *Amor y pedagogía*, that Avito's philosophy of life and pedagogy had not changed after Apolodoro's suicide.[41]

The denouement of *Niebla* is just as inconclusive as that of its sister novel *Amor y pedagogía* and, for that matter, also the novel of U. Jugo de la Raza. Because Unamuno never resolved the mystery of God's superiority to man, the actual cause of Augusto's death is deliberately left ambiguous. Liduvina, Víctor, and Domingo all maintain that Augusto committed suicide, while Unamuno insists on authorial intervention. However, in the 1917 essay "Vida, guerra, alma e ideas (Coloquio con Augusto Pérez)," Unamuno himself is in doubt as to how Augusto really perished. He refers to "aquel desgraciado Augusto Pérez, a quien maté o creí haber matado, o mejor dicho, a quien dejé morir o creí haberlo dejado muerto" (5:1090; that unfortunate Augusto Pérez, whom I killed, or believed to have killed, or better yet, whom I left for dead, or believed to have left for dead). This technique of negating beginning and ending, and of placing characters *in medias res*, makes *Niebla* one of the most forward-looking novels of its time, situating the *nivola* among what R. E. Batchelor calls "the modern novel."[42]

While *Niebla* is a culmination of Unamuno's first two novels, it also anticipates his future interest in Oliver Wendell Holmes's theory regarding the existential discrepancy among what a person believes himself to be, what he really is, how he is perceived by others, and—adds Unamuno—what that person would like to be. These ideas will form the core of a second cycle in Unamuno's work, but they were already present in the plans he was developing at a much earlier date. In a letter to Jiménez Ilundain (October 19, 1900), Unamuno remarked that he planned to title a second novel *Todo un hombre* (Every Inch a Man).[43] Tentatively the piece was to portray the world as a stage whose actors cared only for the impression they made on each other: "Cuando el joven héroe va a pegarse un tiro, solo piensa en lo que dirán, estudia largamente las cortas líneas que dejará escritas" (As the young hero is about to shoot himself, he can only think of what people will say, and carefully reviews the few lines he will scribble in farewell). This novel was eventually released in 1902 as *Amor y pedagogía*, but in 1916 Unamuno did publish *Nada menos que todo un hombre*, a short novella that returns to the issues he raised in his early correspondence with Jiménez Ilundain.

In the second half of his life, Unamuno devoted a great deal of energy to the study of the neurotic and splintered male personality. *Nada menos que todo un hombre* inaugurates this new approach to masculine characterization, with special emphasis on the psychological impasse that arises when a protagonist's ego and the *persona* he offers to his public are in mortal conflict. Both this short work and the ageneric *Cómo se hace una novela* explore the defense mechanisms to which a split personality will resort when threatened by warring personality fragments, each faction fighting for supremacy over its competitors.

4. *Nada menos que todo un hombre* and *Cómo se hace una novela*
The Man and the Mask

Nuestro buen amigo don Ramón del Valle-Inclán . . . ¿no fue él mismo, el actor más que autor?, vivió -esto es, se hizo- en escena. Su vida, más que sueño, fue farándula. Actor de sí mismo. (Unamuno, 3:1246)

(Our good friend don Ramón del Valle-Inclán . . . was he not more an actor than an author? He lived—that is, he created himself—in the public eye. More than a dream, his life was show business. He invented himself.)

Nada menos que todo un hombre (1916) initiates Unamuno's new approach to the male personality. In this second stage of his evolution as a novelist, Unamuno abandons his interest in masculine personality development and begins to explore the progressive dissociation of male ego as manifested by the fully mature, yet divided self. His curiosity regarding the splintered ego culminates in the intensely feverish explosion that constitutes *Cómo se hace una novela* (1924–1927). Studied in tandem with this "novel," *Nada menos que todo un hombre* informs the psychological motives operating behind Unamuno's ageneric, autobiographical essay. Approached in this fashion, the emotional content of *Cómo se hace una novela* proves to have been evolving over a period of many years, and acquires a richness of texture it does not normally display when studied in isolation.

The two works share not only a common psychological foundation, but a theoretical one as well. *Nada menos que todo un hombre* forms part of Unamuno's trilogy collected as *Tres novelas ejemplares y un prólogo* (Three Exemplary Novels and a Prologue, 1921). In his prologue to these three short novels, Unamuno observes that what he had intended to be prefatory material had gradually evolved from an essay to a "novel" in its own right: "Y este prólogo es, en cierto modo, otra novela; la novela de mis novelas. Y a la vez la explicación de mi novelería" (2:972; And, in some ways, this prologue is another novel; the novel of my novels, and at the same time, an explanation of my fiction). This prologue, together with Unamuno's subsequent "treatise" on how to write a novel, is essentially a [pre]text that gives don Miguel the opportunity to share with his reader an intimate view of his psychological state of being. In Unamuno's lexicon, *novela* thus acquires a meaning much more intrinsic to "autobiography" than to fiction, and when he queries, "¿Ves . . . por qué las llamo ejemplares a estas novelas?" (2:977; Now do you see why I call these novels exemplary?), Unamuno alerts the reader to the fact that these works are really metaphors, *exempla*, of his personal self.[1]

Like the heroes and heroines of his *Tres novelas ejemplares*, Unamuno, too, was a self-made man. Through his own will power, he gradually constructed a public persona that he felt best enabled him to function in the alien world beyond his intimate being. For Unamuno, wanting to be, or *querer ser*—the conscious exercise of the individual will—was preferable to simply being, or *ser*. Likewise, he considered the willing not to be—*querer no ser*—far superior to *no querer ser*, or a passive not wanting to be (2:971-77). In this way Unamuno began justifying to himself the superiority of the *persona* he came to believe was the only valid and real aspect of his personality.

As absorbed as he was by his multiplicity of selves, it is not surprising that Unamuno would be intrigued by Oliver Wendell Holmes's proposal that when two humans converse, there are actually six beings in attendance. In Unamuno's words: "el que uno es, el que se cree ser y el que le cree otro"—three selves for each interlocutor involved.[2] To Holmes's three interlocutors, Unamuno adds a fourth: "el que quisiera ser. Y que éste, el que uno quiere ser, es en él, en su seno, el creador, y es el real de verdad" (2:973; the person one would like to be. And it is he, the one whom you want to be, who is the creator, the truly real self). According to Unamuno's value system, the self that actively wills its existence is the most authentic, for it is also the one destined to survive in the external world. Furthermore, in his essay "Nuestro yo y el de los demás" (1917), Unamuno also observed that if a man were to be awarded recompense after death, ideally it should consist of God's permission for him to assume in the afterlife the self to which he always aspired during his earthly sojourn (5:1101; cf. 2:973).

Unlike Unamuno and Holmes, both of whom attach least importance to the person that one "is," Jung suggested that "for the purpose of individuation, or self-realization, it is essential for a man to distinguish between what he is and how he appears to oneself and to others" (7:195). In other words, if he wishes to attain authentic selfhood, a man must recognize the "three Johns" he embodies, and separate what he is in actuality, from what he believes himself to be, and from what he believes others believe him to be. Although Unamuno intuited this requisite for wholeness, he was never able to consolidate his personality, most probably fearing integration as a form of metaphysical compromise.[3]

The plurality of selves a man harbors in his psyche is determined by the extent to which his unconscious dissociates itself from consciousness.[4] In the split personality, cleavage occurs between the subject's outward compliance to what he fancies himself to be (or what others believe him to be), and an inner rebellion against having to maintain such compliance. Psychic duality frequently causes a subject to construct a *persona* meant to camouflage internal divisions and to undertake great efforts to sustain the façade that hides a fragmented self.[5] The neurosis that stems from such inner duality often manifests itself outwardly in a disharmony of the personality caused by what Abellán terms a "falta de integración de las distintas capas del sujeto" (a lack of cohesion among the various layers of the personality), or by what Jung called a "failed process of individuation."

The imposition of a manufactured self is always based upon a certain degree of self-deception. In *Nada menos que todo un hombre*, Alejandro Gómez appears to suffer from what Jung termed a "heroic consciousness": one whose Achilles' heel centers on the fact that "somewhere the strong man is weak and does not like to be reminded of his helplessness" (9.1:20–21, cf. 237). To a great extent all human beings, but especially those who are extremely insecure, construct a public personality as a protective shell to hide inner fragility. This is the *persona* "which in reality one is not, but which oneself as well as others think one is" (Jung, 9.1:123).[6] A review of the effect that a progressively dominant *persona* had on Unamuno's psyche is in order if we are to understand the vehemence with which he exploded in 1924–1925. Unamuno's *Diario íntimo* demonstrates with great clarity that his crisis of the 1920s was not an unexpected turn of events. In reference to his religious conversion of 1897, and his own comments regarding the effect this "spectacle" may have had on his friends and reading public, Unamuno wrote at this early date of having to "representar una comedia" or "hacer espectáculo" (8:781–82, 818, 844; put on a show or make a display of himself). Corroborating Jung's theory that a man sacrifices authenticity upon assuming a *persona* more in keeping with his own ambitions, Unamuno noted in his *Diario*:

> ¿Por qué he de matar mi alma, por qué he de ahogarla en sus aspiraciones para aparecer lógico y consecuente ante los demás? . . . Es terrible la esclavitud de la vanagloria. . . . Hay que vivir en la realidad de sí mismo y no en la apariencia que de nosotros se hacen los demás; en nuestro propio y no en el concepto ajeno. (8:816)[7]

> (Why do I insist on killing my soul, on stifling its aspirations in order to appear logical and consistent before others? . . . The slavery of vainglory is terrible. . . . We must live our own reality, and not conform to the image others create for us; we must live out our own destiny, and not the one others may impose upon us.)

In the 1906 essay "Sobre la consecuencia, la sinceridad," Unamuno begins to make a distinction between his "yo profundo, permanente . . . que llaman ahora muchos subliminal . . . y otro yo superficial . . . el supraliminal" (inner, permanent self . . . the one that many today call the subliminal self . . . and the other, superficial or supraliminal, self), finding in contemporary psychological theory an echo of his own ideas regarding the dialogic relations between interiority and exteriority that he first introduced in *En torno al casticismo*. One year later (1907), in an essay suggestively titled "Soliloquio," Unamuno again referred to the two disparate selves he observed in his own psyche: "Y basta, no hablemos más uno con otro, tu yo íntimo y el público. . . . ¿Son realmente dos?" (3:401; Enough! Let us not speak to each other any more, your intimate self and your public self. . . . Are they really two?), indicating that he may have suspected all along that his two personalities were not necessarily mutually exclusive or incompatible. The 1912 "Días de limpieza" is another important document in this regard, as in it Unamuno relates the etymology of the word *persona* to its original function in the classical theater. Its first meaning was that of a resonating mask worn by actors; later it referred directly to the character represented on the stage; for Unamuno it came to signify the "papel que hace uno en el mundo" (8:298; the role one plays in the world). The idea of masks and role-playing surfaced in Unamuno's work again in 1924, both in *Cómo se hace una novela* and in other essays written during his years of exile.[8]

In his role as one of Spain's leading intellectuals and president of its oldest and most prestigious university, Unamuno drew attention to himself by his continuous opposition to the nation's weak and ineffective monarch, Alfonso XIII, and subsequently also to the King's tacit approval of Primo de Rivera's military dictatorship. Unamuno's public denunciations and embarrassments of the government finally proved intolerable to the regime, and on February 20, 1924, ostensibly due to the neglect of his academic responsibilities, Unamuno received an order of deportation to the Canary Islands. After a relatively short stay in Fuerteventura, Unamuno was pardoned by the Spanish government but, out of principle, elected to ignore the "pardon" extended to him, and opted for self-imposed exile in France. In choosing to play the role of a *proscrito,* as he liked to say, Unamuno consciously made a commitment to become a national symbol, a decision not without its consequences, and one that Unamuno ultimately saw as a genuine sacrifice of his intimate spiritual needs. As his absence from home and country dragged on from months into years, Unamuno was forced to reexamine the effect his decision to remain outside Spain was having on his psyche:

> ¿No estaré acaso a punto de sacrificar mi yo íntimo, divino . . . al yo histórico. . . . ¿Por qué obstinarme en no volver a entrar en España? . . . Es que si no me hago mi leyenda me muero del todo. Y si me la hago, también. (8:745)

> (Am I not on the verge, perhaps, of sacrificing my most intimate, divine self . . . to my historic self. . . . Why do I insist so obstinately on not returning to Spain? . . . If I do not create a legend for myself, I will perish altogether. And if I do succeed, the end result is still the same.)

Having accepted the "exile's" role, Unamuno became intensely aware that he had adopted a mask in the construction of which his political supporters often had a greater share than he. Paradoxically, it was Unamuno's personal need to cultivate prestige in the eyes of others that led him to manufacture, and subsequently to maintain, a *persona* from which he could never fully divest himself in later years. Masks and role-playing always engaged Unamuno's curiosity. Of extreme importance to an appreciation of *Cómo se hace una novela* are the essays that comprise *Alrededor del estilo* (On Style). This collection was begun in Fuerteventura, completed in Paris, and published in Madrid's *El Imparcial* in 1924. In "Hombre, persona e individuo," Unamuno returns to his interest in the significance of the word *persona*:

> . . . significó primero la careta o máscara trágica o cómica que llevaba el actor antiguo cuando representaba lo que llamamos un papel . . . y por

fin, trasladando su acepción . . . al teatro mediato y artificial de la vida pública civil, vino a designar el papel que uno hace en la tragicomedia de la historia, el personaje que representa. (7:890)

(. . . it first referred to the tragic or comic masks worn by actors in antiquity when they played a role on stage . . . finally, changing its meaning . . . to the artificial theater of public or civil life, it came to refer to the role one plays in the tragicomedy of history, to the persona one represents in public life.)

Jung, too, formulated his concept of *persona* around the word's original etymology: "This mask . . . I have called the persona, which was the name for the masks worn by actors in antiquity" (6:465). As it did for Unamuno, *persona* in Jung's understanding refers to the façade one adopts when functioning in the external world. Unamuno not only associated *persona* (the actor) with a mask, but he went as far as to accuse Unamuno, the actor, of hypocrisy, or the dishonest representation of his public role.[9] The suspicion that he was practicing self-deception, or acting a role in conflict with his personal needs, caused Unamuno no small amount of anguish. He attempted to resolve this dilemma by accepting a synchronous relationship between exteriority and interiority, *historia* and *intrahistoria*:

> ¡Hipócrita! . . . sé que hipócrita significa actor. ¿Hipócrita? ¡No! Mi papel es mi verdad y debo vivir mi verdad que es mi vida.
> Ahora hago el papel de proscrito. . . .
> ¿Es que represento una comedia, hasta para los míos? ¡Pero no!, es que mi vida y mi verdad son mi papel! (8:746)

> (Hypocrite! . . . I know that hypocrite means actor. Hypocrite? No! My role is my truth, and I must live my truth, which is my life.
> I am now playing the exile's role. . . .
> Could I be putting on a show, even in front of my family? But, no! My truth and life are my role.)

Following this circuitous logic, Unamuno was able to justify the sacrifice of his intimate self by implying that the historical man is actually the genuine article since it is he who exposes his viscera to public scrutiny. This is the man whose insides become his outside, who lives against the backdrop, as Jung was to say, of his biography:

> Pero ¿un hombre histórico?, ¿un hombre de verdad? . . . Este lleva las entrañas en la cara. O dicho de otro modo, su entraña . . . es su extraña . . . lo de fuera; su forma es su fondo. Y de aquí por qué toda expresión de un hombre histórico verdadero es autobiográfica. (8:765)

(But what about a historical man? A real man? . . . He wears his inner-most feelings on his face. His entrails . . . become his extrails . . . his outsides, so to speak; his form becomes his content. Thus every statement made by an authentic, historical man, is autobiographical.)

In this way, history is finally transformed into the preferred, eternal *intrahistoria*. Thus, at the end of his career as a public figure, Unamuno found himself in the preposterous situation of having to admit that "lo que en uno de mis ensayos de *En torno al casticismo* llamé la intra-historia, es la historia misma, su entraña" ("Discurso leído al ser jubilado como catedrático," 9:444–53; what, in one of the essays of *ETC* I called intrahistory, is really the insides of history itself). The mature Unamuno now recognized intrahistory not as distinct from, and superior to history, but as an essential ingredient of its very marrow. In this manner, he was able to elevate public legend (history) to a status of equality with the secluded, intrahistoric self.

As Unamuno became an established public figure, the balance he initially sought to find between his multiple selves was gradually relinquished. His exclamation in the commentary to *Cómo se hace una novela*—"Y sí, hay que entrar para siempre -à jamais- en la histo-ria. ¡Para siempre!" (And yes, one must enter history forever—à ja-mais—forever!)—is a determination Unamuno had made much earlier in his life, most likely in the years preceding, or immediately follow-ing, 1897 (8:723). A speech delivered at the Atheneum of Seville in 1896 furnishes evidence that Unamuno, at this early date, was al-ready quite aware of the potential conflict between his public and private selves. This same text is an uncanny anticipation of his later theories relative to the mutually exploitative relationship between those who seek prestige and those who designate it. Because the essay is of such seminal importance, it is not remiss to quote from it at length:

> El mito es mil veces más verdadero que el personaje histórico, y no pocas, cuando se forma ya aquél en vida de éste, le guía, le domina, le dirije [*sic*]. ¡Cuántos y cuántos grandes hombres no llegan a ser meros instrumentos de la idea que de ellos se ha formado el pueblo a que sirven! Y así, creyendo dirijirlo [*sic*], son en realidad por él dirijidos [sic], meros órganos de su conciencia, indicadores de sus movimientos como el manó-metro de la presión de una máquina. (9:53).

(Myth is a thousand times more authentic than the historical personage. In fact, quite often, when the former arises during the lifetime of the latter, the myth comes to guide the historical man, direct him, even dominate him. Numbers of great men have become mere functionaries of an abstract idea the public may have of them. Thus, believing they guide their people, these men are, in reality, directed by the very people that they pretend to serve; mere instruments of the public conscience, registers of its fluctuations, they resemble a manometer that gauges the pressure of a machine.)

In this essay lies the seed of Unamuno's subsequent efforts to achieve the syncretism of intimate self and public image that culminates in *Cómo se hace una novela*, a work in which don Miguel finally attempts to impose his notion that the self one projects outwardly is no different from the private self contained within.

Unamuno's preoccupation with his "legend," as he called it, did not come to an end with its disgorging in the period 1924–1927 during which *Cómo se hace una novela* was drafted, translated into French, retranslated into Spanish with additions, and finally published in Buenos Aires. In the 1933 essay "Paz en la guerra," Unamuno continues his emphatic, yet paradoxical, assertion that a truly whole man is one that "se compone de muchas, de infinitas piezas," perhaps another attempt to interpret fragmentation in himself as a healthy, even necessary, ontological state. In 1934 Unamuno once again alludes to Oliver Wendell Holmes's conversation between the three Johns and three Thomases, but this time he refers not to John or Thomas specifically, but to the writer as he could be perceived by his public: "que hay el escritor . . . tal cual es, tal cual Dios le conoce; el que él mismo se cree ser y el que le cree —o le supone— su público. . . . ¿Cuáles los auténticos?" (7:1136; there is the author . . . such as he is, such as God knows him to be; then there is the person the author believes himself to be, and the person his public believes—or imagines—him to be. . . . Which one is authentic?). Noteworthy in this passage is Unamuno's interrogative "¿Cuáles los auténticos?," a clear implication that he was convinced more than one of his many selves could be legitimate.

Although Unamuno's self-imposed exile in Paris and Hendaye precipitated an acute psychological crisis, the issue of personal authenticity that lay at its base had been present in his work as early as his first novel. The interior dialogue between the *yo íntimo* and the *yo histórico* exhibited by Pachico Zabalbide continues to take on an increasing complexity throughout Unamuno's lifetime. A duality of perspective also surrounds Unamuno's so-called religious conversion of 1897. Speaking of himself in the third person, Unamuno questioned the sincerity of his return to religious practice: "Pero se percató de que aquello era falso, y volvió a encontrarse desorientado, preso otra vez de la sed de gloria, del ansia de sobrevivir en la historia" (But he became aware that it was false, and once again, he found himself disoriented, a prisoner once more of his thirst for fame, of his longing to survive in history).[10] The decision Unamuno had made in 1897 to guarantee his own immortality, first as a man of letters, and later as a political figure, caused him to sacrifice his *yo íntimo* in favor of an artificial, historical personage. The schism between these two personalities was surely exacerbated by the pressures of exile, and reached full-blown dissociation in *Cómo se hace una novela*, a "fictional" account of the sundering, as Jung would say, of Unamuno's "original character in the interests of a persona more consonant with the subject's own ambitions" (9.1:162).

In his waning years, Unamuno apprehended the tremendous psychological cost of his decision to remain in the public eye. His consequent turmoil compels the deliberation of Jung's theory that fusion with one's *persona* inhibits successful individuation in that it forces a man to live against the background of his biography (Jung, 9.1:123). This procedure involves extraordinary self-sacrifice, the destructive effects of which are seen in the protagonists Unamuno created in the second half of his life. The neuroses these characters, perhaps even the author himself suffer, appear to be founded upon an inability to cope successfully with conscious self-deception. In many instances the psychological problems of these protagonists stem from an over- or undervalued masculinity. Pachico Zabalbide, like Unamuno, chose to replace his authentic, but introverted and "inferior" self, with a consciously imposed, combative personality. He communicated, as did young Unamuno, a strong, opinionated character while carefully disguising those aspects of his personality considered to be overly sensitive, perhaps even feminine. In the case of Alejandro Gómez (*Nada menos que todo un hombre*), the megalomania of an excessive *hombría* (masculinity) serves to camouflage the character's social inferiority and dread of emotional intimacy.

To some extent, it is possible that Unamuno utilized the public suffering of his "querer creer" (desire to believe) not only to gloss the more profound disturbance caused by his inner dualism, but also as a way of conferring a sense of superiority and stamina on the one who suffered so endlessly. Pelayo Fernández draws a parallel between William James's self-willed, almost physiological instinct to believe and Unamuno's "gana" or "hambre de creer" (yearning or hunger for faith).[11] In *La agonía del cristianismo* Unamuno, indeed, translates "gana de creer" into a curiously sexual idiom whereby he relates the will to believe to "ganas" (urge, yearning), and subsequently to the male sex organs: "Y esta voluntad, ¿tiene algo que ver con la virilidad? ¿La virilidad, es fuente de la voluntad . . . ?" (7:329; And this will, has it anything to do with virility? Is virility the source of will . . . ?). Unamuno links the will to believe to masculine sexuality because "lo que en español sale de los órganos de la virilidad no es voluntad, sino el deseo, la gana"; "Creo, quiere decir 'quiero creer,' o mejor, 'tengo ganas de creer,' y representa el momento de virilidad, el del libre albedrío" (7:329, 333; "The real Spanish word to express what issues from the organs of virility, an expression of desire and not will, is *gana*"; " 'I believe' here means 'I want to believe,' or better, 'I have a craving to believe,' and represents the true high point of virility, of free will" [K-N, 5:45; 53]). To support his conclusions, Unamuno refers to the authority of Schopenhauer who, according to him, "considered the male organs to be the focus of willing. . . . The names for these organs never issue from the mouths of Spaniards" (cf. 7:329).[12] Pelayo Fernández further observed that it was from William James that Unamuno assimilated the notion that genuine belief implied a behavioral norm or course of personal conduct.[13] The "will" to believe, more active than the passive acceptance of church dogma characteristic of the "fe del carbonero" (unquestioning faith), is thus related by Unamuno to the notion that the suffering entailed by *querer creer* confers a sense of manliness on the person who agonizes for the sake of faith.

Unamuno's poetry, fiction, essays, and philosophical thought all seem to be metaphorical expressions of his personal anguish in not being able to reconcile his intimate self, sacrificed for the sake of a dubious longevity, and the unpalatable, but necessary "other," constantly maneuvering for a position in the public conscience. When the *persona* overwhelms the ego, as Unamuno feared it did in *Cómo se hace una novela,* and as it does in the case of Alejandro Gómez, a man becomes susceptible to personality fragmentation. This accounts for the role-playing and accusations of hypocrisy that dominate the lives of the protagonists Unamuno created in this stage of his artistic development.

Similarity between the adult Unamuno and his fictional character Alejandro Gómez has generally been overlooked. Like all inferiority complexes, that of Alejandro Gómez stems from the emotional experiences of a rather difficult childhood.[14] It is rather curious that Unamuno would devote *Nada menos que todo un hombre* almost entirely to building Alejandro's megalomaniacal character, mentioning only briefly, in the last paragraphs of the story, his horrible childhood: the beatings he received at the hands of his father, and the exasperation that one day caused the young boy to blandish his fist at an unjust God (2:1036). One comprehends too late to empathize with Alejandro that the mask he constructed as an impenetrable buffer against inhumane treatment was merely his way of camouflaging his emotions and of surviving a "niñez terrible." This early, acquired behavior affects forever after the way Alejandro would perceive, and relate to, the world outside himself.

Unlike Pachico Zabalbide, Alejandro Gómez does not suffer from a youthful, physiological inferiority; rather it is social deficiency that Alejandro experiences within his newly acquired, aristocratic social circle. Although his fortune and marriage to the beautiful Julia Yáñez give him entrée into the upper classes, Alejandro is aware that the aristocracy accepts him only because his money enables them to survive. Beneath the "hombre ambicioso . . . muy voluntarioso, y muy tozudo, y muy reconcentrado [que] alardeaba de plebeyo" (2:1012; ambitious, strong-willed, obstinate, and self-centered man who boasts of his plebeian origins), hides a man who, Unamuno himself admitted, was a "tirano de timidez" and an "orgulloso de humildad" (5:722–23; timid tyrant whose pride masks a concealed humility). Megalomania, a neurosis in which an outwardly extraordinary self-valuation conceals inward inferiority, becomes a defense mechanism that simultaneously disguises Alejandro's social insecurity and his emotional cowardice, traits he evidently considered threateningly feminine. The narrator's comment—"¿Será un . . . ? ¿Sería un cobarde?" (Can he be . . . ? Could he be a coward?)—is affirmed by Julia's hysterical outburst: "¡Cobarde! ¡Cobarde! ¡Cobarde!" when Alejandro chooses to dismiss, or pretends to dismiss, her allegations that she has taken a lover (2:1023, 1027).

As for Unamuno himself, the anonymous, epistolary correspondence left by "M" documents his "temperamento duro y violento . . . también tiene más que un poquito de soberbia, de confianza en su cerebro" ("harsh and violent disposition . . . he is also more than a little proud, and confident of his intellectual prowess"),[15] foreshadowing not only Alejandro's untempered harshness and pride, but also his own special brand of "inteligencia al servicio de su infernal soberbia plebeya" (2:1029; intelligence at the service of a devilish and plebeian pride). The aggressive personalities developed by Unamuno's "héroes de la voluntad" (heroes of the will), perhaps by Unamuno himself, are techniques devised to preserve the ego from any real, or imagined, incursions on the psyche made by one's fellow men. Jung understood this artificially created, alternate self to be a "system of adaptation to the world," one that allowed a man to disguise his complexes and personal insecurities (9.1:122).

Unamuno's aggressive ego did not permit competition on the part of others. In 1907 he commented that "nadie en su fuero interno admite de grado la superioridad ajena" (no one, in his heart of hearts, willingly admits another's superiority). He further observed that no one was entirely free of personal legend, and that having a personal mythology was perhaps more advantageous than not having one at all (8:243–47). Similarly, Alejandro Gómez is very careful to surround himself with an aura of mystery. His favorite expletive—"¿pero yo? ¿Yo? ¿Yo que he sabido hacerlo [su fortuna] por mí mismo, a puño? ¿Yo?" (2:1012; But I? I? I who have known how to make a fortune all by myself, with the strength of my own hand! I?)—resembles the need Cabaleiro Goas saw behind Unamuno's own demand for public esteem. He attributes Unamuno's behavior to an inferiority complex for which Unamuno compensated with an outward "yo hipertrófico" in constant exigency of affirmation by others. By acknowledging that "yo," others thus also became instrumental in its maintenance and re-creation.[16]

As a child, Alejandro Gómez most probably developed his external *persona* as a method of coping with the impact of parental aggression on his still unformed ego. As a millionaire *indiano* returning to Spain a grown man, Alejandro carries the additional burden of having to cope with social stigma based on his lowly origins and proletarian manners. Self-taught from childhood not to display any outward show of emotion, nor to appear dependent upon others, Alejandro's ostentatious display of self-confidence, and the pleasure he seems to derive from rubbing the noses of his blue-blooded debtors in his *plebeyez*, mask his pathological fear of appearing weak and insecure. Such inflation of the personality produced by deeply rooted feelings of inferiority yields the exaggerated sense of self-importance from which Alejandro Gómez appears to suffer. Psychologically speaking, the more an ego identifies with its *persona*, the more a subject becomes what he appears to be. This severing of the original character in favor of an *ad hoc* personality more in keeping with one's ambitions first results in a dissociation of the self, and ultimately reaches a terminal point in complete "de-individualization" (Jung, 7:302–3). As the *persona* absorbs the ego, the subject only minimally recognizes his intimate needs, while demonstrating a maximum adaptation to societal pressures (Jung, 9.1:162).[17]

Alejandro is in the psychologically precarious situation of wanting to adapt to, but at the same time wishing to subjugate, a society that had always rejected him. This society was represented to the child Alejandro first by his parents, and later by the impoverished, yet socially prominent Spanish aristocracy, whose material survival is dependent on the wealth of men such as himself. It is with the latter element that Alejandro develops a relationship of mutual exploitation. The dialectical relationships between the *siervo* (servant) and the *señor* (master) explored in all three of Unamuno's exemplary novels are based on historically accurate economic factors,[18] but, as is the case with many Unamuno protagonists, dialectic exists not only in a character's external milieu, but also within his own, divided personality. As a former *siervo*, Alejandro must swallow his pride to some extent when he courts the decadent aristocracy in order to initiate business relationships with them. But once successfully established, Alejandro continues to be socially vulnerable, having to endure social snobbery at the hands of his new associates. The despised members of the aristocracy possess social acceptability and finesse, which Alejandro, for all his wealth, cannot purchase but also publicly appears not to care for. He achieves psychological compensation by marrying an impoverished, yet socially acceptable, woman who represents the envied and feared mediators of social status. The dependency of Julia's family upon the wealth of their son-in-law changes Alejandro's position, now placing him in the role of master and enabling him to cast a great amount of psychological torture on his wife. He projects upon Julia the anger and cruelty he feels were directed at him by the social class that she represents.

Possessed of an immense cold-bloodedness, Alejandro is intelligent enough to seize opportunities that enable him to create a personal legend and to manipulate others into conferring upon him a grudging fear and respect. Very little is known of his past: "Corrían respecto a él las más fantásticas leyendas" (The most fantastic legends circulated about him), legends that Alejandro takes care not to dispel. When Julia asks Alejandro about his family, he replies: "Mi familia empieza en mí. Yo me he hecho solo" (2:1017; My family begins with me. I am a self-made man). A true "hijo de sus obras," Alejandro is a self-created man psychologically as well. Later, in *Cómo se hace una novela*, Unamuno will carry this idea of self-fabrication even further, as he desperately casts about for confirmation that will validate the legitimacy of his own public legend.

Creating personal legend consists in fostering the notion of personal worth in the minds of others. In the prologue to *San Manuel Bueno, mártir,* Unamuno notes that *"praestigia,* en latín, quiere decir engaño, ilusión" (*praestigia,* in Latin, means deceit, illusion). According to Unamuno, the creation of prestige involves the fabrication of myth or legend—a *persona* that the man who seeks recognition offers to the public for its consumption (2:1119-20). Jung explained the creation of prestige as the result of collective compromise between the individual in pursuit of notoriety and a pliant mass willing to bestow recognition upon a "legendary" figure. Conferral of prestige is thus made possible both by an individual's will to power and by a society's need to seek out a numinous figure upon whom to bestow esteem, and to whom it is willing to submit (Jung, 7:150-51). The manufacturing of a *persona,* as Unamuno implied in "El cultivo de la demótica," and as he would repeat many times in *Cómo se hace una novela,* is not entirely a one-sided affair. Its creation and conferral stem from a dialogic process of mutual sacrifice, either of individuality on the one hand, or of collective independence on the other. Implicit in this type of compromise, however, is also a certain amount of personal gain: of prestige for the individual who seeks it, and social viability for his supporters. Nevertheless, complete sacrifice of the self, or its repression in favor of what others expect, or intend it to be, often has dire consequences for the individual. Relegating the authentic self to an imaginary existence, or to "private games in front of a mirror," accounts for the schizophrenia intrinsic to those who succumb to their public image—a trait that characterizes many protagonists of Unamuno's mature work.[19]

In Jung's opinion, the man who comes closest to achieving self-realization is the one who successfully minimizes the function of his *persona.* On the other hand, someone fused to the false aspects of his mask is known as a "personal man," due to the alienation from his individual needs that he experiences (6:645). The "personal man," just as the one who cannot divest himself of a dominant mother archetype, shoulders a tremendous psychological burden that prevents him from attaining complete individuation (Jung, 7:176). In the case of Alejandro, the assumed mask not only hides social inferiority, but also impedes the expression of feelings and emotion. Alejandro is prevented from recognizing Julia as his anima and mediator of the unconscious mind to consciousness by his rejection of any outward manifestations of love which he considers "frases de novelas sentimentales. Cuanto menos se diga que se le quiere a uno, mejor" (2:1017; phrases from sentimental novels. The less you tell someone you love them, the better). However, it is only when a male accepts the moderating influence of the anima that he can significantly modify the outer shell of his persona (Jung, 7:194–95). Jung discovered that in the case of exaggeratedly virile men the anima is extremely feminine, accounting for the weakness and impressionability of such men (6:468–69). For all his strength and bravado, at the end of his tragic life Alejandro displays uncharacteristic weakness by committing suicide. The attraction of the feminine proves to be stronger than him, and Alejandro prefers to reunite with Julia in death, rather than to continue living without her.

This hermetically closed soul is not the first example of such behavior among Unamuno's male protagonists: both Pedro Antonio Iturriondo (*PG*) and Avito Carrascal (*AP*) are equally as incapable of expressing love and tenderness toward members of their families. The psychological similarity between Avito and Alejandro is especially striking since both protagonists manifest symptoms of unmitigated psychological domination by patriarchal values. Of all Unamuno's male characters these two are the most successful in imposing their individual wills upon the lives of their families, both with tragic consequences: only the death of a loved one can temper their seemingly frigid souls. Beneath their intransigence both men hide inferiority complexes: Avito, his intellectual mediocrity; Alejandro, his social inacceptability. Both men also relate to their wives in much the same way. They consider the feminine insignificant and see their wives simply as means by which to achieve egocentric ends. Avito reduces Marina to nothing more than a bearer of children for his pedagogical experiments, while Julia has no function in the life of Alejandro other than as a precious household ornament.

To ensure the healthy survival of a heterosexual pair, the male partner must willingly relate to his anima, and rescue her, as it were, from repression into the unconscious.[20] Avito and Alejandro, however, are both too insecure in themselves to permit their anima full interaction with their egos. The final result of excluding the feminine from their lives is to condemn the anima figure to an incoherent existence on the fringes of consciousness: Marina retreats into a world of daydreams and fantasy, while Julia suffers a complete emotional breakdown. Initially it is normal for a male to resist the numinosity of his anima, primarily because she represents all the traits a patriarchal value system tends to belittle: irrationality, creativity, earthiness, the instincts, and the unconscious (Jung, 11:75). It is a common reaction on the part of men to fear being "invaded" or "weakened" by a woman's femininity. Only in the integrative stages of individuation is a man able to reclaim and accept the feminine side of himself that he had rejected previously, in the first stages of development.[21]

The union of Alejandro Gómez and Julia Yáñez theoretically presents an ideal *hierosgamos*, or spiritual union of archetypal opposites. Julia's femininity and beauty, coupled with Alejandro's intelligence and ambition, would have made perfect complements had they been permitted normal integration. Like Alejandro, Julia has her own Achilles' heel, being excessively proud, even rather vain. It is she who first verbalizes what, in adapted form, becomes Alejandro's favorite expletive: "yo, Julia Yáñez, ¡nada menos que yo!, le había aceptado por novio" (2:1010; I, Julia Yáñez, no one less than myself; I had accepted him as my beau!). Despite Alejandro's roughshod *persona*, Julia is able to see beyond his mask. Quite early in their acquaintance she intuits that of all her suitors, Alejandro is the most prepared to carry out his promises. Perhaps unconsciously she even intuits the complementary nature of their personalities: "Y al leerlo [el contenido de una carta], se dijo Julia: '¡Este es un hombre! ¿Será mi redentor? ¿Seré yo su redentora?'" (2:1013; And, having read his letter, Julia said to herself: "Here is a real man. Will he be my savior? Will I redeem him?"). Since each represents the other's psychological opposite, Julia and Alejandro might have balanced one another extremely well. While Alejandro represses all internal feelings in favor of an exterior mask, Julia seeks to divest herself of her *persona* and the reputation with which she is saddled as the official beauty of Renada. More than anything else, she would like to secure for herself appreciation as a human being. The great irony of it all is that only Alejandro will come to value her in such a fashion. As a harmonious partnership, the two might have "redeemed" each other's half-formed psyches from oblivion, but due to Alejandro's inability to articulate his love, Julia is condemned to a life of "incertidumbre del amor del hombre [que] la tenía como presa en aquel dorado y espléndido calabozo de puerta abierta" (2:1018; uncertainty in the love of this man who kept her prisoner in a splendid, gilded cage whose doors he left wide open). Alejandro's tragedy lies in his exclusion of the anima archetype and in the mental cruelty he showers upon Julia as a symbol of that archetype. Ironically, Julia will never know that the impetuous wish she expressed to one of her youthful suitors for a double suicide is granted her by the very man whose love she most doubts.

A weakened anima figure cannot perform her redemptive task of stripping the male personality of its mask.[22] For Alejandro, the weakening of his *persona* that should have accompanied a gradual strengthening of his relationship to Julia does not take place. Alejandro's false self becomes a permanently imposed mask hiding fear of personal insecurity and the display of anything that could be interpreted as feminine character traits. The ideal moment in which Alejandro could have begun a retreat from his pathological attachment to the self-imposed *persona* occurs during Julia's affair with the Conde de Bordaviella. But, rather than modifying his personality in response to the psychic and emotional shock of this episode, Alejandro commits Julia to an insane asylum and coerces Bordaviella into silence. This kind of psychological misadaptation to circumstance is known as a "regressive restoration" of the *persona,* and is the only recourse available to a man who "owes the critical failure of his life to his own inflatedness" (Jung, 7:168). Alejandro's "critical failure" is due to the repression of his own humanity, and to his adherence, no matter what the expense, to a perverse understanding of what a "nada menos que todo un hombre" should be.

Before Julia admits to having had an affair with Bordaviella, she asks her husband whether he could ever feel jealousy. Alejandro responds: "¡Bah!, ¡bah!, ¡bah! Los celos son cosas de estúpidos. Sólo los estúpidos pueden ser celosos, porque sólo a ellos les puede faltar su mujer" (2:1018; Only fools are jealous. Only fools can feel jealousy, because only they can be deceived by their wives). Nevertheless, immediately after this exchange between husband and wife takes place, Alejandro begins to refer to Bordaviella as a "mentecato," a "majadero," and a "michino" (2:1019, 1020, 1025; fool, idiot, lapdog). In his important study of jokes and joking as discharges of unconscious sentiment, Freud proposed that "by making our enemy small, inferior, despicable, or comic, we achieve in a roundabout way the enjoyment of overcoming him."[23] In considering Bordaviella less than human, Alejandro is no longer obligated to see his rival as an authentic threat, nor particularly as one whose feelings or needs hold any significance. When the hypothetical affair between Julia and Bordaviella becomes reality, Alejandro's refusal to relinquish the dictates of his *persona* forces him into an even more complex charade. To prove he is immune to gossip, Alejandro insists that Julia entertain her former lover in their home after she is released from the mental asylum. This senseless cruelty proves to be the last thrust necessary to push Julia's already fragile psyche into complete disintegration. When Alejandro is finally able to admit his love for his wife, it is too late to save Julia from surrendering to the *no querer ser* of a passive "not wanting to be."

Senselessly rejected in her lifetime, in death Julia proves to have irresistible magnetism. Contemplating her body in all its physical beauty and splendor, Alejandro "sintió pasar, como una nube de hielo, su vida toda, aquella vida que ocultó a todos, hasta a sí mismo" (2:1036; sensed his whole life passing before him, like an icy cloud, a life he had concealed from everyone, even from himself).[24] Alejandro's tragic flaw is rooted in the submission of his real self to the hubris of a false personality. This flaw is the cornerstone of his blindness and occasions the severe penalty, usually some form of psychological or physical retribution, which such an act necessarily entails (Jung, 7:194). In a desperate attempt to recover the feminine element without which he cannot survive, Alejandro Gómez takes his own life.

A man who consistently identifies with an imaginary, glorified self chooses what Karen Horney calls an "expansive solution" to his neurosis. This type of person determines to "master" the environment around him by proving his ability to overcome any obstacle set in his path while simultaneously making great efforts to hide the appearance of weakness or personal helplessness. Most characteristic of an "expansive solution" to neurosis is the subject's intent to validate his idealized self through the exercise of intelligence and will power.[25] As do all Unamuno's *héroes de la voluntad*, Alejandro Gómez first creates a fictitious self, and then proceeds to control his position through the financial and/or psychological manipulation of those with whom he is in daily contact. What Horney terms the "narcissistic" type of expansive neurotic, presents character traits particularly applicable to Alejandro whose mastery of others centers on his belief that there is "nothing he cannot do and no one he cannot win." This attitude is evident in all aspects of Alejandro's life: his single-handed amassing of wealth, his conquest of Julia, and especially his carefully controlled staging of Julia's commitment and release from the mental asylum. According to Horney, the expansive neurotic is prone to depression and psychotic episodes, frequently ending his life through suicide or intentional self-exposure to fatal accidents. Such, indeed, proves to be the tragic fate of Unamuno's "superman."[26] Although suicide is a negative response to the challenge to surpass one's limitations, Erich Neumann nevertheless argues that an ego which destroys itself by choice is more active, more independent and individual, than one choosing to languish away in resignation.[27] In the end, Alejandro, by electing his own moment and method of death, remains a true Unamunian *héroe de la voluntad.*

Unamuno's inability, or unwillingness, to resolve the problem of "otherness" became an obsession in the second half of his life, and led to its artistic expression in works such as *Nada menos que todo un hombre* (1916), *Abel Sánchez* (1917), and *El otro* (1926). Assimilation of the ego by a social role is also the *magna quaestio* that dominates *Cómo se hace una novela.* Unamuno's personal duality lies in his oscillation between the extraverted and aggressive public figure he had allowed his primary self to become, and the intimate and contemplative "other" he consistently relegated to a subordinate position. In his play *La esfinge* (1898), Unamuno "assassinated" the leading character, Angel, as he was about to retire from a career in the public service. Unlike Angel, Unamuno made the decision in 1897 to relinquish his private life in order to seek an active role in Spanish culture and politics. Twenty-seven years later, the sacrifice this decision entailed became unbearably burdensome to his psyche. This is not to say that Unamuno became mentally ill, but like most people in times of acute crisis, he suffered from personal tensions and dissociations. Unamuno, however, had the advantage of being able to give vent to the unconscious through his creative work. *Cómo se hace una novela* documents the agony that surrounded Unamuno's identity crisis of 1924:

> ¡Mi novela!, ¡mi leyenda! . . . este Unamuno me da vida y muerte, me crea y me destruye, me sostiene y me ahoga. Es mi agonía. ¿Seré como me creo o como se me cree? (8:734)

> (My novel!, my legend! . . . this Unamuno gives me life and gives me death, he creates me and destroys me, he sustains me and suffocates me. He is my agony. Am I as I believe myself to be, or as others believe that I am?)

In *Cómo se hace una novela,* U. Jugo de la Raza does not personify any single, alternative self as do most other Unamuno protagonists; rather he embodies Unamuno's inability to resolve the conflictive situation occasioned by his multiple selves. Anthony Storr maintains that the creative artist often replaces the self with his work. In cases where identification between creator and creation is most thorough, the artist may even find himself unable to complete his project. The creation, in other words, may come to be such a matter of life and death for the artist that he does not have sufficient courage to bring his work to successful completion.[28] The identification between Miguel de Unamuno y Jugo and U. Jugo de la Raza, who dares not conclude his reading of the ominous novel he had found in a Parisian bookstall, presents an analogous case. In this sense, Jugo de la Raza reflects Unamuno's personal inability to complete writing the "novel" in which Jugo himself plays a central role. Don Miguel's inability to complete this novel is thus a metaphor of his personal failure to reconcile the many selves extant in his psyche. Psychological impasse of this type leaves open only the alternative of renouncing a unified, coherent self. Unable, perhaps unwilling, to fully integrate his inner divisions, Unamuno is just as incapable of fashioning characters who enjoy integrated personalities.[29] Don Miguel's conscious choice to eschew personal consistency and wholeness is perhaps a consequence of his imagined need to be all things at all times: "más doloroso sería, acaso, seguir siempre uno mismo, y no más que uno mismo, sin poder ser a la vez otro, sin poder ser a la vez todo lo demás, sin poder serlo todo" (7:191; it would be even more painful, perhaps, to go on being oneself, and only oneself for all time, without simultaneously being able to be someone else, without the ability to become everything else, unable to be everything). Ironically the effect this need had on Unamuno was that of condemning him to a perpetual crisis of authenticity.

In the two years between his retirement as rector of the University of Salamanca (1934) and his death, Unamuno seems to have approached his fragmentation with much less personal anxiety, no doubt the result of age and psychic exhaustion. However, his yearning for inner peace was already present ten years before, in the uncharacteristically melancholy question he posed in *Cómo se hace una novela:* "¿Cuándo se acabará esa contraposición entre acción y contemplación? ¿Cuándo se acabará de comprender que la acción es contemplativa y la contemplación activa?" (8: 765; When will this opposition between action and contemplation cease? When will it finally be understood that action is contemplative and contemplation active?). Toward the end of his life, Unamuno, much like don Manuel Bueno, was evidently exhausted by the daily battle among his various *yos.* "¡Qué bien se está en las Batuecas!," an essay written shortly after the national homage paid to Unamuno at his retirement, shows that he saw withdrawal from public life as an opportunity to "tratar de sacudirme el mito. ¡Cosa fatídica ésta!" (try to shake off the myth. That cursed thing!). He also admitted, with resignation, that one's popularity (or unpopularity, which is essentially the same thing), "nos faja y ciñe y aprieta. . . . Más de un hombre se ha sacrificado a su mito y por no contradecirlo se ha contradicho íntimamente" (8:1218; girds, limits, and oppresses us. . . . More than one man sacrificed himself to his myth, and, in order not to contradict that myth publicly, he is then forced to contradict his most intimate being). Unamuno's prescient comment, made in 1896, that the public manipulates the public servant, and not the other way around (9:53), had undoubtedly been an important factor in determining the outcome of his own life.

The conflict between the self and its increasingly unmanageable "other" pervades Unamuno's mature work. Following on the heels of *Nada menos que todo un hombre,* Unamuno's subsequent novels consistently address the issue of irreconcilable differences between the ego and its rival, shadow personality. In *Abel Sánchez,* Joaquín Monegro's alternate self finally rejects its normal subordination to the ego, and assumes a threateningly independent existence as his rival and consummate nemesis.

5. *Abel Sánchez*
In Pursuit of the Shadow

Enrique David Thoreau . . . dice que a nadie tenemos más derecho para odiar que a nuestro amigo. (Unamuno, 1:1205)

(Henry David Thoreau . . . says that we have no reason to hate anyone more than a friend.)

Very early in his career Unamuno began to express interest in pride and envy, both as personal characteristics, and later, as sociological phenomena endemic to the Spanish people. The first *cuaderno* (notebook) of his personal diary, written sometime in 1897, reveals a concerted effort to analyze the concepts of pride and envy as they related to his own personality. In 1904 Unamuno published "Sobre la soberbia," the first of many essays[1] to address the issue of pride, and one in which he admitted that vanity and envy were not sentiments foreign to his emotional constitution:

> Y es que de ordinario, lo que aborrezco en otros aborrézcolo por sentirlo en mí mismo; y si me hiere aquella púa del prójimo, es porque esa misma púa me está hiriendo en mi interior. Es mi envidia, mi soberbia, mi petulancia, mi codicia, las que me hacen aborrecer la soberbia, la envidia, la petulancia, la codicia ajenas. (1:1205)

> (Ordinarily what I dislike most in others are the same qualities I dislike in myself, and if I am wounded by the barb of a fellow man, it is because the same barb is stabbing my own insides. It is my own envy, my pride, my arrogance, my greed, which make me detest the pride, the envy, the arrogance, and the greed of others.)

As Unamuno acknowledged, the repugnant qualities he criticized in others were also those that he found most unpalatable in himself. A

106

typical psychological reaction to this kind of admission is to relegate the negative character traits one perceives in the self to an unconscious existence in what Jung called the "shadow personality" (9.1:284–85). The function of the shadow is to represent not only the rejected, negative side of the psyche to the ego, but also those qualities one dislikes most in others. These incompatibilities are normally projected out of the self onto someone who seems to embody the unwelcome character traits.[2] In his study of existential envy in Rousseau and Unamuno, Gregory Ulmer observed, "The envy of which Rousseau felt himself the object . . . is, in part, the projection of his own shadow, of his envious desires for recognition."[3] This could also be said of Unamuno, who by 1907 was no longer assessing his own pride and envy, but projecting them onto his countrymen: "¡La envidia! Esta, ésta es la terrible plaga de nuestras sociedades; ésta es la íntima gangrena del alma española" (3:284; Envy! This is the terrible scourge of our society; this is the intimate gangrene of the Spanish soul).

Unamuno was always inclined to view the success and fame of another with suspicion and as potentially diminishing to his own glory and personal achievement.[4] For him, survival was guaranteed only by an aggressive invasion of his fellow man. This kind of self-expansion was accomplished by ingesting the potential rival in an effort to augment the self. Thus, an early Unamuno protagonist, Dr. Montarco, counters accusations of being proud and aloof as having nothing to do with his true personality:

> Sí, sé que me tienen por desdeñoso de los demás, pero se equivocan. Es que no los tengo por aquello en que se tienen ellos mismos. . . . No, amigo mío, no!, el hombre que trata de sobreponerse a los demás es que busca salvarse; el que procura hundir en el olvido los nombres ajenos es que quiere se conserve el suyo en la memoria de las gentes, porque sabe que la posteridad tiene un cedazo muy cerrado. (1:1130)

> (I know they think I am disdainful of others, but they are wrong. The fact is merely that I don't have the same opinion of them that they have of themselves. . . . For the truth is . . . that when a man tries to get ahead of others he is simply trying to save himself. When a man tries to sink the names of [others into oblivion] he is merely trying to insure that his own is preserved in the memory of living men, because he knows that posterity is a close-meshed sieve which allows few names to get through to other ages. [K-N, 7:236])

As Unamuno's thinly veiled alter ego, Montarco is the first of his fictional characters to voice what becomes a frequently repeated exclamation in the Unamuno canon: *querer serlo todo* (the desire to be everything). This expletive is, curiously enough, not original to Unamuno, but attributed by Montarco to W. H. Rolph, whose book *Problemas biológicos* the doctor is fond of quoting:

> Léalo y verá que no es el crecimiento y la multiplicación de los seres lo que les pide más alimento y les lleva . . . a luchar así, sino que es una tendencia a . . . excederse, a sobrepasar de lo necesario. No es instinto de conservación . . . sino instinto de invasión; no tiramos a mantenernos, sino a ser más, a serlo todo. Es, sirviéndome de una fuerte expresión del padre Alonso Rodríguez, el gran clásico, "apetito de divinidad. . . ." El que no sienta ansias de ser más, llegará a no ser nada. ¡O todo o nada! (1:1131)[5]

> (Read it and you will see that it is not the growth and multiplication of a species which [leads it to require more sustenance and also . . . to struggle, rather it is a tendency to . . .] go beyond the purely necessary. It is not an instinct toward self-preservation . . . but rather an instinct toward invasion. . . . We don't strive to maintain ourselves only, but to be more than we already are; to be everything. [It is, to quote the powerful words of that great man, Father Alonso Rodríguez,] an "appetite for the divine. . . ." Whoever doesn't aspire to be more than he is, will [never amount to anything at all. It is all or nothing!]. [K-N, 7:237])

This compulsion to invade the "other" in order to conserve and to expand the self, together with Unamuno's "herostratic" need to preserve his name in the memory of men, assumes a somewhat hieratic principle in his work. Accordingly, he writes in *Del sentimiento trágico de la vida:* "Mi esfuerzo por imponerme a otro, por ser y vivir yo en él y de él, por hacerle mío—que es lo mismo que hacerme suyo—, es lo que da sentido religioso a la colectividad, a la solidaridad humana" (7:273; "My endeavor to impose myself upon another, to be and live in him, to make him mine, which is the same as making my self his, is what gives religious meaning to our collectivity, to human solidarity" [K-N, 4:302]).

The idea of invasion as a mechanism to preserve the self from potential aggression by the "other" is one of the issues Unamuno considers in *Abel Sánchez*, a novel he subtitled *Una historia de pasión* (The Story of a Passion). The passion in question is undoubtedly Joaquín Monegro's obsessive urge to affirm the superiority of his self over that of others, namely Abel. Comparing his envy of Abel's easily acquired success to Satan's envious aspiration to be the equal of God, Joaquín remarks: "Luzbel aspiraba a ser Dios, y yo, desde muy niño, ¿no aspiré a anular a los demás?" (2:712; Lucifer aspired to be God, and haven't I, since childhood, aspired to annihilate all others?).

During a speech Joaquín offers Abel at the banquet commemorating his famous Cain painting, he makes an observation remarkably similar to Unamuno's "Mi esfuerzo por imponerme a otro . . . por hacerle mío." Joaquín begins his discourse saying that "El [Abel] es nuestro, de todos, él es mío sobre todo, y yo gozando su obra, la hago tan mía como él la hizo suya creándola" (2:716; "He [Abel] belongs to us all, above all he is mine, and I, enriched by his work, try to make this work as much mine as he made it his by the act of creation" [K-N, 6:299-300]). So overwhelming is Joaquín's passionate urge to assert his own sense of self that it blinds him to the fact he had, indeed, successfully overcome Abel by establishing the merit of the Cain painting through the power of his spoken word. Even Abel confesses: "What you have said, Joaquín, is worth more, has greater value, . . . than my painting . . . I did not know what I had accomplished until I heard you. You, and not I, have made my painting, you alone!" (K-N, 6:300). Some of the banquet participants also confirm that "este discurso de Joaquín vale por todos los cuadros del otro. El discurso ha hecho el cuadro" (2:717). Unfortunately the truth of these statements is lost to Joaquín, who devotes a lifetime to pursuing his illusory dream of gaining parity with Abel.

As a novel, *Abel Sánchez* proves to be a rare compendium of Unamunian miscellanea, literary as well as autobiographical, encompassing a largely baroque series of reflections and interior duplications. First, it is a work that recapitulates in fictional guise many of Unamuno's important essays on the themes of pride and envy, while it also anticipates others that Unamuno would write on the same topic at a much later date. Not only is this novel a broadly self-referential hybridization of essay and fiction, but it also claims to be a fictional autobiography edited by a third party. There are moments, however, when Joaquín's *Confesión* mimics Unamuno's *Diario íntimo*, and the novel becomes an excellent example of art imitating life.

An additional series of duplications is sustained when it becomes clear that *Abel Sánchez* is Unamuno's contemporary adaptation of the archetype of unlike brotherhood. That archetypal motifs appear in all of Unamuno's work should be of no surprise since as a Hellenist don Miguel had a greater access than most to a wealth of mythological heritage still extant today in the Western canon. Beneath the surface of the novel is a palimpsest of archetypal material drawn from classical mythology, the Bible, and Romantic literature, sources all of which appear to corroborate Unamuno's personal assessment of the human personality as one continually susceptible to its innate divisiveness. Unamuno frequently associates envy with fraternal rivalry, often choosing the metaphor of civil war, or the motif of unlike brotherhood, to illustrate this concept. His theory that every man harbors within himself both Cain and Abel may be traced to *Paz en la guerra*, where the Carlist War is described as a battle for economic supremacy between urban *cainitas* and rural *abelitas*, while the novel's two protagonists, Pachico Zabalbide and Ignacio Iturriondo, represent two highly disparate facets of the author's youthful personality.

It is in *Abel Sánchez*, however, that to the elementary problem of fraternal discord caused by envy, Unamuno adds the more complex dimension of the problem of personality. In this work fraternal enmity metaphorizes the conflict between the conscious ego and the unconscious contents of a rival, shadow personality. The antagonism between the light and dark sides of the human psyche is a common archetypal motif, and one of the oldest in the history of mankind. While in literature the competition between ego and shadow has long been associated with the metaphor of the hostile, or pursuing double, in psychology the same motif is symbolic of self-division.[6] The coincidence of opposites Unamuno infers the human personality to be, or as he preferred to phrase it, the "problema de la personalidad," acquires an especially prominent role in the fiction he produced after the publication of *Niebla* in 1914.

Otto Rank suggests that authors most attracted to the theme of the double are also those most concerned with articulating the universal theme of the self's relation to itself.[7] Unamuno's growing fascination with twins and personality splitting perhaps had its basis in his own inability to resolve successfully the now famous conflict between his contemplative, but suppressed "other," and the aggressive public figure the novelist permitted to become his dominant personality. Certainly the many works of literature in which Unamuno elects to study the effects of psychological dualism on the personality disclose an attempt to analyze, through literature, the dual tendencies found in his own psyche.

Legends associated with the theme of self-duplication most likely originated as defense mechanisms against the threat of death, but the twin, or double, also appears in folklore as a reminder of death's imminence.[8] The principle of doubling that twins represent has also been regarded as an anthropomorphic representation of ego cleavage, causing twins to be the subjects of superstition and taboo in the mores of primitive cultures. The assumption that one twin was of divine origin while the other was of mortal descent had its roots in the supposed adultery of their mother, and was probably modeled on the dual paternity of the Dioscuric gods, Castor and Pollux.[9] Throughout its history, the double has also aroused paranoid ideas of pursuit, to which a frequent solution is eradication of the bothersome reflection.[10] In *Abel Sánchez*, Joaquín insists to his rival, Abel: "Me amargaste la juventud, que me has perseguido la vida toda" (2:755; You embittered my youth, you have persecuted me all my life). To his wife, Antonia, Joaquín confesses: "No puedo olvidarle . . . me persigue. . . . Su fama y su gloria me siguen a todas partes" (2:708; I cannot forget him . . . he hounds me. . . . His fame and his glory follow me everywhere). Consistent with Rank's observation that the double is frequently responsible for eliminating his alter ego, Joaquín is ultimately accountable for precipitating Abel's fatal heart attack.

It seems evident that the ominous aspects surrounding the mythology of the double and its psychological correlative, persecution by the "other," are present in each one of Unamuno's works that concerns personality duplication. The death of one's double is a denouement that also occurs in the short stories "El que se enterró" and "Artemio Heautontimouroumenos," the short novel *El marqués de Lumbría*, the play *El otro*, and both prose and dramatic renditions of *Tulio Montalbán y Julio Macedo*. The works described here all address the problem of mutually exclusive dichotomies found in the same self, each unwilling to reach a compromise satisfactory to the rival, thus making reconciliation impossible. Only the elimination of one of the antagonists involved brings a temporary, if misleading, solution to the problem—misleading since the pursued frequently perishes within a short while of his pursuer. The conclusion Unamuno appears to draw from his fictional examinations of doubling, is that the psyche can only function completely in the presence of a complementary opposite upon which it depends to provide its sought-for wholeness.

In literature, the double is habitually portrayed as the protagonist's sibling who personifies that part of the ego which becomes detached and assumes an independence threatening to the protagonist. In his study of the double, Rank concludes that this motif occurs with greatest frequency in the work of those authors who themselves experienced sibling rivalry.[11] One could argue that Unamuno's interest in the archetype of hostile brothers may be explained, first, as a reflection of his personal quest to somehow forge a truce from among the plurality of his many selves, but also by the lack of empathy between himself and his younger brother, Felix, who could never quite adjust to Miguel's growing renown. [12] In addition to biographical evidence documenting friction between the Unamuno brothers, don Miguel made a revealing observation in the prologue to his novel *La tía Tula*, that the sibling rivalry he described in *Abel Sánchez* may have been based on personal experience:

> En mi novela *Abel Sánchez* intenté escarbar en ciertos sótanos y escondrijos del corazón, en ciertas catacumbas del alma, adonde no gustan descender los más de los mortales. Creen que en esas catacumbas hay muertos, a los que lo mejor es no visitar, y esos muertos, sin embargo, nos gobiernan. Es la herencia de Caín. (2:1043)

> (In my novel *Abel Sánchez* I attempted to delve into certain hiding places of the heart and catacombs of the soul where most mortals fear to tread. [They believe that the dead, who are better left alone, dwell in those catacombs; it is these dead, however, who continue to govern our lives. It is a bequest left to us by Cain.] [K-N, 7:10])

In 1926, Unamuno published the play *El otro*, in which one brother murders his identical twin. Indistinguishable from each other, it is either Cosme or Damián whose body lies unidentified in the catacombs of the other's "basement," and from there, unseen and unheard, determines the action of the play. The "other," that is, the shadow, implies Unamuno, directs the behavior of the conscious ego from the depths of our unconscious. Cosmas and Damian, Jacob and Esau, Abel and Cain have long been traditional symbols of the archetype of unlike brothers, and as such are paradigmatic of the split personality. [13] Especially suggestive is Unamuno's frequent use of these pairs in his work as metaphorical expressions of psychological dualism. In the case of *Abel Sánchez*, however, the Old Testament archetype of rival siblings is only the tip of the mythological iceberg upon which the novel rests. In order to appreciate Unamuno's adaptation of the Cain/Abel legend, it is necessary to look beyond its genesis in Judeo-Christian tradition.

The notion of doubling appears to derive from the Persian physicians Cosmas and Damian who suffered martyrdom for their conversion to Christianity. [14] Cosmas and Damian, the names Unamuno gave to the rival twins of his play *El otro*, are also thought to be the Christian equivalents of the Dioscuric gods, Castor and Pollux, who in antiquity symbolized the principle of dualism: of light and dark, sun and moon, mortality and immortality.[15] Although the brothers were both sons of Leda, Castor was fathered by the mortal Tyndareus, while Pollux and his twin sister, Helen, were the children of Zeus. After Castor's untimely death, Zeus allowed Pollux to join his brother in the heavens, placing them both in the constellation Gemini, the zodiacal sign of duality. A further connection between the Dioscuri and *Abel Sánchez* is provided by the gods' infamous sister, Helen of Troy. Married to Menelaus, Helen allowed herself to be carried off by Paris, son of the king of Troy. Her abduction was instrumental in causing, if not the oldest extant archetype of fraternal warfare, then certainly its most notorious and legendary exponent. It is likewise significant that Unamuno would have chosen the name *Helena* for his heroine rather than the more familiar Spanish rendering— *Elena*—of the same name, obviously intending the reader to make a connection between his Helena and the heroine of Greek legend.

The mythological triangle Paris-Helen-Menelaus is mirrored by the Unamunian triangle Abel-Helena-Joaquín, the latter-day Helen flanked by the hostile brothers Abel and Cain, each vying for her favors. Thus, when Abel researches the Bible for a new painting he plans to execute, Joaquín pointedly inquires whether in this case Helena could not also serve as a source of inspiration. Puzzled, since in the biblical story of the archetypal fratricide no woman plays a significant role, Abel queries: "¿Mi mujer? En esta tragedia no hubo mujer" (2:711; My wife? In this tragedy there wasn't any woman). Joaquín's reply that "En toda tragedia la hay, Abel" (In every tragedy there is, Abel) is most likely a reference to the similarity between the mythological war inspired by Helen of Troy between the Greeks and their Trojan kinsmen, and the discord Helena has sown between Abel and Joaquín, the "hermanos de crianza" of *Abel Sánchez*.

Unamuno's beautiful and vain Helena displays a personality remarkably similar to the Helen of Greek legend. Like her mythological counterpart, Unamuno's heroine is as unaware as she is unconcerned by the passions she stirs in men, and both the Homeric and Unamunian women show an astonishingly passive acceptance of their destinies as professional *femmes fatales*. The sphinxlike *pava real* (peacock) that Joaquín and Abel conclude Helena to be, is described by Unamuno as a quasi-divine being who posed for her portrait "solemne y fría, henchida de desdén, como una diosa llevada por el destino" (2:693; solemn and cold, disdainful, like a goddess on the wings on destiny). In fact, it is quite likely that Unamuno had Helen of Troy very much in mind when he created the heroine of his novel.

Contemporaneous with *Abel Sánchez* is an essay, "Las coplas de Calaínos" (May 21, 1917), in which Unamuno translates a passage of the *Iliad* highly reminiscent of his fictional Helena: "No hay que indignarse de que los troyanos y los aqueos de buenas perneras sufran tanto tiempo dolores por semejante mujer, parécese en su figura terriblemente a las diosas inmortales" (3:1008; We should not become indignant when the Trojans and the strong-legged Greeks endure so much grief at the hands of such a woman. Her face has a terrifying resemblance to those of the immortal goddesses). Homer's description of Helen of Troy resembles Unamuno's own of Helena as a semi-divine creature whose portrait takes a provincial city by storm, and who now strolls its avenues "como un inmortal viviente . . . ¿no había acaso nacido para eso?" (2:695; as an immortal made flesh . . . was she not born to play just such a role?).

Unamuno's retelling of this Greek legend, however, replaces the brothers Castor and Pollux with the more familiar Old Testament siblings, Abel and Cain. While in the Bible, Abel and Cain are portrayed as two independent personalities, for Unamuno the duo represents different sides of the same psychological coin. His Cain is a demonic and rebellious individual, while Abel, the biblical tender of sheep, personifies the innocent and contemplative personality traits customarily associated with the Lamb of God. Fraternal enmity as a biblical theme reappears in the New Testament dichotomy of Satan and Christ. Milton, whose epic poem plays an important role in Unamuno's novel, establishes this antagonistic, yet clearly dependent relationship, in Satan's challenge to Christ: ". . . in what degree or meaning thou art called / the Son of God, which bears no single sense; / The Son of God I also am or was / And if I was, I am; relation stands."[16]

A similar relationship between Christ and the Antichrist was also perceived by Jung, for whom the pair symbolized a polarity of psychic characteristics in need of reconciliation (9.2:81). "Since Satan, like Christ," observes Jung, "is a son of God, it is evident that we have here the archetype of the hostile brothers" (11:173, n. 19). Jung's study of Christ's dual nature showed that, like the Dioscuric gods, Christ was associated with the constellation Gemini, the sun having been in Gemini during His birth (9.2:810). The birth itself occurred in the Age of Pisces, the two fishes, represented in the zodiac as twin fishes moving in opposite directions (Jung, 9.2:90–91). Furthermore, early Christians adopted the fish as a cryptogrammic symbol of their new faith, while Christ himself was referred to as a "fisher of souls." Jung also noted that double fishes had long been symbolic of the dual, and specifically antithetical nature of the self, and thought Christ to represent the completely individuated man, or one who successfully integrated his dichotomous nature (9.2:145).

Unamuno reproduces the New Testament archetype of good and evil siblings in his novel, endowing Joaquín with a demonic personality, while allocating the superficially innocent and submissive character traits to Abel. The sulfurous fumes of hell and the association of Joaquín with Satan are reinforced in the first chapter of the novel when Abel insists that Joaquín curb his jealous anger by using the verb *sulfurar* on two occasions in the same confrontation: "No te sulfures así, ten paciencia"; "No te sulfures te he dicho" (2:695, 696). This association is strengthened at the end of the same chapter, which concludes with an excerpt from Joaquín's diary in which he observes, "Aquella noche nací al infierno de mi vida" (2:697; "That night I was born to my life's hell" [K-N, 6:264]). From that moment on, references to Joaquín's life as a living hell, and to the demonic qualities of his personality, continue with great insistence throughout the course of the novel.

The representation of Cain as Satan's ally reached its apogee in Romantic literary iconography, which frequently describes both figures as unjustly doomed and excessively maligned creatures.[17] The Romantics are also generally credited with anticipating certain theories of depth psychology, particularly those of C. G. Jung, whose concept of individuation is based on the integration of psychological polarities. Nineteenth-century fascination with doubling as a psychological phenomenon is attributed to the Romantics' oversimplification of Johann Gottlieb Fichte's (1762–1814) ontology of the Ego and the non-Ego, erroneously interpreted as being a theory of split consciousness. It was from Fichte that the idea of light and dark aspects of the soul was derived, and it appears that popularizations of the German philosopher's thought may have also been responsible for the ever-increasing use of the double in nineteenth-century literature.[18]

Finisecular interest in the double can be traced to the neo-Romantic revival that swept through Europe at the end of the nineteenth and the beginning of the twentieth centuries.[19] The coincidence of vision between Jung and Unamuno is therefore partially attributable to their participation in the neo-Romantic movement.[20] Given their essentially romantic and somewhat mystical dispositions, it is hardly surprising that Jung and Unamuno would have shared an interest in the double motif, one of the most popular in Romantic literature. Anticipating Jung, the Romantics subscribed to the notion that true human struggle lay in the urge to integrate good and evil: true evil lodged in the opposition of psychic opposites; true good in their reconciliation. Thus, for the Romantics, the "Christ/Satan" dichotomy symbolized precisely such a need for psychic integration.[21] The dualism that pervades these Romantic beliefs anticipates the integration of psychic polarities upon which Jungian psychology is based. As established by Jung, the keystone of analytical psychology was the process of individuation, consisting in the recognition of one's dark personality (the shadow) and, in the case of men, its assimilation to consciousness through the mediating role of the female anima. According to the Swiss psychiatrist, then, the self was essentially a *coincidentia oppositorum*, containing light and dark aspects simultaneously (5:368), and like the Romantics, Jung saw the resolution of dipsychism as the prerequisite for mental stability and a successful process of individuation.

Unamuno elaborates similar ideas in all his novels that address the problem of personality, or what he understood to be the presence of conflictive psychological tendencies within a single human mind. Much like the Romantics, and his contemporary C. G. Jung, Unamuno articulated the light and dark aspects of the soul through the symbolic indivisibility of Christ and Satan. The "Puerta" segment of *El Cristo de Velázquez* expresses this notion with unmistakable clarity:

> ¡Pobre Luzbel, estrella de la tarde,
> en sombra de tinieblas convertido,
> caído desde el cielo como un rayo!
> ¡Dale, Señor, tu mano, y se derrita
> su sombra en las tinieblas de tu Padre,
> y vuelva a ser lucero matutino!
>
> (6:439–40)

> Poor Luzbel, star of the evening,
> turned into the shadow of darkness,
> fallen from heaven like a lightening flash!
> Give him Thy hand, oh Lord, and may
> his shadow melt into the darkness of Thy Father,
> and he once again become the morning star!

Because of his transgression, Lucifer, once the fabled morning star, is banished from heaven to the shadows of hell. Unamuno, however, pleads with Christ for reconciliation between the two brothers ("Dale, Señor, tu mano") who, as an integrated unit, once more will come to signify a felicitous restitution of opposites in the grace of God, the Father.

As captivated as he was by the phenomenology of psychological dualism, it is hardly surprising that Unamuno would have been attracted to Lord Byron's exegesis of the Cain/Abel legend. Jeffrey Burton Russell suggests that Byron interpreted the biblical fratricide as an attack made by Cain/Lucifer on his unintegrated, rival self, or the Abel/Jehovah facet of his own personality.[22] Although Unamuno denied the influence of Byron's *Cain: A Mystery* (1821) on *Abel Sánchez* (2:685), he, very much like Byron, equates Cain with Satan, and his empathetic portrayal of Cain as predestined to do evil, damned a priori by God to a fall he could not evade, is typically Byronic in spirit.[23] Unamuno's pity of Cain is confirmed unequivocally by Joaquín during his famous banquet speech: "¡Pobre Caín!," he exclaims, "Nuestro Abel Sánchez admira a Caín como Milton admiraba a Satán . . . porque admirar es amar y amar es compadecer. Nuestro Abel ha sentido toda la miseria, toda *la desgracia inmerecida* del que mató al primer Abel" (2:716, emphasis added; "[Poor Cain.] Our Abel Sánchez admires Cain just as Milton admired Satan . . . for to admire is to love and to love is to pity. Our Abel has sensed all the misery, all the [*undeserved*] misfortune of the one who killed the first Abel" [K-N, 6:300).[24] Although in this instance Unamuno compares Milton's admiration of Satan's tragic majesty to Abel's admiration of Cain, Byron's psychological approach to the Cain/Abel myth could not have but stimulated a responsive chord in Unamuno. Not only is Byron's *Cain* read and discussed by the antagonists of *Abel Sánchez*, but Unamuno himself conveys an interpretation of the Old Testament fratricide analogous to Byron's view of the same rivalry as an embodiment of split personality.

In addition to the inspiration Unamuno found in classical mythology and the Romantic view of Cain and Abel as representative of ego cleavage, he may have also been inspired by Robert Louis Stevenson's novel *The Strange Case of Dr. Jekyll and Mr. Hyde.* Unamuno's familiarity with Stevenson's work is suggested by his story "Artemio Heautontimouroumenos" (March 1918), in which an evocative parallel is drawn between Dr. Jekyll, Mr. Hyde, and the divided Artemio:

Artemio A. Silva se lanzó a su vida pública . . . llevando en sí, como todo hijo de hombre y mujer, por lo menos dos yos, acaso más, pero reunidos en torno de estos dos que le acaudillaban. Llevaba su ángel bueno y su ángel malo, o como habría dicho Pascal, su ángel y su bestia. Eran como el doctor Jekyll y el Mr. Hyde del maravilloso relato de Stevenson, relato que nadie que quiera saber algo de los abismos del alma humana debe ignorar. (2:877)[25]

(Artemio A. Silva began life . . . bearing within himself, as do all children born of man and woman, at least two selves, perhaps more, but the lesser ones always grouped around the two in command. Artemio bore within him a guardian angel and a black angel or, as Pascal would have said, his angel and his personal demon. These two were like the Dr. Jekyll and Mr. Hyde of Stevenson's marvelous story, a story anyone interested in knowing something about the depths of the human soul should not ignore.)

As does Stevenson, Unamuno intuits that split personality occurs when the ego rejects its shadow by denying it access to consciousness and a participation in the adult self. Under these circumstances the shadow splinters away from the personality and assumes a rival existence as an autonomous psychic entity (Jung, 9.1:279). Unlike Unamuno, who typically projected his unpalatable qualities onto those outside himself, Joaquín presents the more infrequent case in which the positive qualities that normally compose the ego are rejected, while the negative traits of the shadow are permitted to surface, and to seize hold of the ego (Jung, 5:66). In these rare cases, the positive characteristics of the ego are repressed, causing the ego to assume the negative features customarily associated with the shadow archetype (Jung, 9.2:8).

Although it is normal to discharge psychic incompatibilities by projecting them onto others, it is possible to reject in the same fashion the positive values one feels to be alien, or inaccessible, to the self (Jung, 6:457). Those parts of his personality that Joaquín rejects as nonexistent, namely kindness, vocational success, and a need to love and be loved in return, are projected onto Abel, who is none other than the positive, but repressed half of Joaquín's divided ego. Jung called this process of becoming one's opposite *enantiodromia* (5:375). Inversion of this type is frequently associated with a repression of the shadow personality which, if left unresolved, may lead the alternate self to overwhelm, and finally to destroy the ego.[26]

From a very young age Joaquín falls into a pattern of believing himself to be repulsive, and he begins to play the role of the *antipático* he fantasizes his playmates imagine him to be: "Ya desde entonces era él [Abel] simpático, no sabía por qué y antipático yo . . . y me dejaban solo. Desde niño me aislaban mis amigos" (2:689; For some unknown reason, already in those days, Abel was the agreeable one, and I the disagreeable one . . . and I was left alone. Since the days of my childhood I was isolated by my friends). Through the process of *enantiodromia* Joaquín accepts the negative *persona* created for him by others, becoming what Unamuno called (quoting Oliver Wendell Holmes), the "el que le creen los otros" (2:973; the person others believe one to be).

Unamuno, however, goes to great lengths to show Joaquín's sense of justice and equanimity toward the less fortunate, the persecuted, and the outcast. In the same manner he carefully insinuates enough subtle cruelties and egotistical traits into Abel's character to prevent him from becoming entirely a stereotype of innocence. It is Joaquín who succors the Aragonese beggar whom Abel humiliates and turns away; it is also Joaquín who expresses genuine astonishment when the same beggar claims readiness to give his own life for that of his benefactor: "¿Querer ser yo? ¡No lo comprendo! . . . ni siquiera comprendo que nadie quiera ser otro. Ser otro es dejar de ser uno, de serse el que se es" (2:741; You want to be me? I don't understand! . . . I don't understand how anyone could want to be someone else. To be someone else is to cease being the person who you are).[27] It had never occurred to Joaquín that someone could envy him, a despicable man devoured by hate, and that it would be an envy quite different in nature from that which he felt for Abel. Whereas the Aragonese beggar would like to assume Joaquín's identity, Joaquín would rather possess what Abel has so easily acquired: the beautiful Helena, social acceptance, professional acclaim, and a male child.

The generosity of Joaquín's spirit imparts a human dimension to his character, corroborating Unamuno's empathy for the Cain/Satan figure. In Unamuno's view it is Cain's openly rebellious nature that makes him more honorable than the Abel-type personality with its quietly calculating passivity: "Desconfío del que no lucha," wrote Unamuno in 1904, "y veo siempre un mayor enemigo en el que se me somete que en el que me resiste" (1:1208; I mistrust anyone who does not struggle, and I always see a greater enemy in the person who yields before me than in the one who resists me). The fictional variation on this theme appears in Unamuno's description of Joaquín and Abel as young boys: ". . . parecía dominar e iniciarlo todo Joaquín, el más voluntarioso; pero era Abel quien, pareciendo ceder, hacía la suya siempre. Y es que le importaba más no obedecer que mandar" (2:689; ". . . it was Joaquín, the more willful of the two, who seemed to initiate . . . and dominate everything. Still, Abel, appearing to yield, really always did as he pleased. The truth was that he found not obeying more important than commanding" [K-N, 6:249]). Many years later, Abel's own son confirms the hypocritical nature of his father's personality:

Pero mi padre no siente la pintura ni nada. Es de corcho, maestro. . . . No vive más que para su gloria. Todo eso de que la desprecia es farsa. . . . No busca más que el aplauso. Y es un egoísta. . . . No quiere a nadie. (2:735)

([But my father does not feel painting or anything else. He is made of cork. . . .] he lives only for his own glory. All that talk about despising fame is a farce . . . he seeks only applause. And he is an egoist. . . . He doesn't love anyone else. [K-N, 6:333])

Unamuno always maintained that the *abelitas* were as responsible for their downfall as were the *cainitas*, arguing that *abelitas* surreptitiously cultivated envy in the *cainitas*, and thus provoked them to their vengeful behavior. Joaquín insinuates as much to Abel during their discussion of the latter's research for his painting:

¡Ah!, pero ¿tú crees que los afortunados no tienen culpa de ello? La tienen de no ocultar . . . todo favor gratuito. . . . Porque no me cabe duda de que Abel restregaría a los hocicos de Caín su gracia, le azuzaría con el humo de sus ovejas. . . . Los que se creen justos suelen ser unos arrogantes que van a deprimir a los otros con la ostentación de su justicia. (2:710–11)

([Ah, but do you think that the fortunate] are not to blame? The truth is that they are to blame for not concealing . . . every gratuitous favor. . . . For I have no doubt that Abel flaunted his favor [in the face of Cain, taunted him with the smoke of his burnt offerings]. . . . Those who believe themselves to be . . . just, tend to be supremely arrogant people bent on crushing others [with] the ostentation of their justice." [K-N, 6:289])

In the essay "La ciudad de Henoc" (1933), Unamuno would employ almost identical turns of phrase to again cast aspersions on the *abelita* majority that he portrayed as responsible for the bloodthirsty actions of the *cainitas*:

. . . es que el envidiado suele darse a provocar la envidia; es que el perseguido busca que se le persiga; es que el atacado de manía persecutoria incita a la manía perseguidora del otro. Es que en las democracias las masas de instintos rebañegos [los abelitas] no hacen sino azuzar a los solitarios de instintos lobunos. ¿De qué parte está la envidia? (7:1094)

(. . . the envied tend to provoke envy; the pursued look for persecution; those who suffer from a persecution mania incite that mania in others. It's that in democracies, the majority possesses a herdlike instinct and cannot help rousing the carnivorous appetites of the lone wolf. In which of the two, then, does envy reside?)

At Salamanca, Unamuno was frequently the victim of political and pedagogical intrigue often based on petty academic rivalries. Academic promotion, for example, to which Unamuno was a notable exception, was laboriously slow in his time, and tremendous rancor would have been directed at an *arriviste* such as Unamuno, who not only advanced quickly in his profession, but also enjoyed successes outside the academy. Henri Ellenberger makes an interesting observation regarding Léon Daudet's (1867–1942) description of *invidia* as professional resentment arising among writers, adding that Daudet's remarks "would be equally applicable to university scholars of his period."[28] It should come as no surprise, then, that in *Abel Sánchez*, the first major work of fiction Unamuno published after he was summarily dismissed as rector of the University of Salamanca in 1914, the novelist would feel a natural empathy for the Cain figure as a controversial, though undeservedly misunderstood individual. He clearly imagined Cain as an aggressive and historically oriented character who, like himself, was as much a victim of his own envious nature as he was the object of envy and persecution by others.

There are striking parallels between Joaquín's journal entries and the conscious awareness of personal agony put on public display in Unamuno's *Diario íntimo*, written some twenty years prior to *Abel Sánchez*. Accordingly, Ricardo Gullón's observation that "la representación del drama que Monegro ha montado para sí y para sus íntimos, haciendo—como Unamuno hacía—espectáculo de su alma" should not be taken lightly.[29] (The stage play put on by Monegro not only for his own benefit, but also for that of his family, making—as did Unamuno—a spectacle of his soul). Unamuno noted in his diary that "La vanagloria se viste de humildad. Con razón dirían que sólo busco notoriedad, y es que es vanidad dar a conocer mis crisis" (8:804; Vainglory masquerades as humility. Those who say I seek only fame are right because it is vanity that leads me to make my personal crises public). In the same vein, Joaquín writes in his *Confesión* that personal vanity causes him to make a public spectacle of his most "intimate and revolting pain. . . . This very Diary, is it not something more than simply giving vent to my feelings?" (2:711).

Joaquín admits he harbors a secret hope that someday his child, or grandchildren, might publish the *Confesión* so that those who knew him would be overcome by "admiración . . . ante aquel héroe de la angustia tenebrosa que pasó sin que le conocieran en todo su fondo los que con él convivieron" (2:746; awe . . . before such a dark and anguished hero who passed through life without revealing his innermost secrets to those who knew him well). In the same tone Unamuno asks himself: "¿Acaso mientras he escrito ciertas cartas no ha pasado por mi mente la idea de que el destinatario las guardara? . . . ¡Funesta vanidad que sacrifica el alma al nombre!" (8:845; As I wrote some of my letters, did it not occur to me that, perhaps, the addressee might keep some of them? . . . It is an ill-starred vanity that sacrifices the soul for the sake of renown!). Making direct reference to the *Diario* itself, Unamuno again voices the same concern: "Estos mismos cuadernillos ¿no son una vanidad? ¿Para qué los escribo? ¿He sabido, acaso, tenerlos ocultos como fue mi primer propósito?" (8:846; These very notebooks, are they not a vanity? For whose sake do I keep them? Have I managed to hide them away as I had first intended?).

Both Monegro's and Unamuno's journals reveal an awareness that suffering confers an aura of superiority on the one who experiences emotional distress: "¿Por qué he de creerme superior a los demás hasta en mi capacidad para la tribulación y la lucha? Estoy muy enfermo y enfermo de 'yoismo,'" writes Unamuno (8:845; Why do I believe myself superior to others, even in my capacity for tribulation and struggle? I am very ill, and ill with "ego-itis"). In his *Confesión*, Joaquín echoes his maker: "Me figuro que habría quien desee tener un tumor pestífero como no le ha tenido ninguno para hombrearse con él. Esta misma Confesión ¿no es algo más que un desahogo?" (2:711; I imagine that there could be people who might wish to have the most noxious of tumors, such as no one has had before, just so they can act the man about their misfortunes. This selfsame Diary, is it not something more than a mere airing of my personal anguish?).

There is also a coincidence between Unamuno's recognition that his religious conversion may be the subject of wagging tongues, and Joaquín's anticipation of a similar reaction to his religious conversion on the part of his colleagues. Unamuno confesses in the *Diario íntimo:* ". . . se han percatado de mi cambio, hasta algunos periódicos han hablado de él, me he creado una nueva posición. Y ¿no es ésta una nueva esclavitud? . . . ¿Por qué me inquieto tanto de los demás?" (8:844; . . . they have noticed a change in me, even some newspapers have spoken of it. I've created a new status for myself. And, is this not a new form of slavery? . . . Why do I bother with the opinions of others?). Joaquín initially resists his wife's suggestion that he turn to religion, inquiring: "¿Y qué dirán los que conocen mis ideas? . . . [pero] empezó a frecuentar el templo, algo demasiado a las claras, como en son de desafío a los que conocían sus ideas irreligiosas" (2:719; And what will those who know my convictions say? . . . yet he began to frequent church services somewhat too conspicuously, as if to provoke those who were familiar with his lack of religious belief).

The correspondence of some key portions of Unamuno's *Diario íntimo* with Monegro's *Confesión* provides evidence that Unamuno saw himself and Joaquín as sharing a common destiny. To a great extent both of them exposed, or hoped to expose, their private lives to the mirror of public scrutiny. But while the mature Unamuno only suspected he had become the *persona* his public had invented, Joaquín, as Gullón correctly implied, is instrumental in creating his dour, envious self and in staging the drama of his rivalry with Abel by succumbing to the insinuations of a demon he himself had invented.[30]

Considerable effort is required to face the self-scrutiny necessary to initiate a dialogue with one's shadow personality. Joaquín's tragedy lies in being unable to muster enough self-confidence to assimilate his "demonio de la guarda" (guardian devil), and to overcome the resistance he feels toward acknowledging the self that hates Abel.[31] The deadlock that arises between Joaquín's rejected ego and his dominant, but negative shadow personality, is due in large part to his conscious effort to repress his hate for Abel. Rather than accepting this side of himself, and finding ways of reconciling with it, thereby preventing a darkening of his life, Joaquín erroneously attempts to conquer hate through interiorization: ". . . empecé a odiar a Abel con toda mi alma y a proponerme a la vez ocultar ese odio, abonarlo, criarlo, cuidarlo en lo recóndito de las entrañas de mi alma" (2:697; . . . I began to hate Abel with all my soul and, at the same time, to plan to conceal that hate, to cultivate it, tend it, and care for it in the innermost bowels of my soul).

In his seminal essay "Sobre la soberbia," Unamuno notes that the shadow personality becomes damaging to one's psyche only when it is interiorized:

El satánico yo es dañino mientras lo tenemos encerrado, contemplándose a sí mismo y recreándose en esa contemplación; más así que lo echamos fuera y lo esparcimos en la acción, hasta su soberbia puede producir frutos de bendición. (1:1212)

(Our "satanic I" is harmful only while we keep it imprisoned, contemplating itself, and taking delight in that contemplation. As soon as we cast the devil out of ourselves, and channel that energy into action, even envy can produce beneficent results.)

Although Joaquín is capable of recognizing and identifying the characteristics of his shadow, or what Unamuno called the *satánico yo*, he chooses to beat the inner demon into quiescence rather than to accept him through reconciliation. His banquet speech is a last, valiant "lucha gigantesca de aquel alma con su demonio" (2:716). While the speech is a personal and oratorical triumph, it is at the same time a psychological failure since at its conclusion the demon seems to remain at large. Immediately following the banquet, the *satánico yo* insinuates to Joaquín a novel desire to "dedicarse a la oratoria para adquirir en ella gloria con que oscurecer la de su amigo en la pintura" (2:717; devote himself to public speaking as a means of gaining the fame with which to overshadow his friend's renown in painting).

Joaquín's inability or unwillingness to rid himself of his guardian devil is ultimately responsible for robbing him of the energy he needs to pursue the career in medical research that could have won for him a fame and glory equal to that of Abel. Monegro's error lies in his stubborn refusal to seek the solution to his crisis from within himself. He spends a lifetime searching for a "cure" in the actions of others: he marries Antonia "buscando un amparo" (2:706), hoping that she would "sorberle el demonio" (2:717). He later assumes that "una vez padre se me curaría aquello" (2:712), and disappointed that the child Antonia bears him is female, Joaquín determines to use his daughter as "mi vengadora" (2:713). Years later, he convinces Joaquina that she must marry his rival's son if she wishes to help her father survive. In his diary Monegro confesses to his daughter that "Sólo uniendo tu suerte a la suerte del hijo único de quien me ha envenenado la fuente de la vida, sólo mezclando así nuestras sangres, esperaba poder salvarme" (2:742; Only by linking your fate with the only son of the man who contaminated the wellsprings of my life, only by mixing our bloodlines, did I hope for salvation). None of these solutions proves to be adequate, however, since none arises from within Joaquín's personal autonomy, and the guardian devil continues to rule his life. Only on his deathbed does Monegro admit that the cause of his tragedy was his own weakness and lack of moral courage.

In his study of the double as a psychological and literary phenomenon, Otto Rank notes that friction between doubles often revolves around competition for a woman's attentions. Rank further observes that this original conflict is frequently replaced by a series of subsequent persecutory delusions.[32] Unamuno likewise intuited that fraternal competition engendered envy, and envy a persecution complex. As early as 1907, he remarked that "este funesto cáncer de la envidia ha engendrado, por reacción, otra enfermedad, y es la manía persecutoria, la enfermedad del que se cree víctima" (3:285; this noxious cancer of envy has engendered, in turn, another illness, and it is the mania of persecution, an illness common among those who believe themselves to be victims). Unamuno again refers to a similar notion in an essay published during the same time period as *Abel Sánchez:* "Y con ella, con la envidia, la manía persecutoria que es su correlativa. Donde el espíritu propende a envidiar es muy natural que se crea envidiado y perseguido" (3:775; And with it, with envy, comes its correlative, which is the mania of persecution. Whenever a man tends toward envy, it is natural that he believe himself envied and persecuted).

Through the process of projection, Joaquín comes to believe that he is the victim of Abel's envy, "pues se dio en creer que toda la pasión que bajo su aparente impasibiliada de egoísta animaba a Abel era la envidia, la envidia de él, a Joaquín, que por envidia le arrebatara de mozo el afecto de sus compañeros, que por envidia le quitó a Helena" (2:747; Joaquín was convinced that whatever passion animated Abel beneath his apparently impassive and egoistic façade was based on envy; an envy of him, of Joaquín. That it was envy which led Abel to steal the affections of his childhood friends; that it was envy which led Abel to woo Helena away from him). The loss of Helena leads Joaquín to believe his delusions of purposefully inflicted shame, persecution, and imaginary snubs. He becomes convinced that Abel and Helena based their decision to marry solely on the intention of reviling him: "Ellos se casaron por rebajarme, por humillarme, por denigrarme; ellos se casaron por burlarse de mí; ellos se casaron contra mí" (2:707; "They got married only to demean me, to humiliate and denigrate me; they married to mock me; they married [to thwart me]" [K-N, 6:283]).

Consistent with Rank's observation that the original conflict between doubles over a woman tends to be replaced by other delusions, the loss of Helena to his rival causes Joaquín to replace his obsessive feelings for his cousin with the new desire of winning a fame and success greater than those enjoyed by Abel. He reverts to the contention of his student days, "insisting on proving to Abel that medicine was also an art, and a fine art at that, in which there was room for poetic inspiration" (2:690). As a grown man, Joaquín plans to dedicate himself to medical research and, through the renown he will acquire, he intends to show Helena that it was he, "el médico, el antipático, quien habría de darle aureola de gloria y no él, no el pintor" (2:700; the doctor, the disagreeable one, who could have bestowed upon her a halo of glory, and not his rival, not the painter).

Rof Carballo, following Melanie Klein, suggests that the most envied of people are those who possess the gift of creativity. He proposes that Lucifer's crime was not pride as is commonly believed, but the envy of God's creative capabilities.[33] It is quite possible that Unamuno may have also inferred a similar connection between the envy motivating Joaquín and his resentment of Abel's artistic talent. Joaquín's attempt to compete with Abel by insisting that he, the medical doctor, is an "artista, un verdadero poeta en su profesion, un clínico genial, creador, intuitivo" (2:704), appears to confirm the relationship Rof Carballo perceived between Satan's envy of God's creative power and the general, human tendency to envy those blessed with creative talent.

As the subject of psychological inquiry, Joaquín demonstrates what Karen Horney calls an "aggressive-vindictive" type of personality: one characterized by a "bitter and pervasive kind of envy" that is rooted in a feeling of being excluded from life.[34] Joaquín notes in his journal, "Fue peor . . . lo que me hicieron todos, todos los que encontré desde que, niño aún y lleno de confianza, busqué el apoyo y el amor de mis semejantes. ¿Por qué me rechazaban? ¿Por qué me acojían [sic] fríamente y como obligados a ello?" (2:746; "Much worse, were the acts of every human being upon whom I have relied for love and support since the days of my childhood. . . . [Why was I rejected? Why would people receive me coldly, as if they were obligated to deal with me?"] [K-N, 6:355]). Like Joaquín, the aggressive-vindictive human being seeks to give his personality coherence through self-aggrandizement and the mastery of others.[35] Because the aggressive-vindictive personality constantly strives to overcome the "other," he condemns himself to live in the future, thereby allowing the present to escape him. This personality type plans to become "the great hero, the persecutor, the leader, the scientist attaining immortal fame."[36] In much the same way, Joaquín is sustained by the hope that his anticipated successes as a medical scientist will prove to those who had rejected him just how mistaken they had been. Joaquín "se creía un espíritu de excepción, y como tal, torturado, y más capaz de dolor que los otros, un alma señalada al nacer por Dios con la señal de los predestinados" (2:746). He speaks incessantly of his intent to punish Helena, and to take revenge on everyone else by winning for himself the reputation of a great scientist, finally surpassing Abel's fame as a painter. Nevertheless Joaquín also recognizes that his obsession with Abel robs him of the time and energy he needs for independent research: ". . . esa misma pasión fangosa, el exceso de mi despecho y mi odio me quitaban serenidad de espíritu. No, no tenía el ánimo para el estudio" (2:704; . . . that same filthy passion, the excess of my ill will and my loathing, deprived me of the necessary serenity of spirit. No, it did not leave me the energy with which I could undertake research).

Despite his better judgment, Joaquín is repeatedly drawn to the Sánchez household, although these visits only serve to exacerbate his emotional instability. There is a certain amount of pleasure in the pain of this masochism since it keeps Joaquín's hatred alive and feeds the envy which, in turn, regulates his behavior and becomes the reason for his existence. Shortly after his marriage, Abel falls gravely ill, and Joaquín accepts Helena's request that he care for her husband. Although tempted to allow his rival to die, Joaquín opts to keep Abel alive: "¡No dejaré yo que se muera, no debo dejarlo; está comprometido mi honor, y luego . . . , necesito que viva! Y al decir este '¡necesito que viva!,' temblábale toda el alma" (2:701; "I will not let him die, I must not [allow that], my honor is at stake, and . . . I need to have him live. And as Joaquín said 'he must live!,' his [entire] soul trembled" [K-N, 6:271]). Obsessed with Abel as a kind of lifeline, Joaquín does, indeed, become the *poseído* that he at first only imagined himself to be.

For one so consumed by envy, recognition by the rival is of utmost importance. The magnetism of the Sánchez household is partially due to the incomprehensible disregard in which Joaquín is held by Abel and Helena. By Joaquín's own admission, the realization that Abel and Helena "don't even think about me, don't even hate me," torments him even more than his envy of Abel's success. Joaquín convinces himself that "ser odiado por él con un odio como yo le tenía, era algo y podía haber sido mi salvación" (2:714; to be hated by him, with a hatred equal to my own, would have already been something, and could have been my salvation). Abel, however, maintains himself above the fray in a morally "superior" position, effectively neutralizing Joaquín's existence by conferring no recognition at all upon him as a "rival."[37] Abel's attitude frustrates Joaquín's sense of self-worth so much that he asks God to instill in Abel a hatred comparable to his own. The prospect of seeing Abel suffer the tortures of envy produces in Joaquín a perverse pleasure "que le hizo temblar hasta los tuétanos del alma, escalofriados. ¡Ser envidiado! . . . ¡Ser envidiado!" (2:728; that made him tremble, chilling him to the very marrow of his soul. To be envied! . . . Oh, to be envied!).

Joaquín's adult fascination with Abel's success and fame as a painter lies in the first blow dealt him by his friend's success with Helena. Perhaps Joaquín's fixation on his cousin may be understood better if we consider the fascination she exerts upon him in the context of her qualities as a quintessential "anima woman." As distinct from the anima archetype, the anima-motivated woman represents all the female mythology men tend to project upon her. A man feels "understood" by this type of woman, believing her to be capable of bringing out his "true nature." In reality, the anima female has little individual personality or feelings for others. Much like Unamuno's Helena, the anima woman is unconscious of the divisive effect her presence has upon men, and she manipulates them without being aware of the consequences of her behavior.[38] When pressed, both Joaquín and Abel must admit that Helena is incapable of love, describing her as "nothing more than a beautiful shell of vanity" (2:271).

According to Jung, Helen of Troy, endowed with "considerable powers of fascination and possession," exemplifies the typical anima female (9.1:28). Perhaps this explains the continuous attraction Helena exercises over Joaquín, regardless of the snubs and sarcasm she aims at him. The anima woman also "offers an excellent hook for anima projections" to men with a passive Eros (Jung, 9.1:88–89). This may account for Abel's rapid empathy with Helena, since he insists that she was the aggressor and he the seduced: "Aunque no lo creas, soy un seducido" (2:696; Although you may not believe me, I was the seduced), he remonstrates before Joaquín, who retorts sarcastically: "¡Pobre víctima! Se pelean por ti las mujeres" (Poor victim! You have women fighting over you). It is the passive Abel, rather than the aggressive Joaquín, who catches Helena's fancy. It is also Abel, the aesthete, who responds to the animal nature of this woman, variously recognizing her as a *pava real*, an *india brava*, a *pantera*, and a *fiera indómita* (2:692–93).

Joaquín's misfortune lies not only in rejecting his innately positive qualities, but also in allowing his anima to remain fixated upon Helena even after she must be ceded to the rival through marriage. Since he imagines himself incapable of loving any woman other than his cousin, Joaquín determines to find a wife as quickly as possible since, given the circumstances, any female would do. His decision confirms Otto Rank's observation that in literature related to the double motif, the protagonist often takes a wife so that she will act as a barrier against persecution by the "other."[39] Joaquín devotes his energies to seeking a woman "en que defenderse de aquel odio que sentía . . . para no ver los ojos infernales del dragón de hielo" (2:702; who would shield him from the hatred he felt . . . from the hellish eyes of the icy dragon). He marries Antonia "buscando en ella un amparo, y la pobre adivinó . . . cómo le era un escudo" (2:706; looking for protection, and the poor woman understood . . . that she functioned as his shield). Unfortunately, Joaquín never allows himself to love Antonia properly. Although he recognizes her superiority to Helena, he continues to be enamored of the "peacock": "Antonia le era muy superior, sin duda, pero la otra era la otra" (Antonia was undoubtedly far superior to her, but the other was the other" (2:721). Antonia, too, feels that between herself and her husband is an invisible wall, and she acknowledges that Joaquín cannot be fully hers since he has not yet become the master of his own destiny (2:706).

The stalemate between a male ego and his shadow is meant to be resolved by the intervention of the anima whose role it is to mediate the contents of the shadow to consciousness, initiating a coalescence of the male psyche. Joaquín's inability to accept Antonia as a mediating force maintains the draw between himself and his *satánico yo*, perpetuating indefinitely his moral conflict with the "other." Had she been permitted to fulfill her role, Antonia could have successfully exercised her "curative" powers. Instead she is reduced to an object used for vengeful purposes: "Pero ¿llegué yo a querer de veras a mi Antonia?," asks Joaquín. "¡Ah!, si hubiera sido capaz de quererla me habría salvado. Era para mí otro instrumento de venganza. Queríala para madre de un hijo" (2:712; But did I ever come to love my Antonia? Oh, if I had only been capable of loving her, she could have saved me. For me, she was just another instrument of revenge. I wanted her to be the mother of a son). Monegro goes through life an unwell man, unwell because of his insistence on separation rather than relatedness, and his fear and hatred of himself.

Hate and rejection of some aspects of the self, personified by the pursuing shadow image or double, often culminate in "suicide by way of death intended for the irksome persecutor."[40] Joaquín's role in Abel's "accidental" death is symbolic of his attempt to remove that part of his psyche which had pursued and tormented him for many years. The act is, of course, futile since the slaying of one's double is only an illusory separation of the negative aspects of the ego

from the self. This characteristic elimination of the "other" is tantamount to suicide since the ego cannot long survive without the complementary presence of its opposite. Abel's death thus represents
Joaquín's own self-destruction: rather than relieving him of the unwelcome pursuit of his double, the rival's demise causes Joaquín to
fall into a deep melancholy, and an "espeso bochorno pesaba sobre la
casa" (2:757; feeling of deep suffocation weighed upon the household). Within one year of Abel's passing, Monegro seems to will his
own: "¿Para qué [vivir]? ¿Para llegar a viejo? . . . calló. No quiso o
no pudo proseguir" (2:759; "What should I live for? To grow old?"
. . . Joaquín fell silent. He could not, or did not wish, to go on).
Joaquín's end becomes imminent when a crucial part of his psyche is
definitively severed and, with it, the reason for his existence.[41]

Joaquín's deathbed confession that Antonia had not been able to
cure him of his malaise because he could not bring himself to love her
honestly, must be taken as a delayed recognition of his failure to
accept Antonia's role as mediatrix. Rather than the ranting of a bitter
man determined to inflict one last insult on his family, Joaquín's
admission is a tremendous, if belated, act of insight, one that he had
resisted all his life. At the moment of death, however, he is able to
confess: "No pudiste curarme, no pudiste hacerme bueno. . . . Y no
pudiste hacerme bueno, porque no te he querido. . . . Si te hubiera
querido me habría curado. . . . Y ahora me duele no haberte querido. Si pudiéramos volver a empezar" (2:758; You could not heal
me, you were unable to make me well. . . . And you could not make
me well because I did not love you. . . . Had I loved you, I could have
been healed. . . . And now I deeply regret not having loved you. If
we could only begin all over again). It has taken Joaquín a lifetime to
recognize his own culpability in the ultimate failure of his life. In the
last moments of that shattered existence Monegro is finally able to
relinquish the claim that his salvation was the responsibility of others, and to accept the reasons for his personal failure as intrinsic to
himself.

Unamuno's interest in doubling and self-duplication may have
been founded upon his personal fear of death. Rank points out that
fear of death is often compensated by a tremendous love of life.[42] For
Unamuno nothing seemed as repugnant as the idea of permanent
annihilation: ". . . nada se me aparecía tan horrible como la nada
misma. Era una furiosa hambre de ser, un apetito de divinidad como
nuestro ascético dijo" (7:114; "nothing seemed as horrible to me as
Nothingness. It was a furious hunger to be, an 'appetite for divinity,'

as one of our ascetics put it" [K-N, 5:12]). In Unamuno's opinion, the very essence of humanity is characterized by "nuestro anhelo de nunca morirnos" (7:113; our desire to live forever). The need to extract guarantees of eternal life from a possibly fictional God may thus account for his fascination with doubling since, to a great extent, the threat of death is mitigated by the existence of a shadow, an alter ego, or one's reflected image.

While Unamuno's "furiosa hambre de ser" seems to imply what Jung perceived as the human striving toward psychic plenitude, what he proves to be seeking is not an existentially tenable coexistence with the "other," but an aggressive kind of self-expansion through the ingestion of all potential rivals.[43] As conceived by Jung, the process of individuation can only be attained through compromise. It consists of a metaphorical smoothing of the rough edges of ego and shadow so that each can adjust more successfully to the other's dimensions. Although in his prose fiction Unamuno seems to describe fairly accurately the human striving toward psychic wholeness, the metaphysical compromise such wholeness implies seems to have made it impossible for him to entertain the viability of psychic totality on the practical level. Unamuno's insistence on being all things at all times, his "esfuerzo por ser más, por serlo todo," placed tremendous limitations on the conciliatory frame of mind necessary for a successful incorporation of opposites to take place within the psyche.

However much Unamuno's "apetito de infinidad y de eternidad" is thought to be indicative of a protean ego, or ontological insecurity, this kind of intensity is the product of a psyche yearning to integrate its multiplicity of selves into a coherent and indissoluble totality. It is conceivable, therefore, that Unamuno's unflagging exploration of the split personality reveals an intent to analyze his own duality through the therapy of literary creation. The solution Unamuno appears to reach in *Abel Sánchez*, however, does not take into account a successful resolution of psychic dualism. Nevertheless, Unamuno appears to find an equivalent of Jung's spiritual *coincidentia oppositorum* in the chiasmus, a rhetorical trope that he transposes from its normally stylistic function to one allowing for the structuring of a novel based on the principle of psychological *enantiodromia*, or the conversion of one thing into its opposite. Essentially, the chiasmus, a rhetorical device Unamuno favors especially in his essays, inverts the word order between two parallel phrases or clauses to yield paradoxical yet complementary meanings. The structural premise of the chiasmus thus permits Unamuno to unite not only antithetical words or symbols, but entire concepts, while simultaneously ensuring that each element involved conserves its "separate but equal" status within the parameters of their temporary union.[44] Adopting the chiasmus to convey the inner dualism of his protagonists seems to be the only possible response on Unamuno's part to the integration of psychological polarities. It is only through the chiasmus—that is, through an intellectual conceit—that Unamuno is able to approach successfully the archetype of individuation that he normally found inadmissible on the existential and ontological levels. Thus his stories of male, and not infrequently female doubling, are but pretexts through which Unamuno seeks to experience the fully integrated, yet perpetually elusive self.

Abel Sánchez presents a good illustration of the case in point. While Joaquín Monegro begins life as an ostensibly cynical doctor, and Abel Sánchez as an intuitive artist, their attributes are quickly reversed. Joaquín develops into an intuitive "artist," while Abel becomes a "scientific" painter and covert cynic. It is Abel who immortalizes on his canvases the patients whose lives Joaquín fails to prolong through the application of medical science: "El, él que con su arte resucita e inmortaliza a los que tú dejas morir por tu torpeza" (2:706; "He, who through his art resurrects and immortalizes those you allow to die because of your [clumsiness]" [K-N, 6:282]). This chiastic juxtaposition may be rendered by the following diagram:

Another chiasmus is constructed around the title of the novel. Although it bears the words "Abel Sánchez," the book is actually about Joaquín Monegro, the character meant to represent the ego personality whose tortured life the novel intends to chronicle. Abel will be remembered by posterity only because Joaquín re-creates him in his diary: ". . . la mayor coyuntura que tienes de perpetuarte," writes Joaquín, "no son tus cuadros, sino es que yo acierte a pintarte con mi pluma tal y como eres" (2:747; "the best chance you have to perpetuate your memory does not lie with your paintings but rather with me, with whether or not I succeed in painting you just as you are, with my pen" [K-N, 6:355]). Joaquín has, in effect, ingested Abel, and Abel becomes a kind of parasite staying alive through the nourishment of Joaquín's words.[45] As Abel becomes the recipient of Joaquín's rejected, positive ego, he acquires a fictional stature greater than that of Joaquín. Without Abel, Joaquín would not have suffered the torments that led him to begin his journal, and without this journal, he has no reason at all to exist as the exceptionally tormented fictional entity that he is, worthy of a reader's attention. Unamuno therefore inverts the normal ego/shadow relationship, as described in the following chiasmus:

By allowing his shadow to replace his ego, Joaquín relinquishes autonomy and permits his conscious life to be manipulated by a threateningly independent alter ego. The novel therefore bears Abel's name since it is Abel who determines the course of events in Joaquín's life.

Like the rhetorical chiasmus that hurls two pairs of unlike, but complementary verbal constructs against each other into momentary union, the splintered facets of Joaquín, the poetic scientist, and Abel, the scientific painter, are simultaneously attracted to, and repelled by each other, sundered by their uncompromising individuality. Although Joaquín and Abel are essentially indivisible, neither is able to surrender autonomy in the interest of a harmonious coexistence. Thus they remain, like Unamuno's own personality, an ego forever at variance with its shadow.

6. *San Manuel Bueno, mártir*
God as Great Mother

¿Dios es macho o hembra? (Unamuno, 7:332)

(Is God male or female?)

San Manuel Bueno, mártir is a thematic and aesthetic reprisal of many ideas Unamuno introduced in his first novel, *Paz en la guerra*. Unlike the *nivola* and its concern for the existential plight of the individual, Unamuno's last important novel marks a return to the unconscious collective life of *intrahistoria*, symbolized by the villagers of Valverde de Lucerna whose perspective on reality does not extend beyond the parameters of their church and saintly priest. However, unlike *Paz en la guerra* in which history assumes the role of protagonist, historic time—represented by Lázaro's rejected, Catholic agrarian syndicate—does not play a crucial role in *San Manuel Bueno, mártir*. [1]

Intrahistoria, as Unamuno portrays it in this novel, supersedes history and finally obliterates its angles and contrasts, just as the snow falling outside Angela's window as she writes her memoir, blurs the contours of lake and mountain, imparting to them, and to her story, a timeless, eternal quality. In its structural and aesthetic resemblance to the Gospels, whose primary intent it was to record the acts of Christ rather than to situate them in time and space, *San Manuel Bueno, mártir* assumes an entirely mythical dimension. The sense of "magic realism" about this novel is created by its profound contact with the archetypes of the collective unconscious, its constant contradictions, double meanings, and ambiguity.

Manuel's story unfolds in the Diocese of Renada, in the village of Valverde de Lucerna. In a 1918 essay "¡Res-nada!," Unamuno explained the paradoxical etymology of what was to become, in 1931, the name of his fictional diocese:

Res, en latín, significa "cosa," y de aquí real=efectivo. . . . Pero nótese que en catalán *res*, que empezó significando algo, ha concluido, como en francés *rien* y en castellano *nada* (cosa nacida), por significar nada.

Cerremos, pues, este peloteo de vocablos con una fórmula comprensiva, y es ésta: ¡res=nada! (7:1386)

(*Res*, in Latin, means "thing," and from that meaning we derive the word real=existent. . . . But, let me point out that in Catalan *res*, which used to mean "thing," evolved to mean *nada*, "no-thing," as do also the words *rien* and *nada* in French and Spanish.

Let me conclude this play on words, then, with a universal formula, and it is the following: thing=no-thing!)

From Unamuno's statement it may be inferred that "Renada" is an ahistorical, double nothing, located nowhere. At the same time, it is *renacida*, twice born, perhaps referring to the resurrection of the past in the village of Valverde de Lucerna at the bottom of the lake.

Manuel's story is told by Angela Carballino, whose name links her to the symbolic function of angels as divine messengers between the seen and unseen worlds.[2] Like the Evangelists, Angela salvages Manuel's story from the vagaries of oral tradition by committing his legend to written form. In the process, however, her version of the story becomes susceptible to subjective interpretation, and her reliability as a narrator is not above reproach. At the beginning of her account Angela first insists, quite emphatically, "De nuestro Don Manuel me acuerdo como si fuese de cosa de ayer" (2:1129; I remember Don Manuel as if it were yesterday); while toward the close of her narration, Angela no longer seems convinced of the accuracy of her vision: "¿Es que esto que estoy aquí contando ha pasado y ha pasado tal y como lo cuento?" (2:1152–53; Did what I am writing about really take place? And did it really happen in the way that I tell it?). What the reader ultimately learns is that Angela's story is an account three times removed from its original source. It was her brother Lázaro who actually took the notes from which Angela now reconstructs her story. Her version, in turn, is transmitted to the reader by one Miguel de Unamuno y Jugo, who found and edited Angela's manuscript.

Continuing the biblical analogy, if Angela is a modern-day evangelist recording the acts of Manuel, then Unamuno becomes a priest of the new religion, mediating the "scriptures" to the general public. Angela's motivation as mediator and messenger is further suspect, since by her own admission the account she leaves behind, should it be discovered by church authorities, would prove to be of irreparable damage to Manuel's reputation as a "saint," and certainly halt the recently initiated process of beatification.

Don Manuel Bueno embodies in himself the unresolved dialogical tensions that found their original expression in Pachico Zabalbide of *Paz en la guerra*. The fundamental difference between the two characters is that Pachico is a much less complex entity, living his duality on an alternating basis. There are really two Pachicos who surface at distinct moments of the novel. In Manuel Bueno, on the other hand, Unamuno was finally able to create a character who forges a truce, although an uneasy one it is, between his public and private, his active and contemplative, his believing and disbelieving selves. Because Manuel lives his duality simultaneously, he is forced to be the jailer of his own conscience, on constant guard as to which self is revealed when, and to whom. Unlike other Unamuno protagonists, however, don Manuel refrains from making a public spectacle of his personal despair, and he is the only character ever created by Unamuno who never questions the sincerity of his duplicity. Nevertheless, existentially speaking, this kind of double life accounts for Manuel's daily martyrdom and is the most probable cause of the "enfermedad traidora [que] le iba minando el cuerpo y el alma," bringing on his untimely death (2:1145; insidious sickness that undermined his body and his soul).

The associations of Manuel Bueno with Christ are many and overt, the most obvious being Angela's observation that "su santo patrono era el mismo Jesús Nuestro Señor" (2:1131; his patron saint was Our Lord Jesus Christ himself), and her constant juxtaposition of "nuestros dos Cristos, el de esta Tierra y el de esta aldea" (2:1147; our two Christs, the one of this Earth, and the one of this village). The coincidence of names—Emmanuel, Immanuel, Manuel, in Hebrew meaning "God with us"—is ironic since God is not with Manuel Bueno at all, as Manuel confesses to his friends Angela and Lázaro. The secondary meaning of his anguished cry, echoing that of Christ on the Cross—"My God, My God, why hast Thou forsaken me?"—again stresses Manuel's distance from the God of his parishioners.

For Jung, Christ exemplified the archetype of the self (9.2:37). Self-actualization occurs when an individual is able to incorporate his psychological dualities into a higher synthesis of unity and wholeness.[3] Jung pointed out the success with which Christ resolved his fundamental dualities: born under the sign of Gemini (the twins), in the Age of Pisces (the two fish), Christ embodied in himself the human tendency to mortality and immortality, the spirit and the flesh, the goodness of holiness and the evil of the Antichrist (9.2:72–94).

Like Christ, Manuel has an asexual, almost androgynous quality about him. To Angela he is both "mi verdadero padre espiritual" and a "varón matriarcal" (2:1129; my true spiritual father and a matriarchal man).[4] Like the title character of Unamuno's play *El hermano Juan*, Manuel is described as being both a father and a mother-figure to his flock. Analytical psychology recognizes the hermaphroditic image as a symbol of psychic wholeness.[5] Although Manuel's androgynous qualities are acknowledged by those around him, the fusion of opposites he is meant to represent is only apparent, and his psyche is far from whole. It is very meaningful that Unamuno chose to invert, or sunder, the hermaphroditic symbol in order to express the inner dualism that constitutes the problem of personality, and to imply the need to heal dissociation between the self and the "other." Manuel, the inverted Christ of Unamuno's novel, remains a fortress divided unto itself. The saint of Valverde de Lucerna is comprised of a historic self, whose good works will be remembered by church officials, and an ahistorical self that will form part of the intimate village history, the immortal sediment living at the bottom of the lake.

Manuel's ahistorical self is personified by Blasillo, the village idiot, who most often represents Manuel's alter ego or, in Jungian terminology, the shadow personality.[6] Blasillo's unintentional *sacrificium intellectus* bestows upon him the ability to accept unquestioningly the tenets of Christian dogma; conversely, Manuel's capacity for reason deprives him of the very faith he longs to have. This is evidenced by the psalter found after his death in which a dried carnation, a hand-lettered cross, and a date witness Manuel's loss of unquestioning faith in Christian teaching (2:1149). As Lázaro relates to his sister the resistance he felt to the conversion for appearances' sake urged upon him by Manuel, he reveals that the priest insinuated: "Toma agua bendita que dijo alguien, y acabarás creyendo" (2:1141; Dip your fingers in holy water and, as someone once said, you will end by believing). This *alguien* to whom Manuel refers was undoubtedly Blaise Pascal, who suggested that the only possible way to achieve true faith was, as Unamuno commented when quoting Pascal directly, through a mindless "s'abêtir dans la foi" ("La fe pascaliana," 7:351). Blasillo's constant physical proximity to Manuel only serves to reinforce Manuel's unrealized desire to be able to "entontecerse en la fe" (stultify reason in faith) as recommended by the Jansenist mathematician and philosopher.[7]

Unamuno's reversal of position regarding his opinion of "la fe del carbonero" (unquestioning faith) is not nearly as much a phenomenon of his mature years as criticism would have us believe. His play *La venda* (1899), for example, addresses the issue of blind faith as necessary to the survival of those who are "limpios de corazón" (pure of heart). Unamuno's *Diario íntimo*, written within the same period of time as *La venda*, also indicates how desperately he longed to be able to sacrifice intellect for the sake of faith. At that early date, Unamuno even prognosticated Manuel's Pascalian "toma agua bendita": "¿Quieres creer? Pues imita desde luego esa vida y llegarás a creer. Condúcete como si creyeras y acabarás creyendo" (8:840; Do you wish to believe? Then lead the life of a believer and you will come to believe. Behave as if you believed and you will end by believing).

The link between Blaise Pascal and Blasillo is established definitively when, immediately following Lázaro's confession to Angela, Blasillo appears in the street calling, "Dios mío, Dios mío, ¿por qué me has abandonado?," while Angela notices that her brother "se estremeció creyendo oír la voz de Don Manuel, acaso de Nuestro Señor Jesucristo" (2:1141, trembled, believing he heard the voice of Don Manuel, or perhaps, even that of our Lord Jesus Christ). At this moment Unamuno's fictional *imitatio Christi* begins to unravel as he inverts the paradigm in such a way that it will corroborate his interpretation of Christ. Through Manuel's confession to Lázaro, Unamuno intimates that Jesus himself also died an unbeliever: ". . . acabó confesándome que creía que más de uno de los más grandes santos, acaso el mayor, había muerto sin creer en la otra vida" (2:1151; he finally confessed to me that he suspected more than one of our greatest saints, perhaps even the greatest, died without believing in the other life).

Not only is God, the Father, absent from the spiritual lives of Manuel and Jesus, abandoned on the Cross, but fathers of flesh and blood are likewise missing from the lives of the characters in this novel. Manuel's father committed suicide, the sons of his sister are orphaned, the father of Angela and Lázaro died while they were both quite young, and the second editor of Manuel's story, Miguel de Unamuno y Jugo, was also left fatherless at a tender age. It has been suggested that at the basis of all Unamuno's creative work is a long history of attempts to substantiate the paternal figure.[8] For Unamuno, the quest for God, and the father, began with the crisis of 1897. He wrote in the *Diario íntimo* that "Ahora se me muestra mi labor de gran parte de estos doce años como una busca de Dios, a quien había perdido" (8:861; Now I see a large part of my work in the last twelve years as a search for God, whom I had lost). That Unamuno also associated God with fatherhood is clearly apparent, once again in the *Diario íntimo:* "Para mí la idea de Dios, entraña la idea de Padre también. El hecho mismo de la creación es, seguramente, un acto estupendo de ternura paternal" (8:874; I think that the concept of God implies that of the Father as well. Surely, the act of creation itself is a marvelous testimony of paternal tenderness).

It was also during the crisis of 1897 that Concha called her husband "hijo mío" (my child), a cry re-created in all the novels that follow *Paz en la guerra.* This episode was likewise immortalized by Unamuno in his autobiographical *Cómo se hace una novela:*

> . . . mi Concha. . . . Mi verdadera madre, sí. En un momento de suprema, de abismática congoja, cuando me vio en las garras del Angel de la Nada, llorar con un llanto sobre-humano, me gritó desde el fondo de sus entrañas maternales . . . "¡hijo mío!" (8:747)

> (. . . my Concha. . . . My real mother, yes. In a moment of supreme, of abysmal anguish, when she saw me in the claws of the Angel of Nothingness, wracked with superhuman weeping, she cried out to me from the depths of her maternal being. . . . My child! [K-N, 6:442])

Unamuno's re-creation of this crucial moment in his life, and his constant reference to Concha's role in it as a "mother," seems to imply that he thought himself much more the son of a "wife-mother" than the progeny of a strong, paternal figure. His search for paternal archetypes culminates in *San Manuel Bueno, mártir,* a novel in which Unamuno emphasizes the lack of earthly fathers while at the same time desperately seeking assurances from an enigmatic, silent God. Manuel, unable to find the Divine Father, devotes his life to providing fathers or husbands to those who are in need of them: he plays the role of father not only to his orphaned nephews, but also to Angela and Lázaro Carballino, and provides an adoptive father for Tía Rabona's illegitimate grandson.

Nevertheless, it seems that the father figure in Unamuno's novels tends to be supplanted by the female archetype, and a matriarchal order rules the novelistic universe.[9] As *San Manuel Bueno, mártir* unfolds, Angela evolves from a daughter prototype to a mother substitute, and in the process she becomes the recipient of an entire series of projected female archetypes. Her function as "deaconess" to Manuel stimulates in Angela "una especie de afecto maternal hacia mi padre espiritual" (2:1138; a kind of maternal affection for my spiritual father). Later, when Manuel asks and receives absolution from Angela, she assumes the numinous qualities characteristic of the Virgin Mary. She is, however, an inverted Mary who intercedes not before Christ on behalf of men, but before God, the Father, on behalf of her son, Manuel. Although Angela remarks that at the moment "se me estremecían las entrañas maternales" (2:1144; maternal feelings quickened within me), she remains a virgin-mother in the literal sense, projecting her feelings of unrealized motherhood upon her spiritual director.[10]

Don Manuel, in turn, projects onto Angela the highest form of the female archetype: as his spiritual guide and confessor, Angela is comparable to the Gnostic Sophia, divine virgin, symbol of wisdom, and partner of the male ego.[11] Sophia is frequently identified with the Holy Ghost, imparting to the concept a feminine, rather than a masculine quality (Jung, 11:114, n. 15). In his essay "Santa Sofía," Unamuno also associates Sophia with the Holy Ghost: "Y esta Santa Sofía, la del culto helénico por excelencia, era el Espíritu Santo; sólo que el Espíritu Santo femenino" (9:1197–98; And this Saint Sophia, the one of Eastern Christianity par excellence, was the Holy Spirit, but a feminine Holy Spirit).[12] Angela's implicit association with Sophia not only identifies her with the most evolved form of the anima archetype, but also reinforces her function as "mediator and messenger" between the "unseen" regions of Manuel's psyche and the "seen" world of his story as she records it for posterity.

Finally convinced by Manuel and Angela that his return to organized religion would be a source of infinite joy to the villagers of Valverde de Lucerna, Lázaro consents to receive communion in a public act of faith. It is this pact undertaken by Manuel and Lázaro "for the common good of the people" that marks the most significant inversion of Unamuno's novelistic *imitatio Christi*. In don Miguel's rendering of the story, an unbelieving Manuel condones offering communion to a Lázaro who denies belief in his own redeemer. An entry from Unamuno's *Diario íntimo* suggests that he experienced a confusion and resistance to religious conversion similar to Lázaro's:

Como se presentó Jesús al templo, a la circunsición, por humildad . . . pienso yo acercarme a la comunión. Pero el ir así, sin fe en el sacramento . . . aceptándolo cual santo símbolo, ¿no será sacrilegio? . . .

No debo obedecer la ley hasta creer en ella como el pueblo. . . . Más que creer, quiero creer.

Pero ¿no tendré tal vez una fe en el sacramento, velada aún para mí y que al recibirlo se me revele? (8:806)

(I will approach communion with humility, just as Jesus went humbly to the temple for circumcision. But to go there like that, without believing in the sacrament . . . merely accepting it as a holy symbol, is that not sacrilege? I must not follow the law of dogma until I believe in it as do the common people. . . .

More than believing, I want to be able to have faith. Perhaps I already have that kind of faith, still veiled to me.

But at the moment I take communion, shall it not be revealed?)

Approximately thirty years after writing this entry in his journal, Unamuno re-created the same type of sacrilegious communion in *San Manuel Bueno, mártir*. So aware is Manuel of his imminent betrayal that he is unable to perform the ceremony without dropping the Host. As expressed by Unamuno, the entire ritual is shrouded in a great deal of biblical imagery:

Don Manuel, tan blanco como la nieve . . . y temblando como tiembla el lago cuando le hostiga el cierzo, se le acercó con la sagrada forma en la mano, y de tal modo le temblaba ésta . . . que se le cayó la forma a tiempo que le daba un vahído. (2:1140-41)

(Don Manuel, as white as snow . . . and trembling like the surface of the lake when it is whipped by the north wind, drew near Lázaro with the holy wafer in his hand, and it shook so violently . . . that the wafer fell to the ground.)

It is Lázaro who retrieves the Host, and as he consumes it, a cock crows, ostensibly signaling the arrival of dawn.

The *cierzo*, a north wind, traditionally signifies the devil—both Job (26:7) and Saint Augustine associate the north wind, and the North generally, with the Antichrist, who makes his appearance behind the doubting Christ of Valverde as he convinces (tempts) Lázaro to play the role of a believer (Jung, 9.2:100). The crowing cock recalls Saint Peter's triple denial of Christ, and once again refers to the betrayal perpetrated by Manuel and Lázaro. Further study of the cock's symbolism uncovers an even more profound allusion. Having crowed at Peter's denial of Christ, the cock is regarded as an incarnation of the devil whose presence as north wind and crowing cock reinforces the sense of sacrilege about Lázaro's communion. Associated with the dawn and a rising sun, the crowing cock may also suggest passage from one psychic state to another, vigilance, or resurrection.[13] Unamuno's modern Lazarus, however, is only apparently ransomed from the world of unbelievers: his religious "conversion" is, in reality, a feigned passage into the sphere of unconsciousness that is advocated by his personal Christ.

In San Manuel, Unamuno creates a protagonist who embodies in one self the dialogic personality he often preferred to express as two distinct fictional characters: Pachico/Ignacio, Carolina/Luisa, Berta/Raquel, Cosme/Damián, Joaquín/Abel. Unable to reconcile his duality, Manuel is obliged to live a Janus-like existence, torn between playing the role of a saint as he appears to the villagers, and living the life of an unbeliever, as he knows himself to be in his own mind.[14] As in *Cómo se hace una novela*, the agony resulting from Manuel's split personality is another example of the larger dilemma that concerned Unamuno. In the 1932 prologue to *San Manuel Bueno, mártir* Unamuno observes, "he creído darme cuenta de que tanto a Don Manuel y a Lázaro Carballino . . . lo que les atosigaba era el pavoroso problema de la personalidad, si uno es lo que es y seguirá siendo lo que es" (2:1122; I believe I have come to the realization that both Don Manuel and Lázaro Carballino . . . were tormented by the terrifying problem of personality, whether we are what we appear to be, and whether or not we will continue being what we are). Unable to resolve the tragic rift between the demands of his calling and his personal convictions, Manuel's life becomes a living hell in which the intimate self is willingly sacrificed to a public *persona*. Under these conditions, clinical evidence might show Manuel to suffer from a neurosis in which unintegrated personality fragments splinter away from the ego and assume an independent existence.[15]

Jung dedicated a large part of his research to the analysis of psychic disturbances resulting from contemporary man's rationalization of his faith. He maintained that the rationalization of religious provisions leads to an uneasiness within the self, and as the religious function of the psyche is replaced by self-consciousness, belief in redemption becomes relativized (9.2:109, 256). When the instinctive need to believe is repressed or disturbed, serious injury to psychic health can be expected to follow.[16] When there is a dissociation between outward behavior and a person's most true, intimate desires, an attempt will be made to preserve inner peace by ignoring those innermost spiritual needs. The repression that this procedure implies will often find its outlet in the display of morbid symptoms, as in Manuel's urge to drown himself in the lake of Valverde de Lucerna.[17]

The lake and mountain of Valverde are additional examples of the polysemic symbolism so important to this novel. Always mentioned contiguously with Manuel, the lake and mountain are theriomorphic representations of the self, and are therefore analogous to him (Jung, 9.1:219; 9.2:226). Manuel's crest of hair resembles the "Peña del Buitre" which is reflected in the lake, whose blue color is reminiscent of the color of Manuel's eyes. The very duality of the lake, its surface and its depths, also reflects the historic and intrahistoric facets of Manuel's personality. Tradition has it that lake bottoms are harbors where dead souls continue to live. Most likely this notion stems from ancient belief in which the human life cycle was thought to imitate the "birth-death-rebirth" cycle of the sun, which sets in the oceans of the west each evening and rises from them again at dawn the following day.[18] Thus apparently, a solar mythology accounts for the local stories in Valverde de Lucerna of a mythical village at the bottom of the lake where the dead form part of a living sediment, and where the current villagers can expect to find everlasting life.[19]

Water surfaces are additionally symbolic of mirrors, having the capacity to reveal one's unconscious objectively. While a reflection may emphasize self-alienation, it can simultaneously foster an urge to reunite the self with the "other," reflected on the surface of a mirror or a body of water.[20] The suicide who ends his life by drowning is essentially attempting a reunion with his self by returning to the amniotic waters of the Great Mother where he existed in a state of wholeness before birth.[21] In Unamuno's work this urge to reunite opposites by throwing oneself into a body of water is first seen in the hypnotic effect the waters of the Seine exercised upon U. Jugo de la Raza: "las aguas del Sena, parécele que esas aguas no corren, que son las de un espejo inmóvil"; "He tenido que agarrarme al parapeto"; "he sentido ganas de arrojarme al Sena, al espejo" (8:735; the waters of the Seine seemed immobile to him, smooth like a mirror; I had to hold on to the parapet, feeling an irrepressible desire to throw myself into the Seine, into the mirror). In *San Manuel Bueno, mártir,* the quiet backwater of the lake extends a similar temptation to Manuel: "¡Y cómo me llama esa agua que con su aparente quietud . . . espeja al cielo! Mi vida, Lázaro, es una especie de suicidio continuo, un combate contra el suicidio, que es igual" (2:1144; "And how that water beckons me with its apparent calm . . . mirroring the sky! My life, Lázaro, is a kind of continual suicide, or battle against suicide, which is the same thing").

The vessel-like character of any body of water relates it to the maternal function of protection and containment, while its liquid properties recall the fluids of birth, sexuality, and blood that are commonly associated with the female. The Great Mother archetype, whether expressed by water, earth, cave, mountain, village, or city, bears an even greater symbolic meaning as the "womb of night or the unconscious."[22] Manuel's relationship to both mountain and lake confirms the maternal qualities that Angela observes about him. As a "varón matriarcal" (matriarchal man), the priest fulfills a maternal function by sheltering his flock in an unconscious state of existence, and by voluntarily sacrificing his own well-being so that others may live in peace. Ironically Manuel himself longs for peaceful, untrammeled sleep in a mother's arms. His temptation to commit suicide by drowning reflects a basic need to resolve the contradictory tendencies of his personality by escaping them through psychological assimilation to the Mother, whose womb is a gateway into the peace of the unconscious. At the bottom of the lake life is immortalized, perhaps even reconstituted, in the burgeoning fluids of the Mother.

Manuel channels his tendency to suicide toward a frenetic involvement in village life through which he hopes to take refuge from his tortured mind. The therapeutic value of creative or physical activity has long been recognized as an aid in the release of mental tension.[23] Thus Manuel's involvement in all aspects of village life becomes his own form of "opium," a way of drugging himself into exhaustion. Similar to his oblique reference to Blaise Pascal earlier in the novel, Unamuno borrows and inverts, as is his custom, Karl Marx's notion that religion is nothing more than a drug used to lull the masses into indifference. For Manuel, however, "opium" has a positive connotation:

> Sí, ya sé que uno de esos caudillos de la que llaman la revolución social ha dicho que la religión es el opio del pueblo. Opio . . . Opio . . . Opio, sí. Démosle opio, y que duerma y que sueñe. Yo mismo con esta mi loca actividad me estoy administrando opio. (2:1146)

> (I know well enough that one of those leaders of what they call the Social Revolution said that religion is the opium of the people. Opium . . . Opium . . . Yes, opium it is. [Let us give them opium, so that they may sleep and dream.] I, myself, with my mad activity am giving myself opium. [K-N, 7:166])

Thus "opium" acquires several meanings in Unamuno's novel: for the villagers it consists of religion; for Manuel it refers to his church ministry and physical activity; while for Unamuno it alludes to the cathartic effect of literary creation, which enables him to examine his psychological conflicts in fictional contexts.[24]

Inherent to Manuel's religion of opium is a direct contradiction of Jesus's call to individuation and consciousness. Manuel is a fisher of souls for the purpose of keeping them in ignorance of the horrible truth of human destiny, which he suspects is "acaso algo terrible, algo mortal; la gente sencilla no podría vivir con ella" (2:1142; perhaps something terrible, something mortal; simple people could not live with its revelation). Those souls, such as Lázaro's, that Manuel cannot convince dogmatically are recruited to maintain an appearance of faith and to function as apostles of the new creed. As Lázaro points out, this does not make Manuel a hypocrite; rather he is a saint whose daily self-torture enables the majority to live in peace and happiness. Echoing Unamuno's remark, made many years before, that the truth is "lo que hace vivir, no lo que hace pensar" (3:210), Manuel observes that authentic faith is one that engenders and prolongs spiritual life (2:1142).

This tendency on the part of Unamuno toward conservative ideological positions seems to nullify the Unamuno of *Del sentimiento trágico de la vida*, who stated his "mission" to be one of shattering "la fe de unos y de otros y de los terceros . . . es hacer que vivan todos inquietos y anhelantes" (7:297–98; "the faith of men, left, right, and center . . . to make all men live a life of restless longing" [K-N, 4:349]). However, it cannot be stressed enough that *San Manuel Bueno, mártir* is essentially a recapitulation of ideological positions already held by Unamuno in some of his earliest work. Pachico Zabalbide, for example, displays a dual personality, one facet of which finishes its fictional trajectory completely immersed in the maternal element. There is also the Unamuno who wrote in 1898, "¿No es crueldad turbar la calma de los sencillos, y turbarla por una idea?," clearly anticipating by many years Manuel's attitude toward his parishioners (7:942). In a letter to González Trilla (December 12, 1909), Unamuno offers an objection to "el liberalismo francés, ese horrendo y tiránico jacobinismo ateo que persigue todo sentimiento cristiano, que conspira a arrancar del alma del pueblo la fe en otra vida" (French liberalism, that horrid and tyrannic, atheistic Jacobinism that persecutes all Christian sentiment and conspires to uproot belief in the other life from the souls of the common people).[25]

Manuel's advocacy of unconsciousness as a cure for spiritual turmoil once again establishes a direct link between him and the maternal archetype. While Christ taught separation from the collective, especially from the mother, as part of the individuation process, His modern incarnation seeks out the feminine element as a refuge for himself and his people. Exhausted physically and psychologically by many years of daily battle with himself, Manuel prepares to leave the world of the living. His death is a celebration of his final apotheosis as a female symbol. The priest asks to breathe his last inside the church, to be interred in a casket fashioned from a "nogal matriarcal" (matriarchal walnut tree), and he symbolically passes away just as his congregation begins to recite the passage from the Creed reaffirming the resurrection of the flesh and everlasting life (2:1149). When inhabited by a god or godlike being, such as a priest or mythical hero who transcends the ego personality, a place of worship can be representative of the self (Jung, 9.2:225). In this light the villagers' identification of Manuel with the Church, and his subsequent displacement in their minds of an intangible Christ, becomes readily comprehensible. Furthermore, the Church is traditionally a symbol of the Mother: one speaks of Mother Church and of its interior as her womb (Jung, 5:213, 245). Unamuno himself once referred to the need to shelter incipient faith within the "útero materno en el seno de la Iglesia, nuestra madre" (8:876). San Manuel's identification with the female symbols lake, mountain, and church links him inextricably to a matriarchal order rather than to the masculine world of consciousness and paternal values, and to Christ the redeemer, who, in His role as the typical sun hero overcomes death by descending to the chthonic underworld where he conquers the Mother and is able to ascend, like the rising sun, to perpetual life.

Manuel's request to die in the womb of his church, and to be interred in a casket made of planks from the "nogal matriarcal" beneath which he had played as a child, becomes an allegorical return to the Great Mother.[26] In its association with life and immortality, the wooden casket also has a multiple feminine significance. Christ was crucified on a wooden cross known as the "Tree of Life," but in its relation to the symbolism of coffin or bed, the Cross is also referred to as the "Tree of Death."[27] The association of the Cross with the Trees of both Life and Death also surfaces in Unamuno's *Cancionero*, once more presenting him an opportunity to imply that "Nacer es una muerte / morir un nacimiento" (6:1110; To be born is to die, to die is to be reborn):

> sueña Manuel, nuestro sueño;
> tu cuna está hecha del leño
> de la Cruz.
>
> (6:1164)

(dream, Manuel, our dream;
your cradle is made from the
wood of the Cross.)

Christ's cradle, a bed of life, is made of the same material from which the Cross, His bed of death, will also be fashioned. Convinced as he is that there is no life after death as taught by the Church (2:1147), Manuel is nevertheless moved to request death in her womb, and burial in a wooden casket, thereby assuring himself a symbolic delivery to the Mother Vessel, the agent of death as she is also that of rebirth.

Whether Manuel dies a believer or not will never be ascertained. There are as many allusions to support the belief that he did, as there are to uphold a negative conclusion. As he was wont to do, Unamuno's solution to the problem was to offer no conclusions at all. What does stand out with great clarity, however, is that through its ambiguity and noncommittal point of view, the novel became a tool with which the "editor," Unamuno, hiding behind Angela's pen, offered himself consolation. The relationship between Angela and Unamuno is quite delicate: she may, in fact, be the projection not only of Manuel's anima, but also of that of Unamuno.[28] If such is the case, then Angela's role as mediator and messenger now assumes a triple significance: not only does she record Manuel's story for posterity while simultaneously functioning as his anima and spiritual guide, she is also instrumental in the articulation of Unamuno's thinking as it had been developing prior to the actual writing of this final, major work. In this way Angela is the means by which Unamuno mediates his psyche to consciousness—that is, to the text that he "edits."

Having begun *San Manuel Bueno, mártir* in mid-1930, Unamuno wrote the novel in a matter of a few months, completing it by November of the same year.[29] Anthony Storr, a psychiatrist who studied the creative process in artists, suggests that in some cases creative work produced in relatively short spans of time may articulate concepts that had actually been gestating for much longer periods in the minds of their creators.[30] It is intriguing to entertain the possibility that Unamuno's insinuation Manuel could have died a believer, is perhaps indicative of a subliminal faith incubating in his own unconscious long before he was able to imply its existence in this novel. The biography that Unamuno and Angela, in her role as the author's anima, "produce" at the ends of their lives, is thus the enunciation of heretofore unconscious psychic contents that through the act of writing are mediated to conscious realization.[31] Both "editors" are therefore mediators not only of San Manuel's story but also of their own spiritual uncertainties.[32] As interpreters of San Manuel's life, Angela and Unamuno have the opportunity to project their own psychic confusions onto the character whose "biography" they create. One may therefore venture to suggest that Angela's supposition Manuel and Lázaro may have seen the light of faith at the moment of death, might also be an expression of Unamuno's personal hope that at the end of his life he, too, might share a similar experience: "y creo," writes Angela, "que Dios Nuestro Señor, por no sé qué sagrados y no escudriñaderos designios, les hizo creerse incrédulos. Y que acaso en el acabamiento de su tránsito se les cayó la venda" (2:1152; ["I believe that the Lord, our Father,]—as part of I know not what sacred and inscrutable purpose—[made them] believe they were unbelievers. [But, perhaps, at the moment of their passing, the blindfold fell away"] [K-N, 7:177]).

This possibility is prepared for earlier in the novel when Manuel offers consecrated ground to a suicide who, he was sure, repented of his sins at the moment of death.[33] While alive, don Manuel once recalled the story of Moses who was denied entry into the Promised Land because he had once doubted the bidding of God. Here Unamuno interpolates the episode of his namesake, Saint Michael the Archangel, who ransomed Moses's body from eternal damnation, and from the devil's custody, by informing the Antichrist that "El Señor te reprenda" (The Lord reproaches you). To this, Unamuno adds the following editorial comment: "Y el que quiera entender, que entienda" (2:1153; And may he who wishes to understand, understand). Evidently, neither Manuel nor Unamuno subscribed to the gratuitous condemnation of the unbeliever.

Following Angela's assertion regarding Manuel's sublimated belief, her enigmatic query—"Y yo, ¿creo?" (And I, do I believe)—reiterates Unamuno's conviction that a faith which does not doubt is a dead faith, an echo of his cry "¡Creo, Señor; socorre mi incredulidad!" (Lord, I believe; help Thou my unbelief! [Mark 9:23]).[34] Unamuno maintained throughout his life that the essence of faith is built upon doubt, observing in *Del sentimiento trágico de la vida* that the questions "El '¿y si hay?' y el '¿y si no hay?' son las bases de nuestra vida íntima" (7:179; "suppose there is? and suppose there is not? form the bases of our intimate spiritual life").[35] Life, for Unamuno, was sustained by its own interior dialogue between the desire to believe and the lack of faith. He cultivated this pendular oscillation not because he was a hypocrite, nor because he was a *farsante*, but because such vacillation was indispensable to his ontological and existential survival. Resolution of the dilemma favoring either conclusion, wrote Unamuno to Pedro Jiménez Ilundain, would leave open only the alternative of desperate suicide.[36] Since suicide for Manuel Bueno and Miguel de Unamuno was obviously an untenable proposition, it would seem that, on the unconscious level at least, they both may have doubted their categorical denial of the resurrection of the flesh. For Unamuno the possibility of a life after death, and curiosity about what tomorrow might bring, was sufficient motivation to stay alive: "Los espectadores no saben lo que pasa en el último trance y como éste es único y nadie ha vuelto a contarlo, nada sabemos. . . . ¿Y no vale acaso vivir para este acto único? ¿Vivir para morir?" (8:807; Bystanders have no idea what actually transpires during the death agony. Since we experience death only once in our lives, and since no one has returned from the dead to tell of this experience, we know nothing about this moment. Is it not worth living just to have this experience? To live in order to die?).

What is important about *San Manuel Bueno, mártir* is that the novel focuses attention on the fundamental paradox inherent to Christian teaching as understood by modern man. At the same time that Christ, the hero of solar mythology, anthropomorphizes the archetype of the conscious, individuated self, He also demands His followers sacrifice their ratiocinative faculties. With the advent of Modernism, its questioning of traditional values, and the increasingly unimportant role spiritual life would play in a progressively materialistic society, belief in a historical Christ who conquered death through resurrection was no longer possible for the majority of thinking men and women. Lázaro and Manuel are certainly the descendants of the *maladie du siècle* which, according Unamuno, had its roots in Rousseau and Sénancour, and amounted to nothing less than a "pérdida de la fe en la inmortalidad del alma, en la finalidad humana del Universo" (7:284; loss of faith in the immortality of the soul, in the human finality of the Universe).[37] For those incapable of a *sacrificium intellectus*, only a mythical Christ exists, a folk hero who sacrificed himself for the sake of maintaining an illusion. As a mortal who died without believing in life after death, He merits the prayers and commendations of the living, or so implies Manuel to Angela while celebrating his last communion: " 'Reza, hija mía, reza por nosotros.' Y luego, algo tan extraordinario que lo llevo en el corazón como el más grande misterio, y fue que me dijo con voz que parecía

de otro mundo: '. . . y reza también por Nuestro Señor Jesucristo' "
(2: 1147; " 'Pray, my child, pray for us all.' And then, something so
extraordinary happened that I carry it now in my heart as the greatest
of mysteries: he [leaned] over and said, in a voice which seemed [to
come from the other world]: '. . . and pray, too, for our Lord Jesus
Christ' " [K-N, 7:167]).

Unable to abandon God, the Father, as an intellectual problem,
Manuel advocates the superiority of an unconscious existence in the
chthonic world of the archetypal feminine. By espousing matriarchal
values, Manuel completes the circle of Unamuno protagonists in
whom archetypal domination by Nature, and the urge to unconsciousness, is indicative of the psychological immaturity that characterizes a masculine ego in an arrested state of development. Consonant with this type of personality is a psychological rejection of the
male spiritual principle that typically devalues the feminine as negative and evil.[38] In Manuel's new theology, the notion of apocatastasis—the restoration to wholeness through God—is not related to
Christian dogma, but to the heterodox idea of reconstitution in the
mother's womb, a symbol of the collective unconscious. The phenomenology of this special brand of apocatastasis in Unamuno's work
can be traced to its primitive form in the concept of *intrahistoria*, as
described in *En torno al casticismo* and *Paz en la guerra*, where Unamuno postulates the sedimentation of a living tradition into the collective unconscious. Upon this dynamic sediment of inherited thought
patterns each subsequent generation is to build its future. For Unamuno *intrahistoria* came to signify the eternal return of the past,
immortalized in the recurrence of moral values and traditional manners of apperception.

Finding its metaphorical expression in *En torno al casticismo* as "el
fondo mismo del mar . . . la sustancia del progreso, la verdadera tradición" (1:793; the very bottom of the sea . . . the sustenance of
progress, of authentic tradition), *intrahistoria* makes contact with
Jungian psychology which links the stable qualities of the sea and
tradition to the collective unconscious, represented anthropomor-
phically by the female. In *Del sentimiento trágico de la vida*, Unamuno
interprets the concept of eternal return as Nietzsche's own form of
"opium," referring to it as a "cómica ocurrencia de vuelta eterna que
brotó de las trágicas entrañas de Nietzsche, hambriento de inmortalidad concreta y temporal" ("Religión, mitología de ultratumba y
apocatástasis," 7:245; "comical notion of the eternal recurrence
which issued from the tragic voice of [Nietzsche, from his hunger for

a concrete and temporal immortality"] [K-N, 4:252]). While Unamuno saw *eterno retorno* for the self-deception that it was, he also
related it to the Christian belief in apocatastasis, and admitted that it
provided him the only hope he had against permanent dissolution in
the void: "Sin embargo, sí, hay que anhelarla [la apocatástasis], por
absurda que nos parezca; es más, hay que creer en ella, de una manera o de otra, para vivir" (7:261; However, as absurd as it may
seem, we must long for apocatastasis; and more than longing, we
must believe in it, one way or another, in order to survive).

The importance of the *pueblo* and of tradition as integral compo-
nents of *intrahistoria* is also a salient feature of Unamuno's last important novel. However, in its definitive avatar, *intrahistoria* is no longer a
passive harboring of tradition in the collective, but a potential resurrection offered to man through apocatastatic union with the Great
Womb and its capacity to generate an infinity of births. Unamuno
implies as much in the prologue to *San Manuel Bueno, mártir* in
which he suggests, "Don Manuel Bueno busca, al ir a morirse, fundir—o sea salvar—su personalidad en la de su pueblo" (2:1123; Don
Manuel Bueno seeks to meld—rather, to preserve—his personality in
that of his people). From the mythical village of Valverde de Lucerna
which lies submerged in the amniotic waters of the "lecho del lago,"
bells and voices of the deceased are heard in periodic communication
with the living through whom they once again return to the activity
of the surrounding banks: "en nosotros resucitaban en la comunión
de los santos" (2:1133; they came to life in us, in a communion of
saints).

Unamuno's last great novel is his most unreserved tribute to the
infinite powers of Woman. By confirming the superiority of the
Mother, the Godhead in Unamuno's hands becomes Female, and
apocatastasis lies not with God, the unsubstantiated Father, but in
the womb of the Great Mother. Unamuno, in fact, intimated as early
as 1924 that his may be a female God as seen in the inverted Lord's
prayer he included in a fragment of the long poem *Teresa*:

> Madre nuestra, que estás en la tierra,
> y que tienes mi paz en tu reino,
> ¡ábreme ya tus brazos y acoje [*sic*]
> mi vida en tu seno!
>
> (6:581)

> (Our Mother, who art of the earth,
> and who keeps my peace in Her kingdom,

> open thy arms to me
> and gather me to thy breast!)

Like the Gospels that it sometimes emulates, Unamuno's mystery-in-modern-dress contains everything and nothing simultaneously:

> . . . bien sé que en lo que se cuenta en este relato no pasa nada; mas espero que sea porque en ello todo se queda, como se quedan los lagos y las montañas, y las santas almas sencillas asentadas más allá de la fe y de la desesperación que . . . en los lagos y las montañas, fuera de la historia, en divina novela, se cobijaron. (2:1154)

> (I am well aware that no action takes place in this story that I tell. But I hope it is because everything remains encompassed in it, like the lakes and the mountains, and the blessed simple souls gathered beyond faith and desperation, sheltered in the lakes and the mountains, in a divine novel, beyond the fringes of history.)

These last words from *San Manuel Bueno, mártir* return full circle to a notion Unamuno first introduced in *En torno al casticismo* some thirty years previously: "Pero lo que pasa queda, porque hay algo que sirve de sustento al perpetuo flujo de las cosas" (1:792; But what appears to be transitory remains with us, because there is always something that serves to sustain the perpetual flow of things).

What lies beneath the historical surface of this "divine novel" in which nothing takes place, is an intense activity of archetypal images and collective mythology gleaned from the past experience of Unamuno's personal *intrahistoria*. The final solution to the problem of personal immortality that don Miguel seems to offer in this novel is one of an eternal cycle of *desnacer* and *desmorir* in the Mother's womb which reconstitutes and resurrects the past into a dynamic future. This circular structure imparts to the entire body of Unamuno's work the appearance of a gigantic uroboric circle, in which the serpent's head and tail constantly pursue each other forward, into an infinity of rebirths and self-replications.

Conclusion

Sí, tus obras, a pesar de su aparente variedad . . . no son, si bien te fijas, más que un sólo pensamiento fundamental que va desarrollándose en múltiples formas. (Unamuno, 3:399)

(Yes, your work, in spite of its apparent variety . . . is not, if you examine it closely, more than a single, fundamental thought, developed in multiple forms.)

The entire corpus of Unamuno's novels is, first and foremost, the story of attempted and failed processes of individuation. Unable to extricate himself from psychological dependence upon the Mother, the Unamuno protagonist chooses to take on the role of a son before the wife-mother figure. In these circumstances, a woman who represents the anima archetype can never entirely separate from the mother-imago, and is thus deprived of her liberating function. A typical result of such involution is the truncation of a masculine individuation process, leaving the male in an arrested state of psychological development in which the "Feminine is preponderant over the Masculine, the unconscious over the ego and consciousness."[1]

While the most prevalent interpretation of the mother's role in Unamuno's work accepts Blanco Aguinaga's assertion that "la madre es . . . el refugio primero y último en que el hombre se entrega al buen sueño de dormir,"[2] a psychological evaluation of the mother-figure in don Miguel's novels discloses that, contrary to popular belief, his is a devouring Mother who overwhelms the protagonist with the power of her magnetic numinosity. Unable to resist her, the Unamuno hero ends his fictional existence in total dissolution within the uroboric circle. Therefore the genuine female archetype operative in don Miguel's personal unconscious proves to be a negative variant of the Great and Good Mother.[3]

Because the human urge toward self-completion is the most basic of archetypes, it is impossible for Unamuno not to have responded to its activity and not to have attempted fulfilling its promptings through fictive ventures aimed at realizing some form of self-totality. However, when the instincts and archetypes of the unconscious are repressed, or left incomplete, neurosis is often the final outcome. Unable to achieve psychological wholeness, the Unamuno protagonist, especially in the author's mature work, is a man who suffers from ontological illness. His inability to stabilize the adult psyche ultimately produces a splintered personality, or what Unamuno himself called the "problema de la personalidad."

Literary psychology, without pretending to engage in therapeutic aims, adapts psychological theory to the study of what a literary work might reveal about the author who creates it. The autobiographical nature of Unamuno's writing supports my contention that his masculine characters represent personal conflicts which don Miguel may have suffered and sought to give tangible form in his literature. I have attempted to evaluate the phenomenological aspect of Unamuno's psyche as it is transposed to, or refracted in the finished work of art, and to show that each phase of the novelist's psychological evolution has a corresponding, fictional equivalent.

The repetitive quality of all that Unamuno created can be accounted for by the unflagging determination with which his psyche pursued an outlet through literature, be it philosophical essay or prose fiction. It is only when we isolate the mother-complex operating at the level of Unamuno's unconscious, that we can begin to understand the monomaniacal pursuit of self-discovery which comprises the bulk of his work. Unamuno himself was the first to recognize and to explain this tendency: "No faltará lector que . . . se diga: ¡pero nunca ha hecho usted otra cosa que hablar de sí mimso! Puede ser, pero es que mi costante [sic] esfuerzo es convertirme en categoría trascendente, universal y eterna. . . . Yo investigo mi yo, pero mi yo concreto, personal, viviente y sufriente" (8:300; I do not lack readers who . . . say to themselves: "you never do anything but speak of yourself!" That may be true, but it is because I always strive to become something transcendent, universal, eternal. . . . I study my self, my concrete, intimate, living, and suffering self).

Unamuno's religious and psychological crisis of 1897 gave birth to a *persona* suffering outwardly from existential and ontological insecurity, focusing public attention on the *agonista* while at the same time deflecting notice away from the dissociations belonging to his intimate self. Nevertheless, a study of recurring, unconsciously willed rhetorical devices such as patterns of metaphor, symbolic association, and archetypes expressed through the language of reworked mythoi, enables the critic to unmask an author's most profound, inner being. The personal myth that Unamuno created in his extraverted and contentious public *persona* was but compensation for what he perceived as the inadequacies of his true personality. This artificially created public *persona* aspired to camouflage the author's autochthonous self, one that habitually embarked upon endless imaginary regressions to the mother's womb.

Unamuno's inability to believe fully in the resurrection of the flesh and his "continua obsesión" with the "pavoroso problema de tras la tumba"[4] led him to abandon the Heavenly Father, incapable of providing him the same assurances of immortality as did the Great Mother. For Unamuno the perpetually cyclical aspect of feminine nature was more reliable than a God, who in his estimation "se calla. He aquí el fondo de la tragedia universal. Dios se calla. Y se calla porque es ateo" (8:742; is silent. Here is the bottom line of the universal tragedy. God is silent. And He is silent because He is an atheist). Since it is only the Mother who extends hope of perpetual life to man, Unamuno's secondary personality opts for immersion in uroboric union with her, rather than relying on an unconditional faith in the teachings of a suspect, patriarchal religion.

In the context of Jung's proposal that any work of art can be the adaptation of ancient mythoi to contemporary sensibility, Unamuno's return to the Mother is not unique in and of itself. At the foundation of many world religions lies the belief in personal renewal through symbolic death, followed by a regression to the female underworld and a final ascension to a patriarchal society of light and consciousness. In all its metamorphoses, however, the rebirth myth fundamentally centers on a figurative death that must occur if the personality involved is to experience a process of maturation and renewal: symbolically the old self must die before a new one can be born. What is unique to Unamuno's recasting of this motif is that the symbols of transformation which normally accompany the hero's symbolic death and resurrection are wholly absent from his literary idiom.

As does any creative artist, Unamuno takes the liberty of giving his (in)versions of collective mythology personal interpretation. While the hero of a typical rebirth mythologem responds positively to the

challenge of reentry to the paternal world of struggle and consciousness, Unamuno's protagonists consistently elect to remain in psychologically involuted conditions within the "realm of the mothers."
Thus death in Unamuno's fiction is symbolic not of enlightenment
and personality renewal, but of a permanent escape from life. Although the mother's womb undeniably extends the possibility of rebirth to him, this is an option the Unamuno hero invariably chooses
to leave unexplored. Even Christ, in Unamuno's view, prefers not to
return to the world of the living since only death awaits Him there, as
it awaits all mortals at the end of life's trajectory:

> Este Cristo, inmortal como la muerte,
> no resucita; ¿para qué?, no espera
> sino la muerte misma.
>
> (6:517)
>
> (This Christ, like death, immortal,
> does not come back to life; what for?
> nothing but death itself awaits him there.)

Myths closely associated psychologically with a return to mother's
womb are characteristic of what Northrop Frye called a "comic society in its last stages of disintegration."[5] A product of *fin-de-siècle*
social and political unrest, Unamuno lived in a time of constant
change and fluctuation not only in Europe, but in his own country as
well. As a child he experienced Third Carlist War and the Restoration; as an adult, he endured the dictatorship of Primo de Rivera, the
first World War, six years of exile in France, followed by his return to
the Spanish Republic, and finally, the tragic, first six months of the
Spanish Civil War. The society he portrayed, and often criticized in
his novels, is frequently a subtle reflection of the disarray and final
collapse of a formerly stable organization whose values had been
founded upon a patriarchally oriented community. *Paz en la guerra*
pokes gentle humor at anachronistic Carlist ideals; the grotesquely
comic *Amor y pedagogía* ridicules the intelligentsia's, and Unamuno's
own, turn-of-the-century fascination with positivism. The same attitude continues in Unamuno's burlesque characterization of Antolín
S. Paparrigópulos, the social scientist of *Niebla*, a novel that also
comments indirectly on the useless and parasitic lives of the Spanish
señorito, exemplified by Víctor Goti and Augusto Pérez. *Abel Sánchez* is Unamuno's rendition of what he considered to be the Spanish
national malady: hate and envy. The three short novels of *Tres novelas
ejemplares y un prólogo* show a powerless and bankrupt aristocracy

giving way before a novel system of social alliances created by the increasing visibility of a newly rich, bourgeois element in Spanish society.[6] Finally, *San Manuel Bueno, mártir* represents the dissolution of the Old World and the comfort of its heretofore unchallenged values and beliefs.

In his quest for stability, Unamuno replaced a decaying patriarchal society with the matriarchal archetype. A symbol of eternity, equilibrium, and regeneration, Woman is the only cohesive element remaining to the brotherhood of man. For Unamuno, it was Concha, his own *esposa-madre*, who provided stability amid the permutations of daily life. He referred to her as "mi compañera, / mi costumbre, / tú me diste repetición verdadera, / que a todo cambio resiste, / y es sustancia permanente" (6:1377, no. 1606; my companion, my habit, you gave me true immortality, which resists all change, my eternal substance).

Fortunately for posterity, Miguel de Unamuno's talent and indomitable creative drive enabled him to elevate his personal obsession with the Mother to universal planes of meaning through the use of collectively recognized forms of artistic and symbolic expression. "What are geniuses and heroes," he exclaimed, "but men who have brought the universal substratum of humanity to a higher degree of expression than others?"[7] By transcending the topical and the quotidian, Unamuno succeeded in assuring himself the immortality he struggled so valiantly to claim during more than half a century of literary praxis.

Notes

INTRODUCTION

1. Carlos Feal Deibe, *Unamuno: El otro y don Juan*, 78.
2. See Carlos Blanco Aguinaga, *El Unamuno contemplativo*, 97–98, and Paul R. Olson, "The Novelistic Logos in Unamuno's *Amor y pedagogía*," 265.
3. Leon Edel, *The Modern Psychological Novel*, 60. Edel, a proponent of psychological approaches to literature, believes that "literary study (that is, biography and criticism) can no longer afford to close its eyes and look away from psychological truths in literary works: they are part of the truths sought in literature and biography" (ix–x). Rather than applying psychiatry to literature, Edel's "literary psychology" aims to show how "the artist triumphs over anxieties . . . all the ills of body and mind, and acquires a . . . positive urge to create" (216–17).
4. Charles Mauron, *Des métaphores obsédantes au mythe personnel: Introduction a la psychocritique*, 321.
5. Erich Neumann, *The Great Mother: An Analysis of the Archetype*, 95.
6. Mauron, *Métaphores obsédantes*, 336.
7. Antonio Moreno, *Jung, Gods, and Modern Man*, 22.
8. A representative critical consensus may be found in José Luis Abellán, *Miguel de Unamuno a la luz de la psicología: una interpretación de Unamuno desde la psicología individual*, 168; R. E. Batchelor, *Unamuno Novelist: A European Perspective*, 21; Hernán Benítez, *El drama religioso de Unamuno*, 51; Luis Granjel, *Retrato de Unamuno*, 289, 293; Ricardo Gullón, *Autobiografías de Unamuno*; Julián Marías, *Miguel de Unamuno*, 93; and Victor Ouimette, *Reason Aflame: Unamuno and the Heroic Will*, 131.
9. James Olney, *Metaphors of Self: The Meaning of Autobiography*, 3; also see p. 155 and Jung, 4:336
10. Carl Gustav Jung, *Memories, Dreams, Reflections*, 3.
11. Leon Livingstone, "Autobiografía y autofantasía en la Generación del 98," 301.
12. C. G. Jung and Marie L. von Franz, eds., *Man and His Symbols*, 125.
13. Ann B. Ulanov, *The Feminine in Jungian Psychology and in Christian Theology*, 31.

14. Mauron, *Métaphores obsédantes*, 213.

15. Blanco Aguinaga, *El Unamuno contemplativo*, 27, n. 6, and 45.

16. Feal Deibe, *El otro y don Juan*, 44.

17. Neumann, *Great Mother*, 34, n. 18. Neumann observes that the Romantics were especially distinguished by this type of psychological constitution, being particularly susceptible to the magnetism of the unconscious and the Great Mother (p. 53, n. 6). Due to his penchant for emotional self-exposure and a preference for the confessional literary genres popular during the Romantic era, Unamuno himself has frequently been labeled a latent Romantic (see Armando Zubizarreta, *Unamuno en su nivola*, 234, and Edmund King, "What is Spanish Romanticism?," 10–11; also Unamuno, 9:816). The arguments of these critics are further sustained if we note the tendency the Unamuno protagonist has toward self-immolation and uroboric incest, trends that Neumann views as coincidental with the Romantic psyche.

18. Jolande Jacobi, *The Way of Individuation*, 70.

19. Anthony Storr, *The Dynamics of Creation*, 203. Cf. Anne Clancier: "[el] desequilibrio de una personalidad, ligado a unos conflictos inconscientes, puede encontrar una salida en la creación literaria" (*Psicoanálisis, literatura, crítica*, 85).

20. Benito Brancaforte, "El objeto del deseo en *San Manuel Bueno, mártir*," 136.

21. Referring to Unamuno's masculine characters in particular, Livingstone observes: "¿Son realmente 'héroes de la voluntad,' como él [Unamuno] mantiene, o simples sublimaciones de los deseos latentes o frustrados de su autor?" ("Autobiografía y autofantasía," 301).

22. Harriet Stevens, "El Unamuno múltiple," 273, n. 15. Cf. Blanco Aguinaga, *El Unamuno contemplativo*, 153, n. 15, and Angel R. Fernández y González, *Unamuno en su espejo*, 121.

23. See especially Antonio Sánchez Barbudo, *Estudios sobre Galdós, Unamuno y Machado*.

24. Granjel confirms Unamuno's personality as an introverted intuitive type (*Retrato de Unamuno*, 167). Cf. poem LXXXVI, in which Unamuno exclaims: "¡Soy una voz, soy una voz tan sólo / que clama en el desierto!" (1912; 6:895). For a personal account of his isolation and loneliness, also see the essay "Ramplonería" (1:1239–50).

CHAPTER 1: *En torno al casticismo*

1. To consider just some critical points of view: H. R. Ramsden (*The 1898 Movement in Spain*) and Donald L. Shaw (*The Generation of 1898 in Spain*) focus on the influence of Taine and Spencer; Carlos Clavería (*Temas de Unamuno*) on that of Carlyle; Pedro Ribas ("El Volksgeist de Hegel y la intrahistoria de Unamuno") on that of Hegel, while José Alberich ("Sobre el positivismo de Unamuno") considers the general effects positivism had upon Unamuno's early thought.

2. Pelayo Hipólito Fernández, *Miguel de Unamuno y William James: un paralelo pragmático*, 21–22; cf. 115, 117.

3. The citations themselves are listed by Fernández, ibid., 15–17, and refer to the following Unamuno essays: "La regeneración del teatro español" (1896; 1:902–3, n. 1); a letter to Clarín dated May 10, 1900 (quoted in Adolfo Alas, ed., *Epistolario a Clarín*, 101); "La España de hoy, vista por Rubén Darío" (1901; 4:756); Unamuno's letter to Federico Urales regarding his study of physiological psychology. First published in Urales's *La evolución de la filosofía en España*, the essay is now titled "Principales influencias extranjeras en mi obra" (9:816–18); "Ciudad y campo" (1902; 1:1031–42); "Contra el purismo" (1903; 1:1063–73); "Cientificismo" (1907; 3: 353).

4. Cf. William James, *The Principles of Psychology*, 2:1055–66.

5. Sergio Fernández Larraín, ed., *Cartas inéditas de Unamuno*, 165. Also see "El inglés y el alemán": "empecé a aprender el inglés . . . cuando pasaba de los veintiocho años" (that is, in late 1892 [4:532]).

6. These French translations of James's articles can be located in *A List of the Published Writings of William James*, rpt. from *Psychological Review* 18 (March 1911). *The Principles of Psychology* was first published in French, in abridged form, as *Précis de psychologie*, trans. E. Baudin and G. Bertier (Paris: M. Rivière, 1909. See *A List of Published Writings*, 164). The Spanish translation of James appeared as *Principios de psicología*, trans. Domingo Barnés, ed. Daniel Jorro (Madrid: Luis Faure, 1909).

7. Unamuno was especially familiar with the associationists Alexander Bain, John Stuart Mill, and Wilhelm Wundt, many of whose works are in the Salamanca library (see Mario J. Valdés and María Elena de Valdés, *An Unamuno Sourcebook: A Catalogue of Readings and Acquisitions with an Introductory Essay on Unamuno's Dialectical Inquiry*, 20, 163, 261). On the importance of Mill's three principle associationist treatises, all of which Unamuno had read, see Daniel N. Robinson, *Toward a Science of Human Nature: Essays on the Psychologies of Mill, Hegel, Wundt, and James*, 53.

8. James, *Principles*, 1:566. For Bain, see Robert I. Watson, ed., *The Great Psychologists*, 217.

9. Alexander Bain, *Mind and Body*, 31. The laws of associationist psychology of perception focus on the theory that every thought activates another; a simple impression compounds into more complex ones; mental stimulation effects bodily changes in a chain reaction of thought processes that, in turn, affect a man's volitional capabilities. Cf. Robinson, *Toward a Science of Human Nature*, 183, and Klaus-Peter Koepping, *Adolf Bastian and the Psychic Unity of Mankind: The Foundations of Anthropology in Nineteenth Century Germany*, 71.

10. Bain, *Mind*, 13.

11. Ibid. Unamuno apparently continued to subscribe to this belief well after he published *ETC*. In "Sobre el determinismo en la novela," he observed, "Surge la historia externa de la interna: como lo psicológico de lo fisiológico" (1898; 9:772). This statement recalls the belief held by Bain, Ribot, and Wundt that psychological phenomena are necessarily linked to a general physiology of the human body.

12. James, *Principles*, 1:233. See 1:569 for James's acknowledgment of the theory of discrimination.

13. Ibid., 1:568.

14. The German Volksgeist theorists Waitz, Steinthal, and Lazarus, with whose work Unamuno was well acquainted, were all students of Herbart, and Unamuno may have come into contact with Herbart's thought through theirs. In his view of society as an "organic whole, ruled by psychological laws that are peculiar to it," Herbart anticipates some important aspects of Volksgeist theory (see Théodule Ribot, *German Psychology of Today*, 51).

15. Henri Ellenberger, *The Discovery of the Unconscious: The History and Evolution of Dynamic Psychiatry*, 312. Lying beneath the threshold of perception, Herbart postulated an "apperception mass," consisting of unconscious representations (ibid., 213). Cf. Unamuno: "la vida de la mente es como un mar eterno . . . un eterno crepúsculo que envuelve días y noches, en que se funden las puestas y las auroras de las ideas. Hay un verdadero tejido conjuntivo intelectual, un fondo intra-conciente [*sic*], en fin" (1:813–14).

16. Pedro Laín Entralgo, *La generación del noventa y ocho*, 151; Carlos Blanco Aguinaga, *El Unamuno contemplativo*, 236; Francisco Fernández Turienzo, ed., *En torno al casticismo*, 49–50, 57–58.

17. Unamuno's genuine interest in psychology is evidenced by the large quantity of books on psychological topics in his library, and by his observation that had he been able to choose a profession according to personal preference, he would have first chosen psychology, political economy, or linguistics (see Fernández Larraín, ed., *Cartas inéditas*, 248).

18. The reference to Freud occurs in "El contra-mismo" (1918; 4:1430). In his library Unamuno had only one volume (*The Psychopathology of Everyday Life*) of López Ballesteros's 1922 translation of Freud (see Valdés and Valdés, *Sourcebook*, 88). In the context of Spain's isolation from the rapid developments within the French and German psychological communities, Unamuno's ignorance of depth psychology is not entirely surprising. As late as 1898 only one psychological journal was published in Spain, and it was devoted to physiological psychology: *Revista frenopática barcelonesa*, published under the auspices of the Manicomio Nuevo Belén (see Antonio Gallego Morrell, *Angel Ganivet: el excéntrico del 98*, 72).

19. Jeffrey B. Russell, *Mephistopheles: The Devil in the Modern World*, 173.

20. Fernández Larraín, ed., *Cartas inéditas*, 141, 207. Cf. the letter to Clarín dated May 1895 in which Unamuno also twice confesses "Yo también tengo mis tendencias místicas" (Alas, ed., *Epistolario a Clarín*, 53).

21. Fernández Larraín, ed., *Cartas inéditas*, 250.

22. Barbara Hannah, *Jung: His Life and Work*, 65. Both Jung and Unamuno were interested in liberal Protestant theology. Ritschl's influence on Unamuno has been studied by Nelson R. Orringer in his *Unamuno y los protestantes liberales (1912): Sobre las fuentes de* Del sentimiento trágico de la vida.

23. Murray Stein, *Jung's Treatment of Christianity: The Psychotherapy of a Religious Tradition*, 25–26.

24. Ellenberger, *Discovery of the Unconscious*, 525.

25. For historians of psychology, see ibid., 657, 726. (Cf. Russell: "The views of Carl G. Jung . . . were prepared for and anticipated by Romanticism"

[*Mephistopheles*, 174]). For Hispanists, see Ciriaco Morón Arroyo, "*San Manuel Bueno, mártir* y el 'sistema' de Unamuno," 240–41, and J. W. Butt, "Unamuno's Idea of Intrahistoria: Its Origins and Significance," 13. Also see Peter G. Earle, "Unamuno and the Theme of History," 328.

26. Butt, "Unamuno's Idea of Intrahistoria," 14. Also partially incomplete is Pérez de la Dehesa's opinion that Unamuno learned Volksgeist theory from Joaquín Costa (*Política y sociedad en el primer Unamuno*, 93–95). Morón Arroyo's observation that "se puede relacionar la intrahistoria con el Volksgeist de los románticos" ("El 'sistema' de Unamuno," 240–41) must also be qualified. Morón Arroyo refers to the specifically Romantic notion of folk, or national, spirit. This should not be confused with the more complex and scientific ideas elaborated half a century later by the Volksgeist theorists. The present study considers the Romantic and Volksgeist notions as separate, but compatible, entities.

27. Ellenberger, *Discovery of the Unconscious*, 201.

28. Philip P. Weiner, ed., *Dictionary of the History of Ideas*, 4:492a

29. Ribas, "El Volksgeist de Hegel," 24–25.

30. Ribas concludes that Volksgeist, as interpreted by Hegel, has no bearing at all upon Unamuno's *intrahistoria* since Unamuno's notion is static and quiescent, while Hegel's is vibrant and dynamic ("El Volksgeist de Hegel," 33). That this judgment is flawed is proved by Unamuno's use of the verb *palpitar* to qualify his *silencioso sedimento*, not only in this particular citation from "Sobre el cultivo de la demótica" (1896), but in many passages of *ETC* as well.

31. Koepping, *Adolf Bastian*, 54, 28. The mentor alluded to is Adolf Bastian (1826–1905). Cf. Jung, 11:50–51. For details regarding Bastian's influence on Jung, see Koepping, *Adolf Bastian*, 140–46.

32. Herder may have appealed to Unamuno for the same reasons as did Carlyle: in his work the German Romantic historian anticipates Carlyle's manner of directly addressing the historical personages whose lives and exploits he chronicles.

33. F. M. Barnard, *Herder's Social and Political Thought. From Enlightenment to Naturalism*, 130, 55.

34. In "Sobre el cultivo de la demótica," an essay complementary to the five of *ETC*, and one in which Unamuno expresses similar ideas in much more cogent fashion, don Miguel contrasts what he calls the "public consciousness" ("lo exterior, lo que costituye [*sic*] la vida histórica: cronicones, periódicos, memorias") with the "public spirit" ("la resultante de la totalidad de la vida del pueblo, con su lecho de tendencias subconcientes [*sic*]" [9:49]).

35. Barnard, *Herder's Thought*, 55. Language as one of the determinants of Volksgeist was a concept generally subscribed to by most Romantics (see ibid., 161).

36. Ibid., 73.

37. It is impossible to determine whether Unamuno had any familiarity with Kropotkine's work before the 1899 edition of *La conquista del pan* housed in his personal library (see Valdés and Valdés, *Sourcebook*, 131). Nevertheless, there are sections of *ETC* that recall the Russian's theory that the "upper classes, by

rising over the masses, had impoverished themselves" (Ellenberger, *Discovery of the Unconscious*, 636).

38. Quoted from an article by Unamuno in *Der Sozialistische Akademiker* (Berlin, July 1896), translated and cited by Butt in "Unamuno's Idea of Intrahistoria," 22–23.

39. Barnard, *Herder's Thought*, 110.

40. Lancelot L. Whyte, *The Unconscious before Freud*, 169–70, and Butt, "Unamuno's Idea of Intrahistoria," 14.

41. See Koepping, *Adolf Bastian*, 55.

42. Jung, however, knew Waitz's *Anthropologie der Natürvolker* (5:318), and references to Steinthal's work in comparative mythology abound in Jung's *Symbols of Transformation* (vol. 5 of *The Collected Works*).

43. In his library Unamuno had an 1877 edition of Eduard von Hartmann's *Philosophie de l'inconscient* (Valdés and Valdés, *Sourcebook*, 111). Although the French edition was not available to me, the English translation contains references to Steinthal and Lazarus on pages 41–42, 294, and 300. Also in Unamuno's library was an 1879 edition of Théodule Ribot's *La psychologie allemande contemporaine, école experimentale*, which devotes an entire chapter to Waitz et al. (ibid., 207).

44. Cf. the 1890 letter to P. Múgica (quoted in Butt, "Unamuno's Idea of Intrahistoria," 17), which also mentions Steinthal, Lazarus, and Waitz as the originators of Völkerpsychologie. References to the three continue in Unamuno's work until approximately 1901 ("El siglo de España," 4:344–45).

45. Fernández Larraín, ed., *Cartas inéditas*, 91.

46. Theodor Waitz, *Introduction to Anthropology*, 239, 273, 277, 282. Cf. Eduard von Hartmann: "Language is produced by unconscious activity" (*Philosophy of the Unconscious*, 1:300).

47. Fernández Larraín, ed., *Cartas inéditas*, 152–53.

48. Unamuno devotes the entire second chapter of *ETC* (esp. 1:807–16) to "desenmarañar hasta qué punto hicieron las circunstancias, el medio ambiente que hoy se dice, al espíritu castellano, y hasta qué punto éste se valió de aquélla (1:804). Although this approach has previously been attributed to the influence of Taine and Spencer, Unamuno might have also acquired the same notion from reading Waitz, who determined that all permanent changes in man, aside from morbid phenomena, are attributable to four causes, one of them being climate (*Introduction to Anthropology*, 34). Unamuno would also have found this confirmed by Ribot, who stated, "For Waitz, all is explained by climate, migrations, and religious ideas, but above all by climate" (*German Psychology of Today*, 58).

49. Weiner, *Dictionary of the History of Ideas*, 3:315a, 4:490a–96b.

50. Leonard Zusne, *Biographical Dictionary of Psychology*, 250–51, 407; Weiner, *Dictionary of the History of Ideas*, 4:495b–96a.

51. Koepping, *Adolf Bastian*, 5, 29. Unamuno chose "demótica" to mean the same kind of "study of man." *Intrahistoria* was to reveal itself "en eventos, leyendas y narraciones, es la que pretende explotar y sacar a luz, haciendo de ella material científico, el folklore, o demótica" (9:53).

52. Koepping, *Adolf Bastian*, 87, 43

53. Otto Rank, *The Myth of the Birth of the Hero, and Other Writings*, 3–4.

54. Koepping, *Adolf Bastian*, 31, 43; quotation from 175–76.

55. Unlike Freud, Jung always recognized the influence of Nietzsche in his work, especially of *Thus Spoke Zarathustra* (*Memories*, 102). Nietzsche thought the unconscious to be an "area of re-enactment" of past stages of life, both of the individual as well as of the species (Ellenberger, *Discovery of the Unconscious*, 273). Of particular interest to Jung was Nietzsche's theory regarding the "atavistic nature" of mankind as manifested in dreams, which Nietzsche thought related the dreamer to the most primitive conditions of human culture (Jung, 11:51). It is in this sense that Nietzsche's eternal return is reminiscent of the cyclical nature of tradition in Unamuno's *intrahistoria* and in Jung's collective unconscious.

56. For Jung, see Ellenberger, *Discovery of the Unconscious*, 542 and 729; for Unamuno, see Valdés and Valdés, *Sourcebook*, 111, 293, 225, 173, 224.

57. Ellenberger, *Discovery of the Unconscious*, 204, 542.

58. Barnard, *Herder's Thought*, 135, 48. More often than not, Unamuno creates fictional characters who suffer from inner dualities, or even divides between two characters of the same sex what normally would be considered traits belonging to the same personality.

59. Ellenberger, *Discovery of the Unconscious*, 203, 201. Unamuno read both Schelling and Friedrich von Hardenburg (Novalis). See Valdés and Valdés, *Sourcebook*, 111, 293.

60. Jules Michelet (1798–1874) and Giuseppe Mazzini (1805–1872), two nationalists with Romantic inclinations, had tremendous influence on Unamuno. Historians have also drawn attention to the impact J. G. Herder's nationalism and notion of *Humanität* had on Mazzini's political thought (see Barnard, *Herder's Thought*, 171). Unamuno's contact with Herder might have been reinforced indirectly by Mazzini, whose influence on Unamuno is especially evident in *CSN*.

61. Fernández Turienzo comes to a similar conclusion: "Unamuno, en contraposición a Freud, . . . no reduce lo inconsciente a lo reprimido" (*ETC*, 56–57).

62. Prior to Jung's articulation of it, this notion of the symbolic expression of the unconscious appeared in E. von Hartmann's *Philosophie de l'inconscient* (Philosophy of the Unconscious) (1:108), a work read by both Jung and Unamuno. Hartmann suggests that the contents of the unconscious express themselves in symbolic form since its revelations would otherwise remain unintelligible to the conscious mind with which it did not share a common sensibility.

63. Cf. Blanco Aguinaga: "Y es que el mar, más aún que el campo o que el monte, es, en su abismo y en su voz, como el seno de la madre" (*El Unamuno contemplativo*, 276). Graphically represented, Unamuno's equation may be expressed in the following manner: "intrahistoria = la tradición = la revelación de lo inconsciente = el fondo mismo del mar (1:795) = la mujer (madre) = la tradición = la intrahistoria.

64. Jung, *Memories*, 74–75.

65. Hannah, *Jung: His Life and Work*, 50–52.

66. Jung, *Memories*, 55.

67. Unamuno's *SMB* is structured on a similar premise: the absence of fathers in the novel (none of the characters has one) becomes analogous to the absence, or questioning of God, in their lives.

68. Jung, *Memories*, 79, 22.

69. Ellenberger, *Discovery of the Unconscious*, 665.

70. Cf. letter to P. Múgica: "Pregunta: ¿Qué cosa es fe? Respuesta: Creer lo que no vimos. No, no es eso fe, no, no" (Fernández Larraín, ed., *Cartas inéditas*, 171). Also "Sobre la filosofía española": "Cultivando la voluntad, convenciéndonos de que la fe es obra de la voluntad y que la fe crea su objeto, así lo crea . . ." (1:1164).

71. Hannah, *Jung: His Life and Work*, 66.

72. Ellenberger, *Discovery of the Unconscious*, 679. Cf. Benítez: "A su lado [de Unamuno] quedaban mudos los interlocutores, pues jamás a nadie cedía el turno ni le permitía meter baza" (*El drama religioso de Unamuno*, 126).

73. Blanco Aguinaga, *El Unamuno contemplativo*, 373.

74. Jung and Unamuno were not acquainted with each other's work. In fact, Jung did not publish his ideas on the collective unconscious in book-length form until 1912 as *Symbols of Transformation* (Jung, *Memories*, 158).

75. Cf. "Sobre el cultivo de la demótica": "Es la historia la memoria de los pueblos, y en ella, como en la de los individuos, yacen inmensidades en el fondo insondable del olvido, mas no allí muertas, sino vivas, obrando allí, y desde allí vivificanco a los pueblos" (9:48).

CHAPTER 2: *Paz en la guerra*

1. Unamuno attributes his ideas regarding the historical novel to Taine and Zola: "[que] pueden servirme de ejemplos de la convergencia entre la novela y la historia. Las novelas de Zola son tan historia como novela las historias de Taine; las ficciones del primero tienden a la realidad de lo histórico tanto como al interés e íntima verdad de lo novelesco los sucesos que el segundo cuenta" (9:772).

2. Apparently the "play within a play" duplication fascinated Unamuno while he was still a young boy. In *Recuerdos de niñez y mocedad* he recalls one of the first times that he attended the theater and the effect that the stage set had upon him: "una especie de escenario dentro del escenario. . . . Me hizo el efecto de un teatro en el teatro y me abrió los ojos" (8:129).

3. Cf. 2:178 and 197 where the Carlist Wars are again spoken of as purely economic conflict. In the abstract, *PG* anticipates the themes of envy and fraternal hatred that will crystallize as the Cain/Abel archetype in Unamuno's mature work (*Abel Sánchez*, *El marqués de Lumbría*, and *El otro*).

4. Unamuno wrote to Clarín on December 31, 1896: "pero la redacción definitiva la hice este verano en una aldea de mi Vizcaya. No he querido repasarla, porque sé lo que me hubiese pasado" (Alas, ed., *Epistolario a Clarín*, 71).

5. This is confirmed by Unamuno's letter to Clarín, dated May 9, 1900: "¿Para qué he de trazar aquí una autobiografía? Si usted ha leído *Paz en la*

guerra . . . allí la encontrará. . . . ¡Ah, que triste es después de una niñez y juventud de fe sencilla haberla perdido en vida ultraterrena, y buscar en nombre, fama y vanagloria un miserable remedo de ella!" (ibid., 86).

6. Cf. 2:162–64, 251–52, and 256–58 for descriptions of the Carlist defeat due to lack of military preparedness.

7. Cf. Ulanov, *The Feminine in Jungian Psychology,* 158, and Blanco Aguinaga, who refers to the "significado último que para Unamuno tiene la idea de la madre como imagen viva del subconsciente" (*El Unamuno contemplativo,* 137).

8. Compare Granjel, *Retrato de Unamuno,* 66; Ulanov, *The Feminine in Jungian Psychology,* 37; Jung, 9.1:96.

9. Ulanov, *The Feminine in Jungian Psychology,* 218; Pedro Laín Entralgo, *Teoría y realidad del otro,* 118.

10. Ulanov, *The Feminine in Jungian Psychology,* 242.

11. This passage is clearly autobiographical since it is lifted almost verbatim from Unamuno's memory of his own preparation for the First Communion: "chicos y chicas juntos . . . ellas en trenzas y de corto, dando tirones a las sayas para tapar lo mejor posible las pantorrillas" (8:128).

12. This is a pattern that will be followed by Rafaela's successors Clarita (*AP*) and Eugenia (*N*). All three young women choose as their lovers men who are vaguely defined, although more stereotypically masculine, than the Unamuno hero. Unamuno's reference to Rafaela's future husband as a *gallito* is, again, drawn from his childhood memory of a certain Luis, who apparently made an impression on don Miguel as a "gallito de la calle, el chico más roncoso del barrio" (8:122).

13. Neumann, *Great Mother,* 45. In his play *El otro* (Act 3), Unamuno explores the analogy of womb, cradle, and tomb. For don Miguel death represents the child's reclamation of Mother, whose womb holds the key to infinite birth. Unamuno's *des-nacer* is similar in principle to what Northrop Frye called the cyclical myth of the dying god. The basic premise of this myth is "that the continuum of identity in the individual life from birth to death is extended from death to rebirth" (*Anatomy of Criticism: Four Essays,* 159).

14. That the association of earth, death, and mother was an archetype active in Unamuno's personal unconscious is evident in his poetry, where there are numerous references to *madre tierra, madre muerte,* and to the earth as a mother whose arms and lap welcome the dead into her fold (6:400–401, 607, 851–52, and poem No. 5 of *Teresa,* 6:581).

15. Following upon the heels of the crisis of 1897, Unamuno's play *La esfinge* (1898) is another autobiographical document of those same years. It bears witness to the fact that Unamuno made a conscious decision to allow his public *persona* to dominate the more intimate self. Angel, the protagonist of the play, decides to retire from a political career, but is felled by a bullet as he is about to embark upon life as a private citizen. It seems that even in literary fantasy, Unamuno could not imagine a successful integration of the public and private facets of his personality. Angel, like Ignacio, represents an *ex-futuro* that may have been, one Unamuno defined as "lo que dejó de ser lo que habría sido" (6:661; that which never became what it could have been).

16. Otto Rank quoted in Roberta Johnson, "Archetypes, Structures and Myth in Unamuno's *El otro*," 34.

17. Cf. Sánchez Barbudo, *Estudios sobre Galdós, Unamuno y Machado*, 72, and Alas, ed., *Epistolario a Clarín*, 53–54.

18. This is confirmed by Unamuno's biographer Emilio Salcedo: "Ha sido un niño solitario y triste, acaso tímido, soñador, introvertido" (*Vida de don Miguel*, 53). In an autobiographical sketch preceding the essay "Principales influencias extranjeras en mi obra" (9:816–18), Unamuno corroborates the statements made by Salcedo, as well as those he makes himself in *Recuerdos de niñez y mocedad*.

19. Manuel Cabaleiro Goas, *Werther, Mischkin y Joaquín Monegro vistos por un psiquiatra: trilogía patográfica*, 240. Cf. Adler's theory that physical weakness often contributes to the feeling that one is inferior to others in natural or physical endowments. In Adler's view this type of inferiority produces in a human being the desire for power and superiority over others (see Edel, *Modern Psychological Novel*, 10).

20. While a university student, Jung underwent a similar personality change. "From the rather reclusive, introverted youth there emerged a more extraverted, gregarious and aggressive young man. So much was he this new person that he often managed to dominate student discussions, to the point of generating dislike and opposition among fellow students" (Stein, *Jung's Treatment of Christianity*, 82–83).

21. "El Unamuno de 1901 a 1903 visto por M," 17, 24.

22. Ibid., 24, 22. Armando Zubizarreta implies that Unamuno's religious crisis triggered the "proceso espiritual que convierte al Unamuno tímido en el Unamuno atrevido y combativo" ("Desconocida antesala de la crisis de Unamuno, 1895–1896," 10).

23. Cabaleiro Goas, *Werther, Mischkin y Joaquín Monegro*, 224.

24. Abellán, *Miguel de Unamuno a la luz de la psicología*, 182–84.

25. Unamuno himself asked: "¿Por qué no he de poder vivir ayer y mañana a un tiempo?" (3:379). Jung superseded even Unamuno when he actually described having had a mystical experience similar to Unamuno's imagined *querer serlo todo* (desire to be everything). He writes in *Memories:* "I can only describe the experience as the ecstasy of a nontemporal state in which past, present and future are one" (295–96).

26. Psychiatry attributes the emergence of Unamuno's *yo hipertrófico* to an insecure ego "que necesita del estímulo de la atención de los que le rodean en cada momento existencial" (Cabaleiro Goas, *Werther, Mischkin y Joaquín Monegro*, 224). Laín Entralgo holds much the same view of Unamuno's overvalued self, which he considers a "signo visible de una secreta inseguridad" (*Teoría y realidad del otro*, 347).

27. Prior to this 1906 essay, Unamuno had already questioned the authority of the Deity in *Vida de Don Quijote y Sancho* (The Life of Don Quijote and Sancho, 1905). In *Niebla* (1914), Unamuno not only questions, but finally challenges his God.

28. This idea is affirmed by Fernández y González who, when referring to

Unamuno's inferiority complex, remarks: "He tried to hide it not only from himself, but from his own consciousness as well" (*Unamuno en su espejo*, 51).

29. Alas, ed., *Epistolario a Clarín*, 100.

30. Carmen Morales, "Unamuno's Concept of Woman," 97–98. Cf. Eduardo Ortega y Gasset who remembers Unamuno stating: "Voy a quitarme mi disfraz, porque quizá es usted lo bastante inocente como para creer en él. Soy un cordero al que le gusta disfrazarse con una piel de león" (*Monodiálogos de Don Miguel de Unamuno*, 144).

31. Although experiencing a similar return to the routine practices of faith, Unamuno went to the other extreme, convinced as he was of the false theatricality of his conversion, rather than of his doubt: "¿Es que no me estoy sugestionando y creando en mí un estado ficticio e insincero? Con esta costante [*sic*] lectura de libros de devoción, . . . ¿no estoy creando una ficción en mí?" (8:844).

32. Apparently Unamuno also perceived in the figure of Christ a similar "totality." In "El Cristo de Velázquez," he refers to Christ as the "Hijo de Hombre, Humanidad Completa" (6:493).

33. Ulanov, *The Feminine in Jungian Psychology*, 63, 143.

34. Cf. Fernández, *Miguel de Unamuno y William James*, 96, and Unamuno's letter to Federico Urales (9:816–18).

35. Unamuno himself once observed: "¿Hay mayor caridad que hacer volver a los hombres en sí?" (8:823). He may have based Pachico's dialogic personality on his readings of Marx, who believed that in order to bring about revolution it was necessary to "perform a dialectic analysis, to come to awareness, and to provoke a revolutionary situation" in one's environment (see Ellenberger, *Discovery of the Unconscious*, 240). The inner dialectic Pachico experiences in the last pages of *PG*, and his resolve to "export" his revolution, may be Unamuno's acknowledgment of the Marxist philosophy with which he was quite involved at the time he wrote his first novel.

36. Unamuno most likely culled this reference to Michelet from the French historian's study *La femme*, which suggests that man and woman are not only incomplete, but also relative beings since they are but two halves of the same whole (*Oeuvres complètes* [Paris: Flammarion, 1860], 35:605).

37. Cf. R. D. Laing, *The Divided Self*, 98. Batchelor offers a categorical appraisal of Unamuno as a schizophrenic (*Unamuno Novelist*, 105). For the quotation from Michelet, see *ETC*, 1:785; *STV*, 7:136; *DI*, 8:822.

38. Blanco Aguinaga had a brilliant insight along these lines, although scant familiarity with psychoanalysis led him to excuse his "fifth-hand Freudianism": "la madre es . . . el refugio primero y último en que el hombre se entrega al buen sueño de dormir, y en él a la continuidad de la Humanidad entera" (*El Unamuno contemplativo*, 173). What Blanco Aguinaga did not understand, however, was that the engulfing capability of the Mother is, psychologically speaking, far from a desirable characteristic.

39. For comparable appraisals of Unamuno's interest in the story of Nicodemus, see Blanco Aguinaga, *El Unamuno contemplativo*, 209, n. 51, and Fernández y González, *Unamuno en su espejo*, 107.

40. Referring to his draft of *PG*, Unamuno wrote to Clarín: "Los pocos a quienes les he enseñado algo de ella me dicen que le domina demasiado el pensamiento de la muerte. Es mi secreta obsesión" (Alas, ed., *Epistolario a Clarín*, 60; The few who have seen parts of the book tell me it is excessively dominated by the thought of death. It is my secret obsession).

CHAPTER 3: *Niebla*

1. Unamuno quoted in Charles Moeller, *Literatura del siglo XX y cristianismo*, 4:61, n. 3.

2. I use *Bildung* in Harold Bloom's sense of "education," or the "shaping of a human being." See *The Anxiety of Influence: A Theory of Poetry*, 54. Cf. Barnard's definition of *Bildung* as a "conscious human development" in *Herder's Thought*, 78.

3. In a letter to Pedro Múgica (September 15, 1904), Unamuno also claims to have written *Vida de Don Quijote y Sancho* "de un tirón y por viviparición." See Fernández Larraín, ed., *Cartas inéditas*, 300.

4. Mario J. Valdés's recent discovery of a manuscript copy of *N* dating from 1907 supports my contention that far from being a spontaneously generated work of fiction, *N* is the fruit of a lengthy period of gestation. See Mario J. Valdés, ed., *Niebla*, 47.

5. Sra. Pérez passed away either six months (2:560) or two years (2:568) prior to the beginning of the novel. This discrepancy is perhaps due to careless editing on Unamuno's part, possibly the victim of his own "a vuela pluma" style.

6. Ulanov, *The Feminine in Jungian Psychology*, 243.

7. Ernest Becker, *The Denial of Death*, 36.

8. Unamuno makes frequent references to Wordsworth's "Ode" in his work. See, for example, *CSN* (8:759); "El niño es el padre del hombre," in Victor Ouimette, ed., *Miguel de Unamuno: ensueño de una patria. Periodismo republicano (1931–1936)*, 107–9; and poem 1545 of the *Cancionero* (6:1359). Unamuno may have also found a similar idea in Soren Kierkegaard's *Fear and Trembling* where the Danish philosopher notes: "He who is willing to work gives birth to his own father" (38).

9. Paul Olson studied Wordsworth's "Ode" in connection with the "incest" Unamuno implied existed in his immediate family circle, his father having married his own niece. See "Sobre las estructuras quiásticas en el pensamiento unamuniano (interpretación de un juego de palabras)," 364–65. Cf. Unamuno: "mi abuela materna -que era a la vez tía paterna mía . . . nos solía decir a sus nietos y sobrinos," etc. (6:934).

10. Cf. *CSN* (8:758) and *Recuerdos de niñez y mocedad*: "Murió mi padre en 1870. . . . Apenas me acuerdo de él y no sé si la imagen que de su figura conservo se debe a sus retratos que animaban las paredes de mi casa" (8:97).

11. Salcedo, *Vida de Don Miguel*, 54.

12. Referring to his mother, Unamuno noted: "Es el único freno que le contiene de escribir muchas cosas que piensa" (Alas, ed., *Epistolario a Clarín*, 89–90). Morales also remarked that Unamuno "became the typical child for

whom only his mother's influence and love counted in life" ("Unamuno's Concept of Woman," 91).

13. Granjel, *Retrato de Unamuno*, 128.

14. Cf. Unamuno's description of Concha as "la madre de mis hijos, mi virgen madre, que no tiene otra novela que mi novela" (8:747).

15. Ulanov, *The Feminine in Jungian Psychology*, 193. Cf. J. H. van der Hoop: "It is an instance of retardation . . . when a boy's emotions continue to be centered upon his mother during his whole life" (*Character and the Unconscious: A Critical Exposition of the Psychology of Freud and Jung*, 86).

16. Wolfgang Lederer, *The Fear of Women*, 68.

17. C. G. Jung quoted in Jacobi, *Way of Individuation*, 105.

18. See Jung, 17:198: "The anima archetype is the eternal image of Woman, the synthesis of all ancestral experiences of the female every man carries within himself."

19. Gullón, *Autobiografías*, 106. Gullón likewise observes the neurotic tendencies in Augusto's personality.

20. Geoffrey Ribbans, "The Development of Unamuno's Novels *Amor y pedagogía* and *Niebla*," 275.

21. Feal Deibe, *El otro y don Juan*, 74.

22. Neumann, *Great Mother*, 128.

23. Becker, *Denial of Death*, 246.

24. To read Eugenia's farewell letter, whose contents he anticipates before opening the envelope, Augusto once again takes refuge in Mother Church (2:659). The archetype of the Church as Mother is also found in Unamuno's *Diario íntimo*, the most personal of his documents. In one passage Unamuno compares incipient religious faith to an "embrión, que empieza en masa indiferenciada. . . . En esta época conviene preservarla [la vida religiosa] como en recogido útero materno en el seno de la Iglesia, nuestra madre" (8:876).

25. The juxtaposition of dog and mother suggests the dog's function as a mother substitute, or alter ego. Unamuno will use the same technique in *SMB*, where allusions to Blaise Pascal are made in conjunction with Blasillo, el bobo—Pascal and Blasillo being symbolic of the two sides of Manuel's personality. Like Orfeo, Blasillo passes away within a short while of his beloved "master."

26. *New Larousse Encyclopedia of Mythology*, 198.

27. Jung and von Franz, eds., *Man and His Symbols*, 145, 206, and Jung, 9.1:366.

28. Jung and von Franz, eds., *Man and His Symbols*, 141–42.

29. Gayana Jurkevich, "The Sun-Hero Revisited: Inverted Archetypes in Unamuno's *Amor y pedagogía*," 300–301.

30. Elizabeth Wright, *Psychoanalytic Criticism: Theory in Practice*, 148.

31. Jung and von Franz, eds., *Man and His Symbols*, 166.

32. Feal Deibe, *El otro y don Juan*, 113–14.

33. These articles do, in fact, exist. On July 24 and 30, 1913, Unamuno published in *La Nación* of Buenos Aires a two-part series titled "Del suicidio en España." These articles are now collected in *Obras completas* (8:523–37).

34. Erich Neumann, *The Origins and History of Consciousness*, 88.

35. Joseph Natoli, ed., *Psychological Perspectives on Literature: Freudian Dissidents and Non-Freudians*, 25.

36. Paul R. Olson, *Unamuno: Niebla*, 33.

37. Frances Wyers notes that "Unamuno not only longs for a mother's love but also dreamed of achieving the mother's role: the commonplaces about literary gestation and the pangs of artistic childbirth become intensely personal in his writings" (*Miguel de Unamuno: The Contrary Self,* xii–xiii).

38. This concept of life as a dream-projection conjured by a demiurge who is subsequently dreamt by someone or something else, finds resonances in Jorge Luis Borges's short story "Las ruinas circulares," and in the following dream reported by Jung in which he saw a yogi: "I realized that he had my face. I started in profound fright, and awoke with the thought: 'Aha, so he is the one who is meditating me. He has a dream and I am it.' I knew that when he awakened, I would no longer be" (*Memories,* 323).

39. In the prologue to *N*, Unamuno's spokesman, Víctor Goti, implies that perhaps Unamuno himself is no more independent than his fictional characters: "estoy por lo menos firmemente persuadido de que carezco de eso que los psicólogos llaman libre albedrío, aunque para mi consuelo creo también que tampoco goza don Miguel de él" (2:543).

40. Rank, *Myth of the Birth*, 140.

41. Cf. "Una conversación con Don Fulgencio" (1915; 5:1051–55); "La santidad inconciente (Conversación con Don Fulgencio)" (1915; 5:1056–59); "Una entrevista con Augusto Pérez" (1915; 8:360–66).

42. Batchelor, *Unamuno Novelist*, 239.

43. Benítez, *El drama religioso de Unamuno*, 321.

CHAPTER 4: *Nada menos que todo un hombre* and *Cómo se hace una novela*

1. Following the same logic, *CSN* is not a book about how to write novels; rather it is one about how to "write" a life. Here Unamuno purposefully confuses the boundaries between fiction and autobiography as he sets out to prove that all novels are autobiographical and all autobiographies are novels. Antedating both *CSN* and the prologue to *Tres novelas ejemplares* is the essay "Una entrevista con Augusto Pérez" (1915), in which Unamuno notes, "Los libros mejores no son sino prólogos. Prólogos de un libro que no se ha de escribir jamás, afortunadamente" (8:360). Here *prólogo* appears to mean something akin to "glimpses" or "previews" of one's "Great Book," or autobiography, which Unamuno feels can never be fully written, or perhaps even completed. However, in *CSN*, he attempts writing just such a "Great Book," insisting throughout that all written material destined to achieve lasting recognition, is primarily autobiographical.

2. In *Autocrat of the Breakfast Table* (New York: Houghton Mifflin, 1891), Oliver Wendell Holmes suggests that when "John" and "Thomas" engage in conversation there are at least three distinct personalities to be recognized on each side: "The real John, known only to his Maker. John's ideal John, never the real one, and often very unlike him. Thomas's ideal John; never the real

John, nor John's John, but often very unlike either" (53). "Of these," elaborates Holmes, "the least important philosophically speaking, is the one that we have called the real person" (54). Apparently Unamuno was in complete agreement with Holmes, since in "Traje y estilo" he not only reiterates an interest in the conversation between the three "Johns" and three "Thomases" but, like Holmes, he also concludes that "lo más propio, lo más íntimo, lo más profundo de uno no es lo que es, sino lo que quiere ser" (3:894).

3. Unamuno would have also found himself in conflict with William James's theory of the complete personality, which approximates that of Jung: "So the seeker of his truest, strongest, deepest self must review the list carefully, and pick out the one on which to stake his salvation" (James, *Principles of Psychology*, 1:295–96).

4. Morris H. Philipson, *Outline of a Jungian Aesthetics*, 37.

5. Laing, *The Divided Self,* 105; Abellán, *Miguel de Unamuno a la luz de la psicología*, 182, 187.

6. Jung attributes his concept of the *persona* partially to Schopenhauer, who also referred to the term as meaning "how one appears to oneself and the world, but not what one is" (Jung, 6:218). Thus Unamuno, who knew the work of Schopenhauer quite well, most likely inferred some of his ideas on the four selves contained in every man from Schopenhauer as well as from Holmes.

7. In communicating with friends, Unamuno made the distinction between whether it was he or the "other" who was speaking. In a letter to Jiménez Ilundain (December 7, 1902), Unamuno objects: "Hay en su carta un párrafo de que protesto, y protesto con toda mi alma, sin disfraz, tal cual soy, no tal cual otros se imaginan que yo sea" (quoted in Benítez, *El drama religioso de Unamuno*, 379).

8. Unamuno's interest in the meaning of the word *persona* shows itself as early as his 1894 essay "La enseñanza del latín," which uses practically the same words to describe *persona* as do all the subsequent essays on the same topic (1:883).

9. According to Unamuno, an actor need not be dishonest as long as he believes in the authenticity of his role and plays it sincerely. Cf. Paul Ilie, *Unamuno: An Existential View of Self and Society,* 78ff.

10. Alas, ed., *Epistolario a Clarín*, 90.

11. Fernández, *Miguel de Unamuno y William James*, 69.

12. Here Unamuno clearly refers to Schopenhauer's belief that "Far more than any other external member of the body the genitals are subject merely to the will . . . the genitals are the real *focus* of the will, and are therefore opposite to the brain, the representative of knowledge . . ." (*The World as Will and Representation*, 1:330; cf. 1:380).

13. Fernández, *Miguel de Unamuno y William James*, 32.

14. Cf. van der Hoop: ". . . one of Freud's most striking discoveries is that the emotional experiences of childhood exercise a predominating influence upon later development" (*Character and the Unconscious*, 61). Also see Friedrich Schürr, who considers *NM* indebted to theories developed in depth psychology ("El amor, problema existencial en la obra de Unamuno," 81).

15. "El Unamuno de 1902 a 1903 visto por M," 19.

16. Cabaleiro Goas, *Werther, Mischkin y Joaquín Monegro*, 222–24. Unamuno himself addressed the issue of his *egotismo* and the *hipertrofia de mi yo* in "La personalidad frente a la realidad" (9:1263).

17. Jung defines inflation as an "expansion of the personality . . . by identification with the persona. . . . It produces an exaggerated sense of one's self-importance and is usually compensated by feelings of inferiority" (*Memories*, 396).

18. See Carlos Blanco Aguinaga, "Aspectos dialécticos de las *Tres novelas ejemplares.*"

19. Laing, *Divided Self*, 105. Unamuno's lifelong fascination with mirrors, reflections, *desdoblamiento*, and monodialogues with the self in front of mirrors is so well known that I need only mention the plays *La esfinge* and *El otro* as examples of two works in which his protagonists attempt to recapture their elusive (authentic?) selves reflected in mirrors placed before them.

20. Ulanov, *The Feminine in Jungian Psychology*, 239.

21. Lederer, *Fear of Women*, 3; Ulanov, *The Feminine in Jungian Psychology*, 70.

22. Moreno, *Jung, Gods, and Modern Man*, 53.

23. Sigmund Freud, *Jokes and Their Relation to the Unconscious*, 103.

24. This is an interesting conclusion on Unamuno's part, particularly if we take into account that he may himself have developed a *persona* as his own technique of disguising personal inferiority, not only from himself, but from others as well. Cf. Fernández y González, *Unamuno en su espejo*, 51.

25. Karen Horney, *The Collected Works of Karen Horney*, 2:191–92.

26. Ibid., 2:194–95. Unamuno himself may have been an expansive neurotic of the narcissistic type. Horney notes the excessive "self-valuation" that distinguishes this kind of person, and the perception they may have of themselves as persons of destiny and leadership. The expansive narcissist often "speaks incessantly of his exploits . . . and needs endless confirmation and devotion" (ibid., 2:194). On Unamuno's need to be esteemed by others, see Fernández y González: "En ello estribó el peligro . . . de falsear la realidad con arreglo al cuadro imaginario del efecto que su personalidad iba a causar en sus actuaciones religiosas, políticas, docentes, creadoras . . ." (*Unamuno en su espejo*, 26).

27. Neumann, *Origins and History of Consciousness*, 97.

28. Storr, *Dynamics of Creation*, 80.

29. Cf. Zubizarreta: "No debe olvidarse que Jugo de la Raza es un personaje autobiográfico creado por Unamuno con extremado rigor simbólico para depositar en él muchos rasgos de la biografía más concreta de sí mismo" (*Unamuno en su nivola*, 216).

CHAPTER 5: *Abel Sánchez*

1. Representative essays on pride and envy include: "El individualismo español" (1903, 1:1085–94); "Sobre la soberbia" (1904, 1:1205–13); "La envidia hispánica" (1907, 3:283–93); "Ni soberbia" (1911, 7:483–85); "Ni

envidiado ni envidioso" (1917, 3:775–77); "La ciudad de Henoc" (1933, 7:1093–95); "Más de la envidia hispánica" (1934, 3:1347–49).

2. Hannah, *Jung: His Life and Work*, 18.

3. Gregory Ulmer, *The Legend of Herostratus: Existential Envy in Rousseau and Unamuno*, 29.

4. Cf. letter from Areilza to Unamuno (November 15, 1905), in which Areilza admonishes don Miguel for his pride and vanity: "No podrá subir mientras no se desprenda de la envidia y de la egolatría que le tienen consumido" (quoted in Clavería, *Temas de Unamuno*, 109, n. 21).

5. Cf. Valdés and Valdés, *Sourcebook*, 291, for Unamuno's holdings of Rolph. The favorite Unamuno expletive, "O todo o nada," surfaces first in *ETC*, and again in a letter to P. Múgica (January 23, 1900), in which Unamuno attributes the expression to Ibsen's character Brand (see Fernández Larraín, ed., *Cartas inéditas*, 270). In *ETC*, Unamuno refers to "O todo o nada" as "la voz de la tentación satánica" (1:787).

6. Neumann, *Origins and History of Consciousness*, 95, and Otto Rank, *The Double: A Psychoanalytic Study*, 12.

7. Rank, *The Double*, xiv.

8. Ibid., 85–86.

9. Mauron, *Métaphores obsédantes*, 293.

10. Rank, *The Double*, 85–86.

11. Ibid., 20, 75.

12. Unamuno's biographer notes that "La verdad es que [los dos hermanos] estuvieron separados de por vida por esa invisible muralla de incomprensión. . . . En la inspiración de *El otro* y *Abel Sánchez* hay que ver la sombra de esta situación fraterna y el sentimiento cainita no como algo atribuido al otro, sino como un temor a ser él mismo un Caín en potencia" (Salcedo, *Vida de Don Miguel*, 340; cf. 213–14, 291).

13. Jacobi, *Way of Individuation*, 40.

14. Gullón, *Autobiografías*, 66.

15. For this, and other passages relevant to the mythology of the Dioscuri, see *New Larousse Encyclopedia of Mythology*, 189–91.

16. John Milton, *Paradise Regained*, 393.

17. For pertinent bibliography concerning the Romantic equation of Cain and Lucifer, see Russell, *Mephistopheles*, 174, and Clavería, *Temas de Unamuno*, 115, n. 34. Jung also remarked that "Cain has a Luciferian nature because of his rebellious progressiveness," and observed that Cain and Abel were the Old Testament prefiguration of Satan and Christ (11:173, n. 19).

18. Rank, *The Double*, 82, and Theodore Ziolkowski, *Disenchanted Images: A Literary Iconology*, 176–79. Cf. Ellenberger: "The entire nineteenth century was preoccupied with the problem of the coexistence of . . . two minds and of their relationship to each other. Hence the concept of 'double-ego' or 'dipsychism'" (*Discovery of the Unconscious*, 145).

19. Russell, *Mephistopheles*, 173.

20. Regarding Unamuno's romantic spirit and his predilection for Romantic

literary genres, see Zubizarreta, *Unamuno en su nívola*, 234, and King, "What is Spanish Romanticism?," 10–11. Unamuno himself commented on his "enorme fondo romántico" in the essay "Principales influencias extranjeras en mi obra" (9:816). For the influence of Romantic psychology on Jung, see Chapter 1, above, 25–27.

21. Russell, *Mephistopheles*, 174.

22. Ibid., 186.

23. For Unamuno's familiarity with Byron's *Cain*, see Clavería, *Temas de Unamuno*, 106–10, and Peter G. Earle, *Unamuno and English Literature*, 87. Unamuno, who was inclined to project his own unconscious tendencies upon others, even imagined that since Byron was capable of writing about a creature such as Cain, the poet himself must have had a personality riddled by envy: "En una ocasión le decía yo a Maurois, el autor de la penetratísma [*sic*] biografía de lord [*sic*] Byron, que acaso éste, el autor del formidable misterio *Cain*, fue un singular envidioso. Envidió a los que no le envidiaban; les envidió el que vivieran libres de envidia, que es otra terrible enfermedad del entendimiento" (4:1312).

24. Unamuno empathizes with the Devil once more in his sonnet "Satán." The last tercet of this poem reveals that Lucifer deserves pity since "es que la vida con insidias / nos rodeas, teniéndola en asedio / mientras ser mortales nos envidias" (6:378). As does Milton in *Paradise Lost*, Unamuno implies in this sonnet, and in *Abel Sánchez*, that envy plays an important role in the character attributes of the Devil.

25. Similar to the Romantic and Jungian views of the human personality as a coincidence of opposites, Stevenson's novella, written in 1886, has been interpreted as the story of a divided psyche battling for integration (see Barbara Hannah, *Striving Towards Wholeness*, 38–71). Ellenberger, *Discovery of the Unconscious*, also notes that the theme of Stevenson's work may have been suggested to the author by the dualism of his own personality (166).

26. Hannah, *Jung: His Life and Work*, 189.

27. Joaquín echoes a statement Unamuno made in *STV:* "para mí, el hacerme otro, rompiendo la unidad y la continuidad de mi vida, es dejar de ser el que soy; es decir, es sencillamente dejar de ser. Y esto no; ¡todo antes que esto!" (7:115).

28. Ellenberger, *Discovery of the Unconscious*, 266. In this respect Unamuno's essay, cum short story, "La locura del Doctor Montarco" (1904; 1:1127–36), is not only prophetic but also a paean against provincial jealousies and the persecution of individual versatility by small-minded men.

29. Gullón, *Autobiografías*, 146.

30. Ibid., 126.

31. In his essay "Sobre la soberbia," Unamuno notes the "fe [en sí mismos] de que carecen los soberbios contemplativos" (1:1213).

32. Rank, *The Double*, 33.

33. J. Rof Carballo, "Envidia y creación," 4.

34. Horney, *Collected Works*, 2:211.

35. Ibid., 2:197 and passim. This is a trait that recalls Doctor Montarco's gospel of self-imposition: ". . . la lucha por la vida, por la sobre-vida más bien,

es ofensiva y no defensiva" (1:1131). In this respect, Joaquín makes an interesting distinction between his childhood personality, "cuando aún no iba a cazar premios," and the adult who now dreams of nothing more than to "superar a los demás." He contrasts his attitude with that of Abel, who "no trató nunca de imponérseme" (2:713).

36. Horney, *Collected Works*, 2:203.

37. Laín Entralgo pointed out that the technique of ignoring one's rival "es la manera más sutil—a veces, la manera más cruel—de impedir que llegue a ser obstáculo" (*Teoría y realidad del otro*, 554).

38. Ulanov, *The Feminine in Jungian Psychology*, 252.

39. Rank, *The Double*, 35, n. 3.

40. Ibid., 33.

41. Feal Deibe interprets Joaquín's rapid decline as a consciously sought death and thus a form of suicide. See *El otro y Don Juan*, 149. Nicholas G. Round also considers Abel's unexpected death a form of self-immolation for Joaquín (*Unamuno: Abel Sánchez*, 44).

42. Rank, *The Double*, 79.

43. This notion first surfaces in Montarco's claim that "no es el crecimiento y la multiplicación de los seres lo que les pide más alimento . . . sino que es una tendencia a sobrepasar de lo necesario. No es instinto de invasión; no tiramos a mantenernos, sino a ser más, a serlo todo" (1:1131). In his 1909 essay "Materialismo popular," Unamuno reiterates that "la esencia del ser, más que el conato a persistir en el ser mismo . . . es el esfuerzo por ser más, por serlo todo: es el apetito de infinidad y de eternidad" (3:367).

44. Paul R. Olson and Thomas Mermall (see bibliography) have studied the significance and function of the chiasmus as a stylistic preference in Unamuno's essays. To my knowledge this is a first attempt to relate Unamuno's use of the chiasmus to his intimate psychological needs.

45. Pertinent to this discussion is Unamuno's essay "La nube de la guerra o la Helena de Eurípides," published in response to World War I. Unamuno chose the Trojan War as a paradigm for armed conflict, which he understood to be nothing less than the desire of one nation to ingest, or to impose itself upon, another: "Y hay personalidad colectiva, étnica, que sabe que no puede conservarse intacta sino imponiéndose. Hay veces en que el invadir es defenderse. Pero los otros no se resignan a ser invadidos, a perecer para que el invasor se conserve" (4:1216).

CHAPTER 6: *San Manuel Bueno, mártir*

1. Cf. the legacy Manuel leaves to Lázaro: ". . . y si puedes detener el sol detenle y no te importe del progreso" (2:1148). The contrast between the priests of *PG* and *SMB* is rather striking: Santa Cruz is a warrior-priest, famous for his leadership and outrageous deeds, while Manuel dedicates his life to keeping his flock as uninvolved with historical reality as possible.

2. Gertrude Jobes, *Dictionary of Mythology, Folklore, and Symbols*, 1:95–96.

3. Moreno, *Jung, Gods, and Modern Man*, 71. That Unamuno also thought of Jesus as a symbolic "whole" is evidenced by one of the last verses in *El Cristo de*

Velázquez, where he speaks of Jesus as the "Hijo del Hombre, Humanidad completa" (6:493).

4. The other religious figure in Unamuno's repertoire of masculine characters is the monk, Juan, of the play *El hermano Juan,* who is also an asexual male, a paradoxical inversion of the Don Juan archetype.

5. Becker, *Denial of Death,* 225.

6. In this sense Blasillo resembles Augusto Pérez's dog, Orfeo, so identified with Augusto's psyche that he passes away within a short while of his master.

7. As a character Blasillo was created by Unamuno a few years prior to his appearance in *SMB:* "Blas, el bobo de la aldea / . . . Blas, que se crió desde niño / sin padre, . . . / reza a la tarde el rosario / y le ayuda a misa al cura" (July 1, 1929, 6:1267).

8. Cf. Douglas M. Carey and Philip G. Williams, "Religious Confession as Perspective and Mediation in Unamuno's *San Manuel Bueno, mártir.*" Also see Carlos París, *Unamuno: estructura de su mundo intelectual,* 98. In the long line of Unamuno's male protagonists, only two, Ignacio Iturriondo and Apolodoro Carrascal, have fathers, and very ineffectual ones at that.

9. In many Unamuno novels a shallowly anchored paternal world gives way to the chthonic, female underworld: Apolodoro, Augusto, Alejandro Gómez, and Don Juan (*Dos madres*) commit suicide or die under very suspicious circumstances. Tristán (*El marqués de Lumbría*) and Ramiro (*La tía Tula*) are dominated by women, while Joaquín Monegro and Manuel Bueno lead lives of constant self-immolation, tantamount to consciously sought death, or suicide, as a way of reentry into the peace of the maternal womb.

10. This projection of "maternidad virginal" could not be otherwise since Angela's editor is one Miguel de Unamuno, for whom all women are potential mothers, or virgin-mothers.

11. Juan Eduardo Cirlot, *Diccionario de símbolos,* 427–28.

12. In *La agonía del cristianismo* Unamuno also noted, "En griego el Espíritu Santo es neutro, pero se identifica con Santa Sofía, la Santa Sabiduría, que es femenino" (7:332).

13. For the symbolism of the cock, see Jobes, *Dictionary of Mythology,* 1:353. Also Cirlot, *Diccionario de símbolos,* 98 and 223, and John Layard, "The Incest Taboo and the Virgin Archetype," 284.

14. *The Diario íntimo* once again confirms that the problem of personality was incubating in Unamuno's psyche at a much earlier date than works such as *CSN* or *El otro* would indicate: "¿Qué es eso de vivir exteriormente como ellos [el pueblo], y asistiendo a sus sacrificios y oraciones, y formar interiormente un reino aparte, y no entrar por la puerta?" (*DI,* 8:816).

15. Abellán, *Miguel de Unamuno a la luz de la psicología,* 187.

16. Jacobi, *Way of Individuation,* 106–10.

17. van der Hoop, *Character and the Unconscious,* 165.

18. Cirlot, *Diccionario de símbolos,* 278–79.

19. In early June 1930, Unamuno visited the lake of Sanabria and the village on its banks. He wrote two poems commemorating his experience and included them in the preface to *SMB.* They are also reproduced in the *Cancionero*

(6:1332, no. 1459; 1334, no. 1463). García Blanco associates the legends surrounding the lake of Sanabria to those brought into Spain by French pilgrims on their way to Santiago de Compostela: ". . . leyendas de raigambre francesa . . . supone que una de las dos campanas de la torre de la iglesia del pueblo sumergido . . . es tañida misteriosamente en la mañana del día de San Juan . . . cuyo son sólo pueden escucharlo los que se hallan en gracia de Dios" (6:1437).

20. Jung and von Franz, eds., *Man and His Symbols*, 205. Unamuno was very much aware of the alienatory capabilities of mirrors. An entry in *DI* shows him to have been fascinated by his own reflection: "Yo recuerdo haberme quedado alguna vez mirándome en el espejo hasta desdoblarme y ver mi propia imagen como un sujeto extraño, y una vez en que estando así pronuncié quedo mi nombre, lo oí como voz extraña que me llamaba" (8:797–98).

21. Marie Bonaparte, "La legende des eaux sans fond," 170.

22. Neumann, *Great Mother*, 44–45, 292.

23. Lionel Trilling, *The Liberal Imagination: Essays on Literature and Society,* 43.

24. In his essay "Freud and Literature," Trilling also refers to literary creation as a "narcotic" (ibid., 43). Similar to Angela's remark that Manuel "huía de la ociosidad y de la soledad" (2:1134), Unamuno wrote to Clarín that during his religious crisis, had it not been for his involvement with family activities and the routine practice of Christian devotions, his life would have become unbearable (see Alas, ed., *Epistolario a Clarín,* 89–90).

25. Quoted in Granjel, *Retrato de Unamuno*, 133. Unamuno's conservative opinions under discussion here seem to contradict the theories proposed by Antonio Regalado (*El siervo y el señor: la dialéctica agónica de Miguel de Unamuno*) and Carlos Blanco Aguinaga (*Juventud del 98*) that the collapse of Unamuno's liberalism and his assimilation to a middle-class, bourgeois ideology were the phenomena of his mature years. Statements such as the one above made to González Trilla demonstrate that a conservative ideological orientation existed in the thinking of a much younger Unamuno.

26. Cf. poem no. 1226 of the *Cancionero* ("El hornero de araya"): "Del tronco del olmo anciano / a cuya sombra-follaje / jugó de niño / hizo de su propia mano / para el término del viaje / con seis tablas el escriño" (6:1278).

27. Neumann, *Great Mother*, 256.

28. Cf. Susan Predmore: "As in *Niebla* where Augusto's supposed independence is, in the long run, subordinate to Unamuno's will, so in this novel, Unamuno interferes with the objectivity of his fictional editor, Angela Carballino" ("*San Manuel Bueno, mártir*: A Jungian Perspective," 23).

29. Anthony N. Zahareas, "Unamuno's Marxian Slip: Religion as Opium of the People," 35, n. 11.

30. Storr, *Dynamics of Creation*, 40.

31. Cf. Eric Gould: ". . . the allegories of reading and writing are parables for coming into consciousness" (*Mythical Intentions in Modern Literature*, 214–15). Also Ulanov: "The anima's function is to mediate the collective unconscious to the ego" (*The Feminine in Jungian Psychology,* 232).

32. Unamuno consistently reversed his position regarding anything he ever

thought, wrote, or said. Insofar as his leaving a "final" testament of his religious beliefs is concerned, the last poem he wrote, three days before his death, communicates a Pascalian kind of nihilism:

> Morir soñando, sí, mas si se sueña
> morir, la muerte es sueño; una ventana
> hacia el vacío . . .
>
> . . . .
> ¿Vivir el sueño no es matar la vida?
> ¿ a qué poner en ello tanto empeño?
>
> aprender lo que al punto al fin se olvida
> escudriñando el implacable ceño
> —cielo desierto—del eterno Dueño?
>
> (*Cancionero*, 6:1424)

Had Unamuno lived longer, he most likely would have reversed himself several times more on this particular issue.

33. The conclusion of *SMB* is corroborated by an entry from *DI:* "¿Por qué nos escandalizamos de que un último arrepentimiento sincero borre una vida de pecados? El que obtiene esa gracia es que fue bueno, es que hizo el mal que no quiso" (8:820).

34. A poem from the *Cancionero* indicates that, although Unamuno always doubted God's existence and questioned Jesus's message of resurrection, he did subscribe to the idea of a basic faith:

> Esperas, fe, contra razón, contra mudanza,
> esperas no sé qué,
> ni tú lo sabes ¡qué fe en la fe!
> ¡qué esperanza!
> (December 12, 1928; 6:1118)

In a poem written on the last birthday he was to celebrate, Unamuno observed: "Un angel, mensajero de la vida, / escoltó mi carrera torturada, / y desde el seno mismo de mi nada / me hiló el hilillo de una fe escondida" (September 29, 1936; 6:1419).

35. Also cf. *STV* (7:180) and "Fe que no duda es fe muerta" in *La agonía del cristianismo* (7:311).

36. Benítez, *El drama religioso de Unamuno*, 307–8.

37. In this regard, Unamuno anticipates "death of God" theology. Cf. J. W. Butt: "Unamuno está seguramente al final de sus días mucho más cercano a los teólogos de la muerte de Dios" (review of *El siervo y el Señor* by Antonio Regalado, 199).

38. Neumann, *Great Mother*, 30, 233. Also see Ulanov, *The Feminine in Jungian Psychology*, 69.

CONCLUSION

1. Neumann, *Great Mother*, 43.
2. Blanco Aguinaga, *El Unamuno contemplativo*, 173.

3. Only Feal Deibe mentions the "aspectos temibles" (frightening aspects) of Unamuno's mother (*El otro y don Juan*, 76, n. 3).

4. Quoted in Fernández Larraín, ed., *Cartas inéditas*, 289.

5. Frye, *Anatomy of Criticism*, 185–86.

6. Cf. Blanco Aguinaga, "Aspectos dialécticos."

7. From "Die erste Bedienung einer wahrahft freien Arbeit" in *Der sozialistische Akademiker* (Berlin, July 1896). Cited and translated by Butt, "Unamuno's Idea of Intrahistoria," 22.

Bibliography

Abellán, José Luis. *Miguel de Unamuno a la luz de la psicología: una interpretación de Unamuno desde la psicología individual.* Madrid: Tecnos, 1964.

Alas, Adolfo, ed. *Epistolario a Clarín.* Madrid: Escorial, 1941.

Alberich, José. "Sobre el positivismo de Unamuno." *Cuadernos de la Cátedra Miguel de Unamuno* 9 (1959): 61–75.

Alvarez Villar, Alfonso. "La psicología de los personajes unamunianos." *Arbor* 61 (1966): 39–56.

Azar, Inés. "La estructura novelesca de *Cómo se hace una novela.*" *MLN* 85 (1970): 184–206.

Bain, Alexander. *Mind and Body.* New York: Humboldt, n.d.

Barnard, F. M. *Herder's Social and Political Thought: From Enlightenment to Naturalism.* Oxford: Clarendon, 1965.

Batchelor, R. E. *Unamuno Novelist: A European Perspective.* Oxford: Dolphin, 1972.

Becker, Ernest. *The Denial of Death.* New York: Free Press, 1973.

Benítez, Hernán. *El drama religioso de Unamuno.* Buenos Aires: Instituto de Publicaciones de la Universidad de Buenos Aires, 1949.

Blanco Aguinaga, Carlos. "Interioridad y exterioridad en Unamuno." *Nueva revista de filología hispánica* 8 (1953): 686–701.

———. "La madre, su regazo y el 'sueño de dormir' en la obra de Unamuno." *Cuadernos de la Cátedra Miguel de Unamuno* 7 (1956): 69–84.

———. "Aspectos dialécticos de las *Tres novelas ejemplares.*" In *Miguel de Unamuno,* edited by Antonio Sánchez Barbudo, 251–71. Madrid: Taurus, 1974.

———. *El Unamuno contemplativo.* 2d ed. Barcelona: Laia, 1975.

———. *Juventud del 98.* 2d ed. Barcelona: Crítica, 1978.

Bleiberg, G., and E. Inman Fox, eds. *Spanish Thought and Letters in the 20th Century.* Nashville: Vanderbilt University Press, 1966.

Bloom, Harold. *The Anxiety of Influence: A Theory of Poetry.* New York: Oxford University Press, 1973.

Bonaparte, Marie. "La legende des eaux sans fond." *Revue française de psychoanalyse* 14 (1950): 164–71.

Boring, Edwin. *A History of Experimental Psychology.* New York: Century, 1929.

Brancaforte, Benito. "El objeto del deseo en *San Manuel Bueno, mártir.*" In *Homenaje a Antonio Sánchez Barbudo: ensayos de literatura española moderna,* edited by Benito Brancaforte et al., 117–38. Madison: University of Wisconsin Press, 1981.

Braun, Lucille. "Ver que me ves: Eyes and Looks in Unamuno's Works." *MLN* 90 (1975): 212–30.

Butt, J. W. "Determinism and the Inadequacy of Unamuno's Radicalism." *Bulletin of Hispanic Studies* 46 (1969): 226–40.

———. "Unamuno's Idea of Intrahistoria: Its Origins and Significance." In *Studies in Modern Spanish Literature and Art Presented to Helen F. Grant,* edited by Nigel Glendinning, 13–24. London: Tamesis, 1972.

———. Review of *El siervo y el señor* by Antonio Regalado. *Cuadernos de la Cátedra Miguel de Unamuno* 22 (1972): 198–200.

———. *Miguel de Unamuno: San Manuel Bueno, mártir.* London: Grant & Cutler / Tamesis, 1981.

Cabaleiro Goas, Manuel. *Werther, Mischkin y Joaquín Monegro vistos por un psiquiatra: trilogía patográfica.* Barcelona: Apolo, 1951.

Carey, Douglas M., and Philip G. Williams. "Religious Confession as Perspective and Mediation in Unamuno's *San Manuel Bueno, mártir.*" *MLN* 91 (1976): 292–310.

Carruthers, Kathie. "Apuntes para un estudio de la mujer y el problema de la personalidad en Unamuno." *Reflexión 2* 1, no. 1 (1972): 105–15.

Ciplijauskaité, Biruté. "El amor y el hogar: dos fuentes de fortaleza en Unamuno." *Cuadernos de la Cátedra Miguel de Unamuno* 11 (1961): 79–90.

Cirlot, Juan Eduardo. *Diccionario de símbolos.* Rev. ed. Barcelona: Labor, 1969.

Clancier, Anne. *Psicoanálisis, literatura, crítica.* Translated by M. J. Arias. Madrid: Cátedra, 1976.

Clavería, Carlos. *Temas de Unamuno.* 2d ed. Madrid: Gredos, 1970.

Díez, Ricardo. *El desarrollo estético de la novela de Unamuno.* Madrid: Playor, 1976.

Durand, Frank. "Search for Reality in *Nada menos que todo un hombre.*" *MLN* 84 (1969): 239–47.

Earle, Peter G. *Unamuno and English Literature.* New York: Hispanic Institute, 1960.

———. "El evolucionismo en el pensamiento de Unamuno." *Cuadernos de la Cátedra Miguel de Unamuno* 14–15 (1964): 19–28.

———. "Unamuno and the Theme of History." *Hispanic Review* 32 (1964): 319–39.

Edel, Leon. *The Modern Psychological Novel.* New York: Grosset and Dunlap, 1964.

Eliade, Mircea. *Rites and Symbols of Initiation: The Mysteries of Birth and Rebirth.* Translated by W. R. Trask. New York: Harper, 1965.

Ellenberger, Henri. *The Discovery of the Unconscious: The History and Evolution of Dynamic Psychiatry.* New York: Basic Books, 1970.

Falconieri, John V. "Sources of Unamuno's *San Manuel Bueno, mártir.*" *Romance Notes* 5 (1963): 18–22.

———. "*San Manuel Bueno, mártir,* Spiritual Autobiography: A Study in Imagery." *Symposium* 17 (1964): 128–41.

Feal Deibe, Carlos. *Unamuno: El otro y don Juan.* Madrid: Planeta / State University of New York at Buffalo, 1976.

Fernández, Pelayo Hipólito. *Miguel de Unamuno y William James: un paralelo pragmático.* Salamanca: n.p., 1961.

———. "Más sobre *San Manuel Bueno, mártir* de Unamuno." *Revista hispánica moderna* 29 (1963): 252–62.

———. *El problema de la personalidad en Unamuno y en* San Manuel Bueno, mártir. Madrid: Mayfe, 1966.

Fernández Larraín, Sergio, ed. *Cartas inéditas de Miguel de Unamuno.* Madrid: Rodas, 1972.

Fernández Turienzo, Francisco. *Unamuno: ansia de Dios y creación literaria.* Madrid: Alcalá, 1966.

———, ed. *En torno al casticismo.* Madrid: Alcalá, 1971.

Fernández y González, Angel R. "Morir y sobrevivir: estructura autobiográfica en *San Manuel Bueno, mártir.*" *Mayurqua* 1 (1968): 3–24.

———. *Unamuno en su espejo.* Valencia: Bello, 1976.

Foster, D. W. "The 'Belle-Dame sans merci' in the Fiction of Miguel de Unamuno." *Symposium* 20 (1966): 321–28.

Franz, Thomas. "Parenthood, Authorship and Immortality in Unamuno's Narratives." *Hispania* 63 (1980): 647–57.

Freud, Sigmund. *Jokes and Their Relation to the Unconscious.* Translated and edited by James Strachey. New York: Norton, 1960.

Frye, Northrop. *Anatomy of Criticism: Four Essays.* Princeton: Princeton University Press, 1973.

Galbis, Ignacio. *Unamuno: tres personajes existenciales.* Barcelona: Hispam, 1975.

Gallego Morrell, Antonio. *Angel Ganivet: el excéntrico del 98.* Granada: Albaicín, 1965.

Girard, René. *Deceit, Desire, and the Novel: Self and Other in Literary Structure.* Translated by Yvonne Freccero. Baltimore: Johns Hopkins University Press, 1965.

Gould, Eric. *Mythical Intentions in Modern Literature.* Princeton: Princeton University Press, 1981.

Granjel, Luis. *Retrato de Unamuno.* Madrid: Guadarrama, 1957.

Gullón, Ricardo. *Autobiografías de Unamuno.* Madrid: Gredos, 1964.

Hannah, Barbara. *Jung: His Life and Work.* New York: Putnam, 1976.

————. *Striving Towards Wholeness.* New York: Putnam / C. G. Jung Foundation, 1971.

Hartmann, Eduard von. *Philosophy of the Unconscious,* 2 volumes. London, 1893.

Horney, Karen. *Neurosis and Human Growth.* Vol. 2 of *The Collected Works of Karen Horney.* New York: Norton, 1950.

Ilie, Paul. "The Structure of Personality in Unamuno." In *Studies in Honor of M. J. Benardete: Essays in Hispanic and Sephardic Culture,* edited by Izaak Langnas, 177–92. New York: Las Américas, 1965.

————. *Unamuno: An Existential View of Self and Society.* Madison: University of Wisconsin Press, 1967.

Jacobi, Jolande. *The Way of Individuation.* Translated by R. F. C. Hull. New York: Harcourt Brace, 1967.

James, William. *The Varieties of Religious Experience.* New Hyde Park: University Books, 1963.

————. *The Principles of Psychology.* Edited by Frederick H. Burkhardt. 3 vols. Cambridge: Harvard University Press, 1981.

Jobes, Gertrude. *Dictionary of Mythology, Folklore, and Symbols.* 3 vols. New York: Scarecrow, 1962.

Johnson, Roberta L. "Archetypes, Structures and Myth in Unamuno's *El otro.*" In *The Analysis of Hispanic Texts,* edited by Isabel Taran et al., 33–47. New York: Bilingual Press, 1976.

Jung, Carl Gustav. *Symbols of Transformation.* Vol. 5 of *The Collected Works of C. G. Jung.* Translated by R. F. C. Hull. Executive editor,

William McGuire. 2d ed. Princeton: Princeton University Press, 1970.

————. *Psychological Types.* Vol. 6 of *The Collected Works of C. G. Jung.* Revised and translated by R. F. C. Hull. Exec. ed., William McGuire. Princeton: Princeton University Press, 1971.

————. *Two Essays on Analytical Psychology.* Vol. 7 of *The Collected Works of C. G. Jung.* 2d ed. Translated by R. F. C. Hull. Exec. ed., William McGuire. Princeton: Princeton University Press, 1972.

————. *The Structure and Dynamics of the Psyche.* Vol. 8 of *The Collected Works of C. G. Jung.* 2d ed. Translated by R. F. C. Hull. Exec. ed., William McGuire. Princeton: Princeton University Press, 1978.

————. *The Archetypes and the Collective Unconscious.* Vol. 9, Part 1, of *The Collected Works of C. G. Jung.* Translated by R. F. C. Hull. Executive editor, William McGuire. New York: Pantheon for The Bollingen Foundation, 1959.

————. *Aion: Researches into the Phenomenology of the Self.* Vol. 9, Part 2, of *The Collected Works of C. G. Jung.* Translated by R. F. C. Hull. Executive editor, William McGuire. Princeton: Princeton University Press, 1970.

————. *Civilization in Transition.* Vol. 10 of *The Collected Works of C. G. Jung.* Translated by R. F. C. Hull. Executive editor, William McGuire. New York: Pantheon for The Bollingen Foundation, 1964.

————. *Psychology and Religion: West and East.* Vol. 11 of *The Collected Works of C. G. Jung.* Translated by R. F. C. Hull. Executive ed., William McGuire. Princeton: Princeton University Press, 1969.

————. *Psychology and Alchemy.* Vol. 12 of *The Collected Works of C. G. Jung.* 2d. ed., rev. Translated by R. F. C. Hull. Executive editor, William McGuire. Princeton: Princeton University Press, 1968.

————. *The Spirit in Man, Art, and Literature.* Vol. 15 of *The Collected Works of C. G. Jung.* Translated by R. F. C. Hull. Executive editor, William McGuire. New York: Pantheon for The Bollingen Foundation, 1966.

————. *The Development of Personality.* Vol. 17 of *The Collected Works of C. G. Jung.* Translated by R. F. C. Hull. Executive editor, William McGuire. New York: Pantheon for The Bollingen Foundation, 1954.

———. *Memories, Dreams, Reflections*. Translated by Richard Winston and Clara Winston. Edited by Aniella Jaffe. New York: Vintage, 1965.

Jung, C. G., and Marie Louise von Franz, eds. *Man and His Symbols*. Garden City: Doubleday, 1964.

Jurkevich, Gayana. "The Sun-Hero Revisited: Inverted Archetypes in Unamuno's *Amor y pedagogía.*" *MLN* 102 (1987): 292–306.

———. "Archetypal Motifs of the Double in Unamuno's *Abel Sánchez.*" *Hispania* 72 (1990): 345–52.

———. "Unamuno's *Intrahistoria* and Jung's Collective Unconscious: Parallels, Convergences, and Common Sources." *Comparative Literature* 43 (1991):43–59.

Kierkegaard, Soren. *Fear and Trembling; The Sickness unto Death.* Translated and edited by Walter Lowrie. New York: Doubleday, 1954.

King, Edmund. "What is Spanish Romanticism?" *Studies in Romanticism* 2 (1962): 1–11.

Kinney, Arthur F. "The Multiple Heroes of *Abel Sánchez.*" *Studies in Short Fiction* 1 (1964): 251–57.

Kirsner, Robert. "The Novel of Unamuno: A Study in Creative Determinism." *Modern Language Journal* 37 (1953): 128–39.

Koepping, Klaus-Peter. *Adolf Bastian and the Psychic Unity of Mankind: The Foundations of Anthropology in Nineteenth Century Germany.* London & New York: University of Queensland Press, 1983.

Lacy, Allen. *Miguel de Unamuno: The Rhetoric of Existence.* The Hague: Mouton, 1967.

Laín Entralgo, Pedro. *La generación del noventa y ocho.* 9th ed. Madrid: Espasa-Calpe, 1979.

———. *Teoría y realidad del otro.* Madrid: Alianza, 1983.

Laing, R. D. *The Divided Self.* New York: Pantheon, 1969.

Landsberg, P. L. *Reflexiones sobre Unamuno.* Barcelona: Cruz del Sur, 1963.

Layard, John. "The Incest Taboo and the Virgin Archetype." *Eranos-Jahrbuch* 12 (1945): 254–307.

Lederer, Wolfgang. *The Fear of Women.* New York: Grune and Stratton, 1968.

Le Galliot, J. *Psychanalyse et langages littéraires: théorie et pratique.* Paris: Fernand Nathan, 1977.

Livingstone, Leon. "Autobiografía y autofantasía en la Generación del 98 (Teoría y práctica del querer ser)." In *Homenaje a Juan López Morillas. De Cadalso a Vicente Aleixandre: estudios sobre lit-*

eratura e historia intelectual españolas, edited by José Amor y Vásquez and A. David Kossof, 293–302. Madrid: Castalia, 1982.

McGaha, Michael. *"Abel Sánchez y la envidia de Unamuno." Cuadernos de la Cátedra Miguel de Unamuno* 21 (1971): 91–102.

Marías, Julian. *Miguel de Unamuno.* Buenos Aires: Emecé, 1953.

Martínez López, Ramón, ed. *Unamuno Centennial Studies.* Austin: University of Texas Press, 1966.

Mauron, Charles. *Des métaphores obsédantes au mythe personnel. Introduction a la psychocritique.* Paris: Corti, 1962.

Mermall, Thomas. "Unamuno's Mystical Rhetoric." In *The Analysis of Hispanic Texts,* edited by Isabel Taran et al., 256–64. New York: Bilingual Press, 1976.

———. "The Chiasmus: Unamuno's Master Trope." *PMLA* 105 (1990): 245–55.

Meyer, François. *La ontología de Miguel de Unamuno.* Translated by C. Goicoechea. Madrid: Gredos, 1962.

Milton, John. *Paradise Lost; Paradise Regained.* Edited by Christopher Ricks. New York: NAL, 1968.

Moeller, Charles. *Literatura del siglo XX y cristianismo.* 4 vols. Translated by V. G. Yebra. Madrid: Gredos, 1960.

Morales, Carmen, Sr. "Unamuno's Concept of Woman." *Fu Jen Studies* 5 (1971): 91–100.

Moreno, Antonio, O.P. *Jung, Gods, and Modern Man.* Notre Dame: University of Notre Dame Press, 1970.

Morón Arroyo, Ciriaco. *"San Manuel Bueno, mártir* y el 'sistema' de Unamuno." *Hispanic Review* 32 (1964): 227–46.

Natoli, Joseph, ed. *Psychological Perspectives on Literature: Freudian Dissidents and Non-Freudians.* Hamden: Archon, 1984.

Neumann, Erich. *The Great Mother: An Analysis of the Archetype.* Translated by Ralph Manheim. New York: Pantheon, 1955.

———. *The Origins and History of Consciousness.* Translated by R. F. C. Hull. 1954. Reprint. Princeton: Princeton University Press, 1969.

New Larousse Encyclopedia of Mythology. Translated by Richard Aldington and Delano Ames. 1959. New York and London: Hamlyn, 1972.

Nicholas, Robert L. *"El proceso de creación en Abel Sánchez."* In *Homenaje a Antonio Sánchez Barbudo,* edited by Benito Brancaforte et al., 167–85. Madison: University of Wisconsin Press, 1981.

Olney, James. *Metaphors of Self: The Meaning of Autobiography.* Princeton: Princeton University Press, 1972.

Olson, Paul R. "The Novelistic Logos in Unamuno's *Amor y pedagogía.*" *MLN* 82 (1969): 248–68.

――――. "*Amor y pedagogía* en la dialéctica interior de Unamuno." In *Actas del Tercer Congreso Internacional de Hispanistas*, edited by Carlos H. Magis, 649–56. Mexico City: Colegio de México, 1970.

――――. "Unamuno's Lacquered Boxes: *Cómo se hace una novela* and the Ontology of Writing." *Revista hispánica moderna* 36 (1970–1971): 186–99.

――――. "Sobre las estructuras quiásticas en el pensamiento unamuniano (interpretación de un juego de palabras)." In *Homenaje a Juan López Morillas*, edited by José Amor y Vásquez and A. David Kossof, 359–68. Madrid: Castalia, 1982.

――――. *Unamuno: Niebla*. London: Grant & Cutler / Tamesis, 1984.

Orringer, Nelson R. *Unamuno y los protestantes liberales (1912): Sobre las fuentes de* Del sentimiento trágico de la vida. Madrid: Gredos, 1985.

Ortega y Gasset, Eduardo. *Monodiálogos de Don Miguel de Unamuno*. New York: Ediciones Ibérica, 1958.

Ouimette, Victor. *Reason Aflame: Unamuno and the Heroic Will*. New Haven: Yale University Press, 1974.

――――, ed. *Miguel de Unamuno. Ensueño de una patria. Periodismo republicano (1931–1936)*. Valencia: Pre-textos, 1984.

Palley, Julian. "Unamuno: The Critique of Progress." *Revista de estudios hispánicos* 10 (May 1976): 237–60.

París, Carlos. "El pensamiento de Unamuno y la ciencia positiva." *Arbor* (May 1952): 11–23.

――――. "La inseguridad ontológica, clave del mundo unamuniano." *Revista de la Universidad de Madrid* 13 (1964): 92–123.

――――. *Unamuno: estructura de su mundo intelectual*. Barcelona: Península, 1968.

Pérez de la Dehesa, Rafael. *Política y sociedad en el primer Unamuno*. Madrid: Ciencia Nueva, 1966.

Philipson, Morris H. *Outline of a Jungian Aesthetics*. Evanston: Northwestern University Press, 1972.

Predmore, R. L. "Flesh and Spirit in the Works of Unamuno." *PMLA* 70 (1955): 587–605.

Predmore, Susan. "*San Manuel Bueno, mártir:* A Jungian Perspective." *Hispanófila* 22 (1978): 15–29.

Putnam, Samuel. "Unamuno y el problema de la personalidad." *Revista hispánica moderna* 1 (1935): 103–10.

Ramsden, H. R. *Angel Ganivet's* Idearium español. Manchester: Manchester University Press, 1967.

———. *The 1898 Movement in Spain*. Manchester: Manchester University Press, 1974.

Rank, Otto. *The Myth of the Birth of the Hero, and Other Writings*. New York: Vintage, 1964.

———. *The Double; A Psychoanalytic Study*. Translated and edited by Harry Tucker. Chapel Hill: University of North Carolina Press, 1971.

Regalado, Antonio. *El siervo y el señor: la dialéctica agónica de Miguel de Unamuno*. Madrid: Gredos, 1968.

Ribas, Pedro. "El Volksgeist de Hegel y la intrahistoria de Unamuno." *Cuadernos de la Cátedra Miguel de Unamuno* 21 (1971): 23–33.

Ribbans, Geoffrey. "The Development of Unamuno's Novels *Amor y pedagogía* and *Niebla*." In *Hispanic Studies in Honor of I. González Llubera*, edited by Francis W. Pierce, 269–85. Oxford: Dolphin, 1959.

———. "Estructura y significado de *Niebla*." *Revista de la Universidad de Madrid* 13 (1964): 211–40.

Ribot, Théodule. *The Diseases of the Will*. Chicago: Open Court, 1894.

———. *German Psychology of Today*. New York: Scribner's, 1899.

Richards, Katherine C. "Unamuno and the 'Other.'" *Kentucky Romance Quarterly* 23 (1976): 439–49.

———. "Unamuno y la paternidad espiritual." *Hispanófila* 83 (1985): 53–60.

Robinson, Daniel N. *Toward a Science of Human Nature: Essays on the Psychologies of Mill, Hegel, Wundt, and James*. New York: Columbia University Press, 1982.

Rof Carballo, J. "Envidia y creación." *Insula* 13, no. 145 (December 15, 1958): 1, 4.

———. "El erotismo en Unamuno." *Revista de Occidente* 7 (1964): 71–96.

Round, Nicholas G. *Unamuno: Abel Sánchez*. London: Grant & Cutler / Tamesis, 1974.

Rubia Barcia, José, and M. A. Zeitlin, eds. *Unamuno: Creator and Creation*. Berkeley & Los Angeles: University of California Press, 1967.

Russell, Jeffrey B. *Mephistopheles: The Devil in the Modern World*. Ithaca: Cornell University Press, 1986.

Salcedo, Emilio. *Vida de Don Miguel*. 2d ed. rev. Salamanca: Anaya, 1970.

Sánchez Barbudo, Antonio. "The Faith of Unamuno: His Unpublished Diary." *Texas Quarterly* 8 (1965): 46–66.

————. *Estudios sobre Galdós, Unamuno y Machado.* 2d ed. Madrid: Guadarrama, 1968.

————, ed. *Miguel de Unamuno.* Madrid: Taurus, 1974.

Schopenhauer, Arthur. *The World as Will and Representation.* 2 vols. Translated by E. F. J. Payne. Indian Hills, Colo.: Falcon's Wing Press, 1958.

Schürr, Friedrich. "El tema del suicidio en la obra de Unamuno." In Vol. 3 of *Studia Philologica: Homenaje a Dámaso Alonso,* 411–17. Madrid: Gredos, 1963.

————. "El amor, problema existencial en la obra de Unamuno." *Cuadernos del idioma* 1 (1965): 63–93.

Seator, Lynette. "Women and Men in the Novels of Unamuno." *Kentucky Romance Quarterly* 27 (1980): 39–55.

Sedwick, Frank. "Unamuno and Womanhood: His Theater." *Hispania* 43 (1960): 309–13.

Shaw, Donald L. *The Generation of 1898 in Spain.* London: E. Benn; New York: Barnes & Noble, 1975.

Shergold, N. D. "Unamuno's Novelistic Technique in *San Manuel Bueno, mártir.*" In *Studies in Modern Spanish Literature and Art,* edited by Nigel Glendinning, 163–80. London: Tamesis, 1972.

Spires, Robert C. *Beyond the Metafictional Mode: Directions in the Modern Spanish Novel.* Lexington: University of Kentucky Press, 1984.

Stein, Murray. *Jung's Treatment of Christianity: The Psychotherapy of a Religious Tradition.* Wilmette, Ill.: Chiron, 1985.

Stevens, Harriet S. "Las novelitas intercaladas en *Niebla.*" *Insula* 16, no. 170 (1961): 1.

————. "El Unamuno múltiple." *Papeles de Son Armadans* 34 (1964): 253–84.

Storr, Anthony. *The Dynamics of Creation.* New York: Atheneum, 1972.

Summerhill, Stephen J. "*San Manuel Bueno, mártir* and the Reader." *Anales de la literatura española contemporánea* 10 (1985): 61–79.

Toro, Fernando de. "Personaje autónomo, lector y autor en Miguel de Unamuno." *Hispania* 64 (1981): 360–65.

Trilling, Lionel. *The Liberal Imagination: Essays on Literature and Society.* Garden City: Doubleday, 1957.

Turner, David G. *Unamuno's Webs of Fatality.* London: Tamesis, 1974.

Ulanov, Ann B. *The Feminine in Jungian Psychology and in Christian Theology.* Evanston: Northwestern University Press, 1971.

Ulmer, Gregory L. *The Legend of Herostratus: Existential Envy in*

Rousseau and Unamuno. Gainesville: University of Florida Press, 1977.

"El Unamuno de 1901 a 1903 visto por M." *Cuadernos de la Cátedra Miguel de Unamuno* 2 (1951): 13-31.

Unamuno y Jugo, Miguel de. *Obras completas.* 9 vols. Edited by Manuel García Blanco. Madrid: Escelicer, 1966-1971.

―――. *Selected Works of Miguel de Unamuno.* 7 vols. Translated and annotated by Anthony Kerrigan and Martin Nozick. Bollingen Series LXXV. Princeton: Princeton University Press, 1967-1984.

Valdés, Mario J. *Death in the Literature of Unamuno.* Urbana: University of Illinois Press, 1966.

―――. "Archetype and Recreation: A Comparative Study of William Blake and Miguel de Unamuno." *University of Toronto Quarterly* 40 (1970): 58-72.

―――. "Metaphysics and the Novel in Unamuno's Last Decade: 1926-1936." *Hispanófila* 15 (1972): 33-44.

―――, ed. *Niebla.* Madrid: Cátedra, 1982.

Valdés, Mario J., and María Elena de Valdés. *An Unamuno Sourcebook: A Catalogue of Readings and Acquisitions with an Introductory Essay on Unamuno's Dialectical Inquiry.* Toronto: University of Toronto Press, 1973.

van der Hoop, J. H. *Character and the Unconscious: A Critical Exposition of the Psychology of Freud and Jung.* Translated by Elizabeth Trevelyan. College Park: McGrath, 1970.

Waitz, Theodor. *Introduction to Anthropology.* London: Longman Green, 1983.

Watson, Robert I., ed. *The Great Psychologists.* 4th ed. Philadelphia: Lippincott, 1978.

Webber, Ruth. "Kierkegaard and the Elaboration of Unamuno's *Niebla.*" *Hispanic Review* 32 (1964): 118-34.

Weber, Frances W. "Unamuno's *Niebla:* From Novel to Dream." *PMLA* 88 (1973): 209-18.

Weiner, Philip P., ed. *Dictionary of the History of Ideas.* 4 vols. New York: Scribner's, 1973.

Whyte, Lancelot L. *The Unconscious before Freud.* London: Tavistock, 1962.

Wright, Elizabeth. *Psychoanalytic Criticism: Theory in Practice.* London and New York: Methuen, 1984.

Wyers, Frances. *Miguel de Unamuno: The Contrary Self.* London: Tamesis, 1976.

Zahareas, Anthony N. "Unamuno's Marxian Slip: Religion as Opium of the People." *Journal of the Midwest Modern Language Association* 17 (1984): 16–37.

Ziolkowski, Theodore. *Disenchanted Images: A Literary Iconology.* Princeton: Princeton University Press, 1977.

Zlotescu-Cioranu, Iona. "Ejemplaridad de las *Tres novelas ejemplares.*" In *Actas del Tercer Congreso Internacional de Hispanistas,* edited by Carlos H. Magis, 955–60. Mexico City: Colegio de México, 1970.

Zubizarreta, Armando. "Aparece un diario íntimo de Unamuno." *Mercurio peruano* 38 (1957): 182–89

———. "Desconocida antesala de la crisis de Unamuno, 1895–1896." *Insula* 13, no. 142 (September 15, 1958): 1, 10.

———. *Unamuno en su nivola.* Madrid: Taurus, 1960.

Zusne, Leonard. *Biographical Dictionary of Psychology.* Westport: Greenwood, 1984.

Index